# GOING
# HOLLYWOOD
## MIDWESTERNERS IN MOVIELAND

### SARA JORDAN-HEINTZ

*To Tiscuses ~
Thanks and happy reading!
Sara Jordan-Heintz*

## PAGE TURNER
### BOOKS INTERNATIONAL

Going Hollywood: Midwesterners in Movieland

Copyright 2019 by Sara Jordan-Heintz

Library of Congress Cataloging-in-Publication Data Names: Jordan-Heintz, Sara, 1990- author. Title: Going Hollywood: Midwesterners in movieland /Sara Jordan-Heintz. Description: Guthrie Center, IA : PageTurner Books International, 2016. Identifiers: LCCN 2016031477 <2016031477> Subjects: LCSH: Motion picture actors and actresses--United States--Biography. Classification: LCC PN2285 .J67 2016 | DDC 791.4302/80922 [B] --dc23 LC record available at https://lccn.loc.gov/2016031477 <https://lccn.loc.gov/2016031477>

First printing 2019
978-0-692-75223-4
www.pageturnerbooks.biz

To Andy, with love

And to all classic film buffs, captivated by the mystique of Hollywood
and its tragic, transcending, beautiful people.

## Acknowledgments

Special thanks to my parents, Julie Campbell-Jordan and
Larry Jordan, for their continued support, encouragement and love.
Thank you dad for all your copyediting and design work that made
this book a reality. I would also like to thank fellow authors
Mark Shaw and David Wayne for their continued championing of
my work. Mary Ann Seberg Shuey, Ann Dandridge, Melissa Galt,
Cathy Katz, Nancy Adams, and Mark Adams-Westin
provided invaluable insights.

*Fame is a bee.*
*It has a song —*
*It has a sting —*
*Ah, too, it has a wing.*

—Emily Dickinson

# Table of Contents

## ABOUT THE AUTHOR

Sara Jordan-Heintz is a writer, editor and 20th century historian. She has experience in journalism, including writing for newspapers, magazines, journals and book editing, beginning in her early teens. She is the associate editor of *Midwest Today* magazine and her celebrity articles written for that publication formed the basis of this book.

Ms. Jordan-Heintz is a 2018 recipient of the Genevieve Mauck Stoufer Outstanding Young Iowa Journalists Award from the Iowa Newspaper Foundation. Many of her articles have been published by the Associated Press, and in 2019, she earned an award from the Iowa Associated Press Media Editors. Her film and pop culture research has been cited in several books. Her debut work of fiction, *A Day Saved is a Day Earned*—a novella set in 1961—is available as an eBook. It was also published in Rod Serling Books' inaugural anthology *Submitted For Your Approval* in 2015.

She holds a Bachelor of Arts degree in American Studies and history from the University of Iowa. She lives in the Midwest with her husband Andy Heintz, whose debut book *Dissidents of the International Left* was recently published by New Internationalist.

# FOREWORD

A S AN INTROVERTED ONLY CHILD GROWING UP IN SMALL-town Iowa, I became fascinated with the glamorous and mystical world cultivated on the sound stages of Hollywood's great studios, decades before I was born. I found myself drawn to the glittering MGM musicals, slapstick comedies of the 1930s, sexy and slinky *film noir* capers of the 1940s, wholesome family films of the 1950s and the changing social mores of the 1960s and '70s. I wanted to be as glamorous and tough as Jane Russell, hobnob with Clark Gable and Carole Lombard, and kiss Rock Hudson.

There was something captivating, and enticing and all the while familiar about sitting in a darkened room watching black and white films fill the screen with old automobiles, art deco furnishings, men in fedoras and ladies in fanciful hats—and a cigarette always at hand. Intimate gatherings required hiring a hat check girl and booking an orchestra to perform in your garden. People evinced refined manners. Women wore sublime gowns designed by Adrian. The men were debonair, opened doors for ladies and never swore in mixed company. The simplicity—even predictability—of some of the plot lines not only appealed to the proverbial "little ole lady from Dubuque" but captivated me as well.

I couldn't get enough.

As I matured, I realized the films of the Studio Era, moving into the 1960s, were the product of censorship and outside pressure to shoot movies with morals to the story, free of profanity and blatant sexuality. They were made to reflect a more innocent period in our nation's history, when *doing the right thing* was the rule, not the exception, and honesty was exalted, not abandoned as it is today.

I revel in modern-day portrayals of television and film characters with more realism. Women swear. People have sex. Marriages crumble. The bad guys sometimes win.

Yet, I find myself beckoned back to the Golden Age time and time again. No matter how long it's been since I popped in a DVD or tuned into Turner Classic Movies, there they are; like long lost friends you can resume a conversation with after lo so many years apart.

For over 25 years, my family has published the glossy regional magazine *Midwest Today*. When I was 15, I became interested in assisting my father plan out the magazine and try my hand at article writing. Every issue, a notable from the Heartland graces the cover, with a well-researched profile found inside. I decided to merge my love of classic films with our Midwest-based format and came up with the concept of profiling a movie star from the past, born or raised in a Midwestern state. **This is just the first volume in what I hope will be a multi-book series featuring famous movie folks from mid-America.**

*Going Hollywood: Midwesterners in Movieland* is the first book of its kind to chronicle the lives of 12 Hollywood legends, all from the Heartland, a region whose wholesome image is in stark contrast to the glamour, glitz, and excesses of Hollywood and its inhabitants. I seek to tell "the story behind the story" of some of Tinseltown's most beloved entertainers.

Leaving behind cities filled with billowing smoke emanating from the tops of factory smokestacks, overcrowded tenements or impoverished rural landscapes, these 12 Midwesterners embarked on journeys which ended up in the place where perky teenagers "get discovered" drinking a soda sitting at Schwab's drug store counter in Hollywood, where there are more movie stars than stars in the heavens and dreams really do come true.

I have pondered the question regarding what qualities did growing up in the middle part of America endow these people with such that they were able to achieve star status? Surely it was not their innate talent alone. I theorize it was an amalgam of factors, such as the Heartland's values, climate, geography, economy and culture. The strong work ethic, religiosity, struggle to overcome obstacles, and the pervasive humility and empathy of Midwest natives all provided these stars with experiences that shaped them as individuals and helped them be ready to shine when opportunity came knocking. They were each unique personalities, to be sure. But they all had traits to which moviegoers could relate.

The celebrities profiled in this tome grew up in difficult economic times. Some no doubt were desperate to escape the Midwest, (the proverbial train whistle at night beckoning them to far-off places, perhaps)? Although the Colorado Gold Rush of 1859 that had induced Americans to shout "Westward, ho!" and the quote attributed to (but never confirmed as having been expounded by) Horace Greeley to "Go west, young man!" had predated the birth of the stars I've written about here, there was still a fascination with California as the land of sunshine and golden opportunities. It remained in the public consciousness well into the 1950s, especially as the interstate highway system began to connect even the remote areas of the nation with both coasts.

So while the Midwest certainly contributed many characteristics to these 12 celebrities, the hardships they encountered in the region incongruously known as "America's bread basket" might have also provided the motivation for them to seek a better life in Tinseltown.

The book kicks off with a profile on Clark Gable, best known for his portrayal of Rhett Butler and hailed as the King of Hollywood. He went from a day laborer on a farm in Ohio to cinematic royalty. The rugged "he-man" image he projected on celluloid was genuine to a certain extent; he enjoyed hunting, fishing, fast cars, and had worked manual labor jobs. But fans didn't know of Gable's intellectual interests —only about his suave playboy ways.

He wed his soul mate, actress Carole Lombard, only to lose her three years into their storybook marriage. More than anything, Gable wanted to be a father, yet he would never know his two children.

Comedienne Carole Lombard, a stunning blonde from Indiana with impossibly high cheekbones, was known as the "The Hoosier Tornado." She never grew out of her tomboy tendencies, even after she became a highly sought after glamorous leading lady. She hunted, fished, played sports, swore like a sailor and was known for her love of practical jokes. Above all else, however, she was devoted to her great love, Gable. Loyal to her country and the cause of defeating the Nazis, Lombard set off on a war bonds selling tour in 1942, never returning home alive.

Long before blonde bombshells Marilyn Monroe and Jayne Mansfield catapulted to superstardom there was Kansas City, Missouri native Jean Harlow. Her sexy figure, bleached locks and feisty speech made her one the most popular movie stars of the 1930s, but her sensual image concealed her deadly health problems.

Spencer Tracy, born and raised in Milwaukee, Wisconsin, became a beloved film star due to his natural acting abilities and relatable Average Joe persona. He made moviegoers believe they weren't watching a scripted scene shot on a soundstage, but rather were in the presence of Spencer Tracy just being Spencer Tracy. In reality, he was the embodiment of Catholic guilt, a man who suffered from alcoholism, insomnia and insecurity.

Michigan City, Indiana native Anne Baxter is best known for her role as the conniving Eve Harrington in the 1950 film *All About Eve*. From the infamous Anne Baxter/Bette Davis feud, to motherhood in the Australian outback, to being the granddaughter of famed architect Frank Lloyd Wright, Baxter's life story is a colorful bricolage. She won an Academy Award for *The Razor's Edge*, appeared in the religious epic *The Ten Commandments*, and enjoyed a 40-year career in film, television and theater.

Jean Seberg had a small-town Lutheran upbringing in the manufacturing city of Marshalltown, Iowa. Despite having no formal acting training, at age 18 she beat out 18,000 other contenders for the role of Joan of Arc in the film *Saint Joan*. She became the darling of French New Wave cinema with her breakout role in the film *Breathless* and appeared alongside Warren Beatty in the psychological thriller *Lilith*. She lived fast and hard in Europe and was preyed upon by the FBI because of her Leftist causes.

Brash, ultra-religious and conservative, Jane Russell paradoxically embraced her sex symbol status. Growing up in the Northern Minnesota town of Bemidji and marrying young, she was discovered by Hollywood billionaire Howard Hughes, who shaped her image and launched her career with the salacious film *The Outlaw*. Russell represented liberated and ballsy women making a stand in a man's world.

Dorothy Dandridge, America's first interracial movie star, who hailed from Cleveland, Ohio believed she could have "captured the world" if she had only been born white. She was an early manifestation of the "Black is Beautiful" mantra, but was never able to break free from the crushing hands of racism and sexism, both on and off the big screen.

Winnetka, Illinois native Rock Hudson made women (and men) swoon whenever he entered a movie scene. In 1957, he was voted the number one "Name Power Star" and his movies with Doris Day captured the essence of the changing sexual mores of the late 1950s and early 1960s. Hudson led a private existence shunning fans and the press and living with a secret he desperately desired to take with him to the grave.

Clarinda, Iowa may best be known as the hometown of swing king Glenn Miller, but a perky, comedic blonde named Marilyn

Maxwell grew up in the small town during the Roaring Twenties. A popular Big Band singer, USO performer and movie actress, she was known on the Paramount lot as "Mrs. Bob Hope." Her long-time relationship with Rock Hudson had parallels to that of the TV sitcom *Will & Grace*.

Jane Wyman, Ronald Reagan's first wife and mother of his eldest two children, was a native of St. Joseph, Missouri whose legacy is shaped by her 50-year-long film and television career. Wyman is also the only spouse of a president to win an Academy Award.

*Going Hollywood: Midwesterners In Movieland's* final chapter belongs to Freeport, Illinois native Louella Parsons, who became famous through her tempestuous reporting on the lives of the beautiful and glamorous players of the movie world.

She broke the most controversial, scandalous and tantalizing Tinseltown stories of her day and blackmailed the most celebrated and famed names in the industry, including some of the subjects featured in this book. Parsons was Hollywood's top—and most feared—gossip columnist for 40 years, a notoriety compounded by mutual animus with rival columnist Hedda Hopper.

I interviewed friends and relations of the aforementioned subjects, gaining an insider perspective into the lives and deaths of these 12 celebrities. In addition, I acquired a collection of books, magazines and newspaper articles, dusting off rare material not read in decades, long forgotten and overlooked—until now.

—*Sara Jordan-Heintz*
*February 2019*

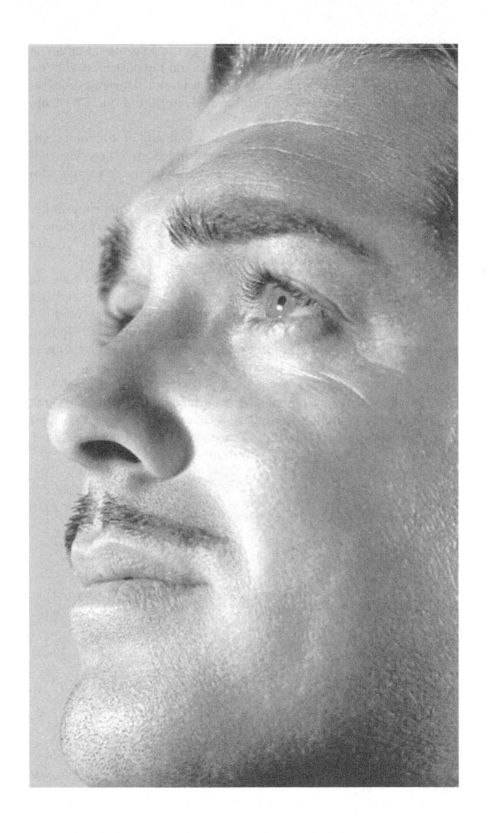

# 1.

# CLARK GABLE:
## *An Enduring Enigma*

CLARK GABLE IS PERHAPS ONE OF THE MOST FAMOUS MOVIE AC-
tors of all time. Invoke his name in conversation and someone is sure to recite Gable's iconic declaration from the end
of Gone With The Wind: "Frankly my dear, I don't give a
damn." But how does a man remain popular so many
decades after that famous line was first uttered? In many ways, Gable
was a walking paradox. He was a deeply guarded man who shunned
the press and preferred the company of blue-collar folks to the Hollywood elite to which he belonged.

The rugged "he-man" image he projected on celluloid was genuine to a certain extent; he enjoyed hunting, fishing, fast cars, and had
worked manual labor jobs. Yet Gable was a closeted intellectual who
refused to be photographed reading a book. He could quote Shake-
speare from memory. The man kept himself immaculately groomed
and outfitted in expensive threads. He showered several times a day
and refused to take baths because he believed them to be unsanitary.
In addition, the actor also shaved his chest and underarm hair.

Gable never met a woman he didn't find attractive (and the
feeling was often mutual), yet he valued the institution of marriage and
walked down the aisle five times—often to women he didn't love, and
against the better judgment of his closest friends and associates. He
wed his soul mate, actress Carole Lombard, only to lose her three years
into their charmed marriage. More than anything, or so he said, Gable
wanted to be a father, yet he never got to know his daughter and died
before his son was born. Gable's wife Kay was pregnant at the time of
his death with what was reported as the actor's first and only child. But
Clark had become a father decades earlier when he had an affair with
co-star Loretta Young, who bamboozled the press by passing the child
off as her adopted daughter. All his life, Gable distanced himself from

the very people who loved and supported him.

William Clark Gable was born on February 1, 1901 in Cadiz, Ohio, a coal-mining town, to William and Adeline Gable. His mother died within the year, and doting relatives raised the child while Mr. Gable sought fortune in the oil business. Two years later, Will married a woman named Jennie Dunlap who proved to be the boy's saving grace.

Jennie saw potential in her stepson. She exposed the boy to classic literature and encouraged him to take up the French horn and singing. "If it hadn't been for Jennie Dunlap, I'd probably be on a farm in Ohio," Gable admitted. She devoted her life to the needs of her step-son, having never had children of her own. This relationship may have been the catalyst for the actor's lifelong attraction to older women and females who mothered him.

Will Gable regarded the arts as effeminate and pushed his son towards a life of tending the farm and helping him work in oil fields.

Cadiz, located in Harrison County, is part of the Seven Ranges of Ohio, a region Congress in 1787 designated as the first part of the wilderness settled during the expansion of the West. An oil boom at the turn of the 20th century and coal mining were the region's main points of industry.

Clark was a well-built youth who grew into a strong and mus-cular man. He could best be described as a "gentle giant" because he never got into schoolyard fights and was cognizant of his awkwardly large hands and bulky frame. For a while Clark obliged and held down a slew of manual labor jobs including carrying water to miners, chop-ping wood and mechanics. He struggled financially but did not let a lack of resources dampen his desire to break into acting. "You're always scared the first few times you find yourself broke," he recalled of the lean years. "Later you just feel interested in what is going to lift you out of it this time."

Now going by Billy Gable, he joined a theater group and ulti-mately made his way out to Portland, Oregon. It was there in late 1923 he made the acquaintance of a Broadway actress and acting coach named Josephine Dillon, 17 years his senior. He ended his relationship with serious girlfriend Franz Dorfler in order to concentrate on study-ing with Dillon.

Although she has often been described as a poor acting coach, that is not true. Miss Dillon was actually a very accomplished stage per-former who appeared in many plays as the lead actress. In the play *The Dawn of Tomorrow*, which ran in 1913, an article in the *Tacoma Times* said that "she has amazed other members of her company with her fine interpretation of the part." Another review described her as an exceptionally talented young actress with a charming personality.

Josephine poured her money and time into making Gable a decent actor. She helped him lower his high-pitched voice, worked on his posture and taught him how to communicate emotion with facial expressions. His teeth were terrible so she paid for dental work. (By age 33, because of a gum infection, Gable had to have most of his teeth removed and replaced by dentures). She would give him her last 25 cents to send him to the movies every week. In 1924, teacher and pupil made their way to Hollywood. Josephine fell in love with her protégé, and Clark fell in love with all the possibilities.

## The Women Behind the Man

Dillon put Clark up at a hotel while he looked for acting jobs. She taught acting classes as a means of paying her young lover's bills. On December 18, 1924 Josephine and Clark married. He was 23, she was 41. One of her friends threw them a party afterward, which Clark spent dancing with a wealthy buxom blonde while Josephine fumed. On their wedding night, Clark merely tipped his hat at his new bride, and went to bed alone.

Gable worked as an extra in silent movies, but his mainstay was stage work where he traveled to San Francisco, Houston and New York City. Oftentimes, Josephine stayed home because there wasn't enough money for her to accompany her young beau. But Clark didn't want for companionship—the leading ladies of the plays kept him company.

Clark made his Broadway debut in *Machinal*. His wife made

**Josephine worked a miracle in transforming Gable (left) into a star (right)**

the trip East to visit him, but the young upstart had other plans. "Clark phoned me to keep out of his life, said he was through with me. I said I was going to California and that he had better become the best actor he could as he could never be a man," Josephine said.

They would remain husband and wife in name only. The first Mrs. Gable later wrote an unpublished memoir chronicling her time as Clark's long-suffering first wife, except she changed their names to Julia and Mark Craven.

Josephine also expressed her thoughts on her husband publicly on occasion: "What went on in Clark's mind that did not concern acting, I do not know, have never known, and will never know—now," she reflected. "What did I think about when we were not talking about his acting, or his career? He never knew, and I have never known whether he ever wondered or cared. As for myself, I put in very little time resenting his silences, or in suspicions of possible other women —but I was often very lonely. Perhaps he was too."

Josephine said "Clark Gable had the furrowed forehead of a man who was overworked and under nourished. He had the straight lipped, set mouth of the do it or die character. He had the narrow, slit-eyed expression of the man who has had to fight things through alone, and who tells nothing."

"[The marriage] was not fun to watch and not fun to live through."

On March 30, 1929, Josephine filed for divorce, citing desertion. By that time, Gable was romantically involved with a thrice-married older woman—Ria Langham.

It was actually Ria's daughter Jana who first became acquainted with the actor when he was appearing in *Huston*, and she played matchmaker. Like Josephine, Ria was also 17 years older than Clark. But unlike the first Mrs. Gable, Ms. Langham was a sophisticate. Money was no object and she gave her lover the star image to go with the talent that Josephine had developed.

Clark was offered a role in the play *The Last Mile*, in the west coast production. He and Ria had seen the Broadway version with Spencer Tracy in the part Clark was to play. Gable was intimidated by Tracy's acting skills and although the two would become friends in Hollywood, they had a healthy rivalry. Gable told the press that he desired to be "half as good as Tracy."

Gable, Ria and her two children moved out to Hollywood to launch Gable's career. He hired famed agent Minna Wallis, sister of movie producer Hal Wallace. With his connection to the Wallaces, he was introduced to MGM mogul Irving Thalberg. Clark Gable signed a movie contract on December 4, 1930. He made 12 films in 1931 alone. In the film *Dance, Fools, Dance* he was paired for the first time with Joan Crawford—the actress he would appear alongside more than any other woman—a total of eight times.

Their friendship blossomed into a romance that was on-again-off-again for decades. Hearst journalist Adela Rogers

Clark with wife #2, wealthy socialite Rita Langham

St. John called the relationship "the affair that nearly burned Hollywood down." St. John befriended Gable and it was speculated that at one time the two were lovers and may have even had a child. "Well, who wouldn't have wanted to have Clark Gable's baby?" was St. John's coy reply.

Joan remained close to Gable for the rest of his life, speaking and writing of how she revered the man. "His manliness came out in so many ways—in the sudden eruption of boisterous laughter, in the capacity for competition, in the need for physical daring, in the total acceptance of life as tragedy and comedy, and in the exceptional ability to establish friendship beyond a thin smile and weak handshake…He was not afraid of life because he was too busy living," Crawford wrote. Ria desired to become the next Mrs. Gable, but Clark was hesitant. She went to MGM publicity man Howard Strickling to tell him that she and Gable were living together and not married. Strickling, who would serve as Gable's right-hand man for years, went into high gear and told the budding star he would have to wed. On June 19, 1931 the couple got hitched.

In 1932, Gable made movies with some of the top actresses in the business: Jean Harlow, Norma Shearer, and a screwball comedienne named Carole Lombard. *No Man of Her Own* was the first and only picture Gable and Lombard made, although years later when the two got together, they expressed interest in making another film.

*Men in White* was the first movie he made with Myrna Loy. A public poll dubbed them the "King and Queen of Hollywood." The Pre-Code film dealt with adultery and abortion. Their next movie, also made in 1934, was a crime saga entitled *Manhattan Melodrama*. This motion picture became infamous because it was the final film seen by the gangster John Dillinger who was shot and killed by federal agents as he exited Chicago's Biograph Theater. Miss Loy scorned the studio for profiting off the movie in relation to the mobster's violent demise.

Gable played roguish men who used and abused women yet the female sex flocked to his films. Celebrity profiler Anne Helen Petersen reflected of Gable, "He looked very much as if someone had taken a swarthy pirate, given him a facial, parted his hair to the side, trimmed his mustache, and put him in tails."

When stars did not comply with the movie studios' demands and expectations, they were loaned out to smaller studios as punishment. In Gable's case, he was sent to "Poverty Row" to star in a movie made at Columbia pictures called *Night Bus*, later renamed *It Happened One Night*. Several actors and actresses had turned down the lead roles. Reluctantly, Claudette Colbert signed on in the female lead. She played Ellie Andrews, an heiress who wed against her father's wishes and took a bus out of town to reunite with her husband. Colbert encountered journalist Peter Warne, played by Gable, who recognized the woman and said if she gave him the exclusive on her story, he would aid and abet. Of course, the characters end up falling in love over the course of their travels. This is the flick with the iconic hitchhiking scene, wherein Colbert lifted up her skirt to reveal a shapely leg in order to stop a car. After filming wrapped, Claudette complained she had "just finished the worst picture in the world."

Yet moviegoers came in droves and to the surprise of Columbia pictures, *It Happened One Night* became its most lucrative film to date. But the biggest shock came when the movie was nominated for five Academy Awards: Best Picture, Director, Actor, Actress, and Screenplay. Gable and Colbert figured it was a long shot that the flick would win in any of those categories. On the night of the awards ceremony —February 27, 1935—Colbert boarded a train out of town, declining her invitation to attend the ceremony.

When it was announced that she had won, studio head Harry Cohn had someone fetch her from the train, which had not yet left the station. Slightly embarrassed by her shabby wardrobe, Claudette Colbert was brought up on stage to accept her Oscar. That evening, Gable became the first actor to win the Academy Award for a comedic portrayal. The movie won every Oscar in which it was nominated. Holding his statuette, white tie and tails—grinning—Clark Gable had officially become a movie star.

## The Call of the Wild

Now a major star earning $3,000 a week, 34 year old Gable was cast in an adventure film based on a novel by Jack London. His co-star was 22 year old actress Loretta Young, who had been appearing on celluloid since she was a child. Cast and crew journeyed to Washington, destination Mount Baker, to begin filming *The Call of the Wild*. A blizzard extended the ten-day shooting schedule for months.

Loretta found the flirtatious married man irresistible. They dined together, frolicked in the snow and fell in love. It was hard to hide their feelings from the 150-person movie team, as well as the ever-inquisitive press.

When the filming was completed, Loretta had to immediately return to Hollywood to film *The Crusades*; Gable was set to star in *Mutiny on the Bounty*. Loretta soon learned she was pregnant. Going to her mother Gladys first with the news, the Catholic Youngs debated what to do. When Gladys broke the news to Clark he replied, "She was a married woman [briefly at age 17]. I thought she knew how to handle herself."

When the petite Loretta began to show, she headed for Europe, citing illness. When she neared her due date, Young returned to the States and stayed in a house owned by the family in Venice, California. Gable separated from Ria and left the country for a trip to South America.

Ria called Loretta incessantly. The fan magazines and papers wanted to hear from the actress as well. Dorothy Manners, a reporter and associate of powerful gossip columnist Louella Parsons, finally got in to see Young in the fall of 1935. Now nine months pregnant, Loretta hid under layers of blankets in a sick bed with a hired nurse by her side. Ms. Manners got her interview.

"This is the truth about Loretta Young's mysterious illness: Hard work, her great popularity that put her to the physical strain of making one picture immediately following another...has aggravated an internal condition from which Loretta has suffered since maturity. It has weakened her, sapped her strength in the great loss of energy; and an eventual operation is the only remedy...She has been surprisingly lucky in not losing too much of her preciously acquired poundage put on during her vacation trip to Europe."

On November 6, 1935 Loretta gave birth to a baby girl she named Judith Young, citing "father unknown" on the birth certificate. Gable again was nominated for an Academy Award for *Mutiny on the Bounty*, but lost, although the film won Best Picture. Loretta feared revealing the truth about the love child would end both their careers.

An Associated Press newspaper article entitled "Loretta Young Now Is Mother—By Adoption" reported that Young took in two young blonde girls, Jane, three years old and Judy, age two. She told the press she decided to adopt two girls because, "We just had to have baby girls in the house again...[My sisters and I] had so much fun growing up together." One of Young's statements may have been a subtle confession. "There's just one thing I can't tell and that is where I got the children. That is a secret I hope I never have to reveal."

In reality, Loretta Young had concocted a delusory scheme wherein she placed Judy in orphanages for 19 months, then told the press she was adopting two children (one baby looked suspicious, but two created a red herring). The other child Jane (if one had existed at all) was "returned" and Judy kept, albeit her age was fudged so as to not coincide with the time frame of the romance.

Loretta gave an interview to Louella Parsons explaining the decision to adopt two children as a single mother. The astute columnist couldn't have possibly believed the fabricated story and yet after the article was printed, the press stopped hounding Loretta about Judy's origins.

But as Judy grew, she looked as though someone had superimposed a photo of Clark Gable and Loretta Young, down to Gable's large ears and Loretta's crooked teeth. "I may have wanted my ears fixed, but my mother wanted it even more," Judy wrote in her memoir *Uncommon Knowledge*. At the tender age of seven, the child had her ears pinned back in an excruciating procedure. "The surgeon erased my connection with my father...I also had prominent buckteeth, just as my mother had had. Instead of waiting until my second teeth came in, my mother took me to an orthodontist, who put braces on my baby teeth."

Gable never contributed financially to their daughter's care. Loretta married Tom Lewis, and while Judy took the man's last name, he never adopted her. No one had ever adopted Judy. Tom shunned the girl after his two sons were born, and Loretta raised her daughter in a stark, loveless home, deeply in denial that she had given birth to Judy. Most likely, Ms. Young suffered from undiagnosed Narcissistic Personality Disorder (NPD), which made Judy Lewis' life a living hell. Having a mother with mental illness may have sparked the girl's lifelong interest in psychology.

In 1937, a British woman named Violet Norton claimed Gable had fathered a child with her in 1922. But Clark had never even been

**Clark Gable was an outdoorsman who liked to get away from the madding crowd**

issued a passport to leave the country. Norton was convicted of using the mail system to defraud the actor and was sentenced to five years in prison or a $10,000 fine. Gable was unscathed. His film *Parnell* bombed at the box office, but instead of slowing down his career, the failure just became a running joke. It seemed no one could dislike Clark Gable for long.

### The King of Hollywood

While *Parnell* was considered a box office bomb (Gable had portrayed Irish politician Charles Stewart Parnell in the role), his subsequent features remain fan favorites. The next movie Gable made, *Saratoga*, paired him for the sixth time with blonde bombshell Jean Harlow. With the film 90 percent completed, Harlow collapsed on the set while filming a scene with Walter Pidgeon. She passed away on June 7, 1937 at the age of 26. Initially, MGM wanted to replace Harlow and re-shoot her scenes but the public decried the move, proclaiming Harlow's last film deserved to be seen. The movie was released several weeks after her death and became MGM's most lucrative motion picture of the year. Her character's final scenes were completed with a body double.

Gable played a daredevil test pilot opposite Myrna Loy in *Test Pilot*. MGM believed putting Gable, Loy and Spencer Tracy in a film together—the studio's top moneymakers—would draw mobs at the movie theaters. *Test Pilot* was a monster hit with Gable and Tracy vying for the audience's attention. Gable and Loy made another aviation flick in 1938 called *Too Hot To Handle*.

In January 1939, MGM released *Idiot's Delight*, a film that put Gable in his only musical role. He performed the Irving Berlin classic *Puttin' on the Ritz*. Despite an all-star cast, including MGM's queen Norma Shearer, the movie lost money at the box office.

Gable was offered his most famous role as Rhett Butler in the movie adaptation of the popular novel *Gone With the Wind*, which was set in the Civil War era. Clark was the first and only choice for the role, as if the

(Top) Gable reading the book, "Gone With the Wind" sitting in his car; and on camera in a love scene with Vivien Leigh

character had been modeled after him, but he rebuked the flattery. "When the book was being written I was a four-dollar-a-day laborer in Oklahoma and not in anybody's mind for anything," Gable quipped.

Producer David O. Selznick considered hundreds of women for the part of Scarlett O'Hara before settling on a relatively unknown British actress named Vivien Leigh. At the time, she was having an affair with the married actor, Laurence Olivier. Vivien had the hardest part of that movie, spending over 120 days filming *Gone With The Wind*, whereas Gable logged a little over 70. There is also strong evidence that Ms. Leigh was a true nymphomaniac whose sexual appetite was insatiable. Still, she complained about having to kiss Clark Gable because his dental problems had given him a bad case of halitosis.

By all accounts, Gable got along well with his co-stars during filming. He was a good friend of actress Hattie McDaniel, (who played the role of the maid Mammy), and as a prank even slipped her a real alcoholic drink during the scene in which they were supposed to be celebrating the birth of Scarlett and Rhett's daughter. Clark Gable almost walked off the set when he learned that the studio facilities were segregated and were designated "White" and "Colored." Gable called the film's director, Victor Fleming, who in turn told the studio, "If you don't get those signs down, you won't get your Rhett Butler." The signs were removed immediately.

Clark's last line in *Gone with the Wind*, "Frankly, my dear, I don't give a damn," is one of the most famous lines in movie history, though it was thought scandalous at the time.

Gable tried to boycott the premiere of the movie in Atlanta, Georgia, because Hattie McDaniel, who was African American, was not allowed to attend. He reportedly only agreed to go after she pleaded with him to do so. Gable remained friends with Ms. McDaniel for years, and always went to her Hollywood parties, especially when she was raising funds during World War II.

Clark was nominated for the third time for Best Actor—he again did not win—although *Gone With the Wind* won Best Picture and several other Oscars. The 1939 cinematic classic holds the record as the most financially successful movie ever made when ticket sales are adjusted for inflation.

Meanwhile, if Loretta Young had hopes that she, Judy, and Clark would be a family, they were dashed when Gable began a whirlwind love affair with Carole Lombard. She was a Liberal free spirit who threw elaborate parties and was a practical joker. Gable had met his match. "You can trust that little screwball with your life or your hopes or your weaknesses, and she wouldn't even know how to think about letting you down," Gable said. "She's more fun than anybody, but she'll take a poke at you if you have it coming and make you like it. If that adds up to love, then I love her."

The couple wed on March 29, 1939 and settled on a ranch in Encino, California. The new Mrs. Gable de-glamorized herself and tried to create domestic bliss. Though seven years his junior, Gable called Carole "Ma" and she in turn referred to him as "Pa."

In 1940, Spencer Tracy penned a lengthy complimentary article entitled "My Pal, Clark Gable" for *Screen Life* magazine. He wrote, "He's so natural, most people can't tell the difference between the on-screen Gable and the off-screen Gable. They think he's playing himself.

He is, up to a certain point…It takes a little art to be natural with a camera in front of you and a microphone over you. Gable has made a fine art of it. If you don't think he's a past master of acting, let me point out that nobody ever takes a scene away from Clark Gable."

Tracy observed of the Gable/Lombard romance, "I think one reason why he fell in love with Carole Lombard was that she had a knack for making him laugh at himself. Like sending him a ballet skirt when she heard he was going to dance in *Idiot's Delight*."

While the couple retreated to their ranch for quiet evenings alone, Gable's movie career remained hot. In 1940 he appeared in three films: *Strange Cargo*, opposite Joan Crawford, *Boom Town* with Claudette Colbert and Hedy Lamarr and *Comrade X* again with

**Carole enjoyed many of the same hobbies as Clark**

Lamarr. Lombard was always suspicious of the attention he gave to other leading ladies. "Yes, I've been known to like ladies...and I do," Gable said in his defense. "But with her, it's different. Everything about her is different than with any other gal."

The following year, the actor starred in *They Met in Bombay*, wherein he and Rosalind Russell played rival jewel thieves on the run in India. Next, he made the western *Honky Tonk* alongside rising star Lana Turner. But the young blonde starlet repeatedly flubbed her lines during rehearsals. Gable complained, "She couldn't read lines. She didn't make them mean anything; it was obvious she was an amateur."

Carole was uncomfortable with the sultry love scenes Gable and Turner filmed, so she stormed the set in order to supervise. Intimidated, Lana would retreat to her dressing room until Mrs. Gable cooled off. Supposedly, Lombard had even taken up her concerns with studio boss Louis B. Mayer, asking him to speak with Turner about her flirtatious behavior. Carole was certain Lana and her husband were sleeping together. Unable to conceive a child and grappling with a husband with a roving eye, Carole set aside her personal disappointments and focused on her new film *To Be Or Not To Be* and agreed to go on the road selling war bonds—in place of Gable—who was the studio's first choice for the job.

Before embarking on the war bonds selling tour in her native Indiana, Carole placed a buxom blonde mannequin in their bed with a note reading, "So you won't be lonely." Clark had a male mannequin made up to present to Carole upon her return.

Astonishingly, Lombard managed to raise over $2 million—an enormous sum in 1942 dollars.

But instead of traveling back West via train, she got impatient and insisted on flying. (It was rumored that Gable was getting cozy with his co-star Lana Turner while filming *Somewhere I'll Find You*). On January 16, 1942, TWA Flight 3 crashed into the side of a mountain in Nevada, killing all 22 people on board, including Carole and her mother. A melted down ruby brooch pinned to her clothing was all that clearly identified the gorgeous blonde's charred remains. It had been a gift from her husband. Gable put the remnants in a locket he wore everyday.

"He was never the same," said actress Esther Williams. "He had been devastated by Carole's death."

Although at age 40, Clark was a bit old for military service, given the ultimate sacrifice his wife had made, Gable didn't feel that he personally had done enough to fulfill his patriotic duty. So he dispatched a telegram to President Franklin D. Roosevelt asking for a role in the war effort. The President replied, "STAY WHERE YOU ARE."

However, the bereaved actor ignored the admonition of the Commander-in-Chief and enlisted in the U.S. Army Air Forces in honor of Carole. He went through the 13 week Officer Candidate school, and was trained as a photographer and aerial gunner.

At first, due to his Hollywood background, Gable was assigned to work on recruitment films at what troops derisively called "Fort Roach" — the Hal Roach Studios in Culver City, California. Other actor colleagues Ronald Reagan, Alan Ladd and Van Heflin remained out of harm's way. But Clark was sent to Polebrook, England, where he joined the 351st Bombardment Group, which began flying bombing missions over the German Third Reich.

It was rumored that Adolf Hitler offered a huge reward to anyone who was able to capture and return Gable to him alive.

Clark—along with a cameraman and sound engineer—followed the crew of a B-17, named "Ain't It Gruesome," through 24 missions, including one where the aircraft was shot up by German Focke Wulf Fw 190 fighters and lost an engine, and the crew had to bail out over a field in England when fog closed in.

During one of the missions he flew on, Clark's plane was badly damaged by flak and attacked by fighters, which knocked out one of the engines and shot up the stabilizer. In the raid on Germany, one crewman was killed and two others were wounded, and flak went through Gable's boot and narrowly missed his head. Upon learning of the close call, MGM begged the Army Air Forces to reassign its most valuable screen actor to non-combat duty. He returned stateside in November 1943 to edit a film he had made for the U.S. military called *Combat America*, which he narrated and that debuted in late 1944.

As part of his assignment to work on recruitment films, Clark Gable officially flew on five combat missions, but veterans recalled he flew on many more. He received the Air Medal and the Distinguished Flying Cross. Fellow actor Capt. Ronald Reagan signed his discharge papers.

From his service, Gable became a more humble, stoic and mature man. "I saw so much in the way of death and destruction that I realized that I hadn't been singled out for grief—that others were suffering and losing their loved ones just as I lost Ma," he said.

In 1945, the King of Hollywood returned to the silver screen in *Adventure*, opposite one of his least favorite leading ladies, Greer

Garson. Gable disliked the fanfare and detested the tag line: Gable's back and Garson's got him!

One would think that Gable and Loretta Young would have avoided each other at all costs, but in 1949 they made a film entitled *Key to the City*. While he had met Judy as a baby, the two had never spoken until she returned home from school one day—age 15—and found the actor sitting in her living room. "It was very unusual for me to be asked about myself, and particularly by a star as big as Clark Gable. It seemed strange for him to be interested in me at all. But I knew that he was, and I trusted what I felt from him," Judy wrote.

**Loretta Young and Gable**

Gable asked the teen about her interests and school, thanked her for the lovely chat, then kissed her on the forehead and left. They never met again. Judy questioned her mother for decades about her birth parents. Loretta didn't confess to being her biological mother and Gable her father until Judy was 31 years old.

Later that year, on December 20th, Gable married British socialite and actress Lady Sylvia Ashley. However, Sylvia was too high-brow for Gable's everyman persona, and they divorced in 1952. "She could be good company," Gable said. "Syl is just the social type, which I am afraid I'm not." Sylvia told the court her rationale for the split: "Mr. Gable did not want to be married to anybody. He told me he didn't wish to be married to me or anyone else."

**Wife #4 Silvia Ashley**

Afterwards he told friends that he must have been drunk when he agreed to marry her. Sylvia received $6,000 in community property, and a portion of her ex-husband's earnings for subsequent films (ten percent for the first year, and seven percent for two years thereafter). Gable was relieved his ex-wife's demand of millions of dollars in alimony was denied.

Then he found love with a blonde model he had dated in the '40s named Kathleen Williams. On June 11, 1955 they wed. Kathleen, or Kay as Clark called her, was content living at the ranch her husband once shared with Carole. Unlike Sylvia, the latest Mrs. Gable did not want to change the home in any way. "Why should I? Carole had great taste," she observed.

Gable continued to make successful screen appearances in the 1950s, including the racecar drama *To Please a Lady*, with Barbara Stanwyck. The Technicolor stunner *Mogambo* was filmed in 1953 alongside Ava Gardner and Grace Kelly. The story was a remake of 1932's *Red Dust*, in which Gable had starred alongside Jean Harlow and Mary Astor.

**With Ava Gardner in *Mogambo*. Clark still had big screen appeal.**

Next, he made *The Tall Men* opposite Jane Russell. She and her husband Robert Waterfield had founded their own production company—Russ-Field Corp.—and recruited Gable to co-produce their next film as a team.

Gable established Gabco Productions, Ltd and took the first production on location to St. George, Utah. Clark starred in the film, called *The King and Four Queens*. Barbara Nichols and Eleanor Parker served as the blonde eye candy. The film was not well received by the public. Gable decided to quit while he was behind and shelved the idea of producing any more motion pictures.

In 1958 the actor made the World War II submarine drama *Run Silent, Run Deep* with Burt Lancaster. Later in the year, Gable appeared in the romantic comedy *Teacher's Pet* co-starring Gig Young, Mamie Van Doren, and Doris Day—the latter assuming the role of Gable's much younger love interest. Clark played the city editor of a metropolitan daily newspaper that rudely turns down Day's invitation to speak to her night-school writing class. He goes undercover as a student in her class and the two wind up teaching each other the merits of their different approaches to journalism.

As television was coming onto the American scene, Gable started to receive offers to appear in TV series, but rejected them outright. At 57, he opined, "Now it's time I acted my age."

His next two films were light comedies. *But Not For Me* teamed the actor with Carroll Baker. *It Started in Naples* put the actor in an Italian cast with the sizzling Sophia Loren.

**With Marilyn Monroe**

Clark's final film, *The Misfits*, was released posthumously. Gable had performed his own stunts, endured the scorching heat of the Nevada desert and tolerated Marilyn Monroe's chronic lateness on the set.

On November 6, 1960, Judy Lewis' 25th birthday, Gable was rushed to the hospital after suffering a heart attack.

"I've asked myself so many times why I didn't just ask my mother point-blank that night if Clark Gable was my father," Judy wrote. "But at the time I felt to do so would have threatened the happy family facade and forced my mother to confess to her 'mortal sin'…We were a family of avoidance."

The legendary actor succumbed ten days later on November 16, 1960—Judy's daughter's first birthday—the grandchild he never knew. Gable is entombed in Forest Lawn Memorial Park beside his beloved Carole Lombard. His widow Kay, in a classy gesture, saw to it that his wishes were respected in this regard.

To add to the tragedy, Kay Gable was expecting their first child together. John Clark Gable was born on March 20, 1961 in the same hospital in which his father had died. Louella Parsons served as god-mother—a woman who had turned a blind eye to the birth of Gable's first child, having not challenged the adoption story—which was out of character for the cutthroat columnist.

Kay released a memoir about her life with Gable in which she expressed a very sexist view of marriage, "I keyed my life entirely to his needs…I believe an important part of marriage for a woman is in doing what her husband wants. So I stocked up on hunting clothes, long, warm underwear, slickers and boots, and wherever he went, I went. I learned to shoot and fish and play golf," she wrote. Mother and child made the rounds with the press garnering sympathy that first-born Judy would never receive.

In August 1961, Jill Winkler Rath, the widow of Otto Winkler, the publicist killed in the Lombard plane crash, sued the Gable estate for $100,000. She claimed Gable promised to pay her a sum of money as compensation for "inducing her husband to accompany Miss Lombard." She alleged Gable had promised her money if she agreed not to file suit against TWA for negligence in the downed flight. Mrs. Rath dropped the suit but re-filed a year later. A Los Angeles Superior Court dismissed the case. Mrs. Rath later learned Gable had settled a claim against the airline for a mere $10 to make the unrest die down.

**Judy Lewis, daughter of Clark Gable, with her mother Loretta Young**

Not until 1994 was it finally publically revealed that Loretta Young's adopted daughter Judy Lewis was actually Loretta and Clark's biological daughter. Upon release of Judy's autobiography in 1994, Loretta disowned her daughter and the two never spoke again. Loretta Young finally confessed the

**Wife #5 Kay Williams**

truth about Judy to her biographer and requested the book be published after her death, which occurred on August 12, 2000.

Judy reflected, "If I could talk to him now, I'd say, 'where were you when I needed you? Why did you stay away?' Then of course, I'd tell him how much I missed him." Despite a tumultuous upbringing, Judy earned Bachelor's and Master's degrees in clinical psychology and worked as a psychotherapist, actress, and producer until her death from cancer on November 25, 2011.

As of the publishing of this book, John Clark Gable does not acknowledge Judy Lewis as his half-sister. His son, Clark James Gable was a one-time host of the reality show *Cheaters*. He passed away unexpectedly in February 2019, age 30.

Clark Gable may have had an average Joe persona, but the mundane was extraordinary whenever he was involved. Fans worshipped him; fellow actors admired him. Yet Gable could never understand what all the fuss was about. "You know, this King stuff is pure bullshit...There's no special light that shines inside me and makes me a star. I'm just a lucky slob from Ohio...On my tombstone they should write, 'He was lucky and he knew it.'"

# 2.
# CAROLE LOMBARD:
## *Unorthodox Angel*

CAROLE LOMBARD — BLONDE, TRIM, WITH CHEEKBONES THAT could cut through glass, was not just another pretty face in the constellation of movie stars. Her passion in life was to make people laugh. Indeed, her screwball comedies *My Man Godfrey* and *Nothing Sacred* secured a loyal contingent of fans eager for escapism during the bleakest years of the Great Depression. Despite her movie star status, Miss Lombard had the common touch and often preferred the company of the prop and cameramen to that of her fellow celebrities. She never forgot a birthday. She threw elaborate parties and played practical jokes, and her Madcap persona made her the queen of the comedy.

A rare feminist during the studio era, she went toe to toe with domineering producers and directors. She was protective of colleagues and would refuse to appear in a film if a favored cameraman or grip didn't get hired. She kept up with the boys. Ever the tomboy, she enjoyed fishing and hunting, drinking and became infamous for her swearing and dirty jokes. Friends dubbed the paradoxical Lombard the "Profane Angel." In 1939 she married Hollywood's most desired man—Clark Gable—and the two became the most talked about couple in the movies. Three years later, Lombard would be dead, killed in the service of her country.

She was born Jane Alice Peters on October 6, 1908 in Fort Wayne, Indiana in the home of parents Frederick Peters and Elizabeth "Bessie" Knight. The city is located less than 20 miles west of the Ohio border, and at the turn of the 20th century, its heartbeat was the urban working class, many of whom immigrated from Ireland and Germany. It was in this city that the domestic refrigerator was invented in 1913.

A spunky child, Jane played stickball with the neighborhood kids and her older siblings Stuart and Frederick. Her athleticism ran the gamut from playing ball to dancing. She tried her hand at acting in the school production of *The Talking Dog*.

With her soft blonde hair and blue eyes, the child was a budding beauty, and her mother set out to turn her little tomboy into a movie star. In 1914, Frederick and Elizabeth's marriage came to a sudden end. Mother and children headed to Los Angeles. Jane was an avid volleyball and tennis player who also went out for broad jumping and swimming and appeared in the school play *Pauvre Sylvie*.

Their next-door neighbors, the Kaufmans, knew some people in the film industry. Silent film director Allan Dwan was visiting one day when he spotted young Jane playing baseball in the street, and asked her if she would like a small role in his upcoming film *A Perfect Crime*. The 12-year-old jumped at the chance, vowing the movie wouldn't be her last. Throughout junior and high school, she took acting and dancing lessons, auditioning like crazy for more movie roles. She also had a brief stint with a theater troupe.

The aspiring actress attended Fairfax High School and was on the track team. She frequented the Coconut Grove nightclub dancing the Charleston. Stories vary as to how her first film contract came to fruition. Some say a talent scout spotted her at a dinner party, others cite the Coconut Grove as the place of discovery. However, in all likelihood mother Elizabeth contacted columnist Louella Parsons who arranged for the young girl to have a screen test at Fox Pictures. In October 1924, Jane was signed to a $75 a week contract and dropped out of high school. Jane's name was changed to Carol Lombard.

The following March, the newly dubbed Carol took the lead role in the motion picture *Marriage in Transit*, opposite Edmund Lowe. Then she appeared in a forgettable Western entitled *Hearts and Spurs* with Charles "Buck" Jones. It was filmed on location near Barstow, California. She was soon told that the director, W.S. Van Dyke, hated tardiness to the set. So the next day, Miss Lombard arrived early. She waited and waited. Finally the director appeared on set. Van Dyke angrily confronted Jones, also tardy. Just then, the director pulled out a pistol and shot Jones, who fell to the ground. Carol ran to the river for water as requested. Upon her return, she found a very jovial Jones and Van Dyke laughing at her naïveté.

She then appeared in *Durand of the Bad Lands*, *The Road to Glory* and had a small uncredited role as a shop girl in the Mary Pickford vehicle *My Best Girl*. But the roles were bit parts and years later she bemoaned, "All I had to do was simper prettily at the hero and scream with terror when he battled with the villain."

Carol decided to add an "e" to the end of her name. Media at the time reported the change was due to the actress' interest in numerology. However, she told writer/director Garson Kanin, "That's a lot of bunk."

Carole was a student of numerology and adhered to the Bahá'í faith. She was a second-generation follower of the Middle Eastern religion that promotes peace among religions, and individual—not group—worship.

"I don't seem to get solemn about it (religion) and some people might not understand," she reflected. "That's why I never talk about it. I think it's all here in the mountains and the desert. I don't think God is a softie, either. In the end, it's better if people are forced back into—well—into being right, before they're too far gone. I think your temple is your everyday living."

While in a car stopped at a red light, the vehicle in front of her kicked into reverse, causing the windshield to shatter. Carole's face was damaged from broken glass. The wound needed 14 stitches during a four-hour-long operation, which she endured without anesthesia. While taking a hiatus from filming, Carole read up on the art of photography, and soon was quite knowledgeable about the best ways to conceal the scar in photographs.

After a year of recovery, Carole took a screen test for Mack Sennett, the man credited for pioneering slapstick comedy films. Miss Lombard secured a film contract and was added to the roster of Sennett's Bathing Beauties—young women who paraded in swim attire for short films and public appearances. Between September 1927 and March 1929, the actress made 15 short flicks.

**Carole at the beach in 1929**

Sennett films were distributed by Pathé Exchange, an independent movie production company that decided to put Lombard in a few of their prominent pictures.

Carole's big break came in the form of Raoul Walsh's

1928 *Me, Gangster*. "While Carole was busy dodging pies all day at the studio, she spent her evenings evading the disapproval of her mother and the ire of two brothers," Dave Keen wrote in *Silver Screen* magazine. "When she finally received an offer from Fox to do a lead in '*Me, Gangster*,' the family ceased their schoolroom campaign and decided to let little sister have her way about the movie nonsense."

Proving herself a capable and charming starlet, she was cast in her first talkie, 1929's *High Voltage*, wherein Lombard played felon Billie Davis. When the bus gets stuck in a blizzard, she and the other jailbirds take advantage of the situation. Other films followed that year, including *Big News* alongside Robert Armstrong. The two played married reporters working for rival papers, and one of them is brought up on murder charges. Lombard and Armstrong reteamed for *The Racketeer*, which featured an early performance from Hedda Hopper in her pre-columnist days.

While never a fan of her work in Westerns, Carole teamed with popular actor Warner Baxter for 1930's *The Arizona Kid*, which proved a boon to her already irradiating career. Later that summer, she appeared in *Fast and Loose* (the first time the actress' name was spelled Carole with an "e") alongside Miriam Hopkins.

In early 1931, Carole made the comedy *It Pays to Advertise*. She was then signed for the film *Man of the World*, written by Herman J. Mankiewicz. In the role, Carole played an American in Paris who is wined and dined by a writer who is merely using her to get at her uncle. William Powell played the dastardly scribe. Lombard teamed up again with the suave Powell for *Ladies Man*, released only a few months later. The young starlet had fallen in love with her co-star, the top male star on the Paramount lot.

### The Odd Couple

Polished, urbane and intellectual, William Horatio Powell was the antithesis of the fun-loving, rough around the edges Lombard. Powell was born in Pittsburgh, Pennsylvania in 1892 and grew up in Kansas City, Missouri.

"I got my first taste of the drama while at Kansas City Central High School," Powell told a reporter. "I appeared in the school's Christmas plays. The first play was *The Rivals*, the second *Captain Jack Absolute*. I was the heart interest in both of them and the girls told me I was a knockout. I believed them!...All ambitions for practicing law vanished with the first curtain call. I burned to act."

After high school, Powell enrolled at the University of Kansas

**Carole with William Powell**

but the stage called him to New York City. In 1920 he made it to Broadway and was offered a film role in 1922's *Sherlock Holmes*. He found his niche playing the villain. His break-through role came in the form of the 1929 flick *The Canary Murder Case*, where he played detective Philo Vance.

Despite a brief courtship and the 16 year age gap, on June 26, 1931 Lombard and Powell got married. Powell's first marriage to Eileen Wilson lasted 15 years, and produced a son named William Powell, Jr. Lombard told *Motion Picture* magazine, "The whole explanation of our marriage and our happiness is that we understand one another," she explained. "I can't see the sense in these so-called modern-marriage pacts, talking things over, planning what one will do in this or that emergency, making charts of emotions. After all, emotional matters cannot be charted. If there is perfect understanding between two people, what is there to plan about?"

Carole settled into her role as doting wife and stepmother. She read the books Powell liked, cooked and cleaned and told friends she planned to spend only a few more years in the movie business before retiring. Powell showered his bride with lavish gifts including star sapphire and diamond jewelry as well as a new Cadillac for Christmas. Carole's mother approved of the union, hoping Powell's sophistication would polish her diamond in the rough daughter. Marrying one of the top movie stars in the country also helped Carole land more movie roles and magazine covers and she enjoyed success with the films *Up Pops the Devil* and *I Take This Woman*.

Lombard kept busy appearing in several movies yearly and was cast in the 1932 romantic drama *No Man of Her Own* opposite Clark Gable in their only film together. The pair sizzled on screen and the motion picture was hailed as Lombard's finest to that point. But Lombard and Gable's relationship was merely professional—their fairy tale romance still years away.

Next, Carole starred in the horror film *Supernatural*, wherein she played a woman possessed by a spirit. *White Woman*, alongside Charles Laughton, followed. But after only two years of wedded life, Powell and Lombard amicably ended their marriage, citing career conflicts. In actuality, the duo had little in common. Biographer Robert D. Matzen described the mismatch. Powell went around "in elite, intellectual circles while Carole bummed around much of the time, giggling with Fieldsie (her secretary/best friend Madalynne Field Lang), salting every sentence with a 'shit' or a 'fuck.'"

In Kanin's memoirs he noted Carole's eagerness to play the part of perfect wife. Carole told Kanin her union with Powell was "when I learned how to put a house together...and how to take care of his clothes...I was the best fuckin' wife you ever saw...a ladylike wife. Because that's how Philo [Powell] wanted it."

Lombard hadn't fit in with Powell's friends, particularly acting buddies Ronald Coleman and Richard Barthelmess, who alongside Powell were known as the "Three Musketeers."

After her divorce from Powell, Lombard bought a Dutch-style home she famously had decorated by her friend William "Billy" Haines, a former film star turned interior designer and antique dealer. In 1933, he had been arrested for public displays of homosexuality.

**Ms. Lombard was a homebody at heart who loved animals**

MGM studio boss Louis B. Mayer told Haines he had to marry a woman or never make another picture again. Haines told Mayer he already regarded himself married to his partner Jimmie Shields, a relationship that lasted almost 50 years.

Lombard's home was Haines' first project, and he enjoyed a patronage from friends such as Joan Crawford and Marion Davies. Haines decorated Lombard's home in a Grecian style with the drawing room done in six shades of blue.

Carole's career continued with the screwball comedy *20th Century* opposite John Barrymore. The movie was directed and produced by Howard Hawks, Carole's second cousin.

In the motion picture *20th Century* circa 1934, Carole played Lily Garland opposite a man she greatly admired, John Barrymore. After the movie's completion, Barrymore gave Carole an autographed picture that read, "To the finest actress I have worked with, bar none." William Fleming of *Shadowplay* magazine said of her film performance, "When you see her, you'll forget the rather restrained and somewhat stilted Lombard of old. You'll see a star blaze out of this scene and that scene, high spots Carole never dreamed of hitting."

## A Second Chance At Love

Lombard re-entered the dating scene, stepping out with screenwriter Robert Riskin, known for writing the films *It Happened One Night* and *Mr. Deeds Goes to Town*. In September 1933, the couple spent an evening at the Coconut Grove. The actress was enchanted by a 25-year-old budding star by the name of Russ Columbo. The next day, she received a dozen yellow roses from the crooner.

Columbo could sing, play the violin and compose music. With his wavy black hair, smoldering good looks and silky baritone, Columbo arrived in Hollywood just as the sound era began, and appeared in films with Gary Cooper, Fay Wray, Franchot Tone, Constance Cummings and Constance Bennett. His credits include *Moulin Rouge*, *Wake Up and Dream* and *Men Without Fear*. His biggest hit songs were *I Can't Do Without You* and *You Call It Madness, I Call It Love*. Universal studios saw Columbo as the next Bing Crosby.

In the first part of 1934, Columbo secured a prime-time radio program that aired on NBC Sunday nights from the famed Roosevelt Hotel in Hollywood. Introduced as "the Romeo of songs, here with songs to delight your ears and heart," Russ would open with the greeting "Good evening, my friends," followed by his theme, *You Call It Madness*, followed by his superb performances of songs like *All of Me*, and plugs for material from current films. Columbo was earning a reputed $500,000 a year—when $50 a week was considered a living wage.

But gossip columnist Hedda Hopper questioned the singer's masculinity, and Carole's involvement with him, insolently claiming "the couple's relationship was based on many things—but not sex." Hopper cited a number of traits which she regarded as unmanly, including the fact that Russ spent time combing his hair and getting a suntan, as well as his habit of carrying around a pocket-mirror to check his appearance.

Carole Lombard was utterly devoted to Russ and tried to help him in his movie career. She invited Columbo to visit sets to observe the film making process and gave him pointers on acting. He repaid this favor by coaching her on the two songs she had to sing in the movie *White Woman*.

Columbo and Lombard could be seen dining and dancing at nightclubs most Wednesday nights.

Russ was eager to marry the glamorous blonde movie star, but she demur-

**Carole adored Russ Columbo**

red. They dated off-and-on throughout 1934, with him also being seen publicly with actress Sally Blane, Loretta Young's sister.

Carole continued seeing Robert Riskin, finding the older man intellectually stimulating. Yet Carole and Russ remained close, believing eventually the two might marry. However, Russ Columbo's promising career and romance with Lombard came to a tragic end on September 2, 1934.

Only two nights before, Carole Lombard had accompanied Russ to the premiere of his first starring film, *Wake Up and Dream*, on Friday, August 31, 1934. On Sunday, Columbo went to the home of a photographer friend named Lansing Brown, Jr. The official version of events is that while sitting across from each other at a desk, Brown struck a match against a Civil War-era percussion-cap and ball pistol, which was used as a paperweight.

According to Brown, "I had a match in my hand and when I clicked, evidently the match caught in between the hammer and the firing pin. There was an explosion. Russ slid to the side of his chair."

When asked by police to demonstrate, Brown held the pistol in his right hand, pulled back the hammer on the weapon, stuck the tip of a wooden match between the hammer and the firing pin and then lowered the hammer of the pistol to supposedly ignite the match. The flare of the match exploded a percussion cap and the gun sent a bullet into Russ Columbo's face. (*Who lights a match that way?*)

"I had the pistol in my hand, snapping the trigger with my thumb and not actually paying much attention to what I was doing," Brown claimed. "I don't know how or why I got the match under the hammer. All I know is that there was the explosion...that's all I remember."

Lansing Brown was never charged, even with involuntary manslaughter.

Brown claimed he had purchased several pistols from an antique store years before and had never bothered to check to see if they were loaded. The bullet struck Columbo in his left eye, lodging in his brain. Surgeons were unable to remove the bullet and the handsome crooner was dead at the age of 26.

The scenario Lansing Brown described was so implausible, the Hollywood rumor mill decreed that Brown and Columbo were lovers and Columbo may have sealed his fate when he announced that he and Lombard were to marry. The truth will never be known as all three took their story to their graves.

At the time of the shooting, Carole was at her Lake Arrowhead cottage with her secretary. Her mother called and told her the news. Lombard flew to his side, but it was too late. She issued a statement saying in part "we planned to have a late supper tonight with my mother and brother at my home. His death shocks me beyond words."

Carole made the funeral arrangements and presented herself as a grieving widow. A believer in fate, the actress said, "I believe that Russ' death was predestined. And I am glad that it came when he was so happy—so happy in our love and in his winning of stardom."

Two day's before the accident, Russ' mother suffered a heart attack and it was decided that she not be told of her son's demise. Carole agreed to go along with the plan. She and family members had telegrams sent to Mrs. Columbo signed from Russ. Rosemary Clooney later bought Brown's house. She suspected Columbo's spirit haunted the premises.

Carole resumed her relationship with Riskin and appeared in a string of films ranging from the gangster comedy *The Gay Bride* to dance pictures *Bolero* and *Rumba*. The actress was paired with Fred MacMurray for *Hands Across the Table*. The next film she released in March 1936 and was entitled *Love Before Breakfast*. It had Preston Foster and Cesar Romero vying for her love. Two months later her next flick exploded at the box office. *The Princess Comes Across* teamed her again with MacMurray. Lombard played a woman from Brooklyn posing as a Swedish princess, styled after MGM's elusive megastar Greta Garbo.

Over at Universal Studios, ex-husband William Powell had signed on to star in a motion picture based on a pulp novel that was published in the May and June editions of *Liberty* magazine. Originally entitled "Irene, the Stubborn Girl," the novel was published in book form and re-titled *My Man Godfrey*.

A glamour pose

The story poked fun at the ultra-rich and their hedonistic ways that continued through the Great Depression. Irene Bullock, played by Lombard, partakes in a scavenger hunt wherein she must find "a forgotten man."

Irene brings down and out Godfrey, played by Powell, back to the party. Feeling sorry for him, he is hired as the family's butler. Godfrey in reality is a Boston blueblood now left broke after the stock market crash. Irene and Godfrey form a bond that leads to a romance. Constance Bennett was originally planned for the role of Irene, but Powell refused to do the movie unless Carole was cast as his leading lady.

*My Man Godfrey* received six Oscar nods, including Lombard being nominated in the Best Actress category, but she lost to Luise Rainer for *The Great Ziegfeld*. Powell was nominated for Best Actor, and lost to Paul Muni for *The Story of Louis Pasteur*.

Powell then introduced Lombard to his agent, Myron Selznick, who was known to negotiate lucrative movie contracts for his clients.

By 1937, Carole was earning $500,000 yearly. Because of the high tax rate of the era, 80 percent of her salary went to taxes, but the outspoken actress came out publically in favor of the system. President Franklin D. Roosevelt sent her a letter of gratitude for her patriotic stance.

*Swing High, Swing Low* was her third pairing with MacMurray, who played an aspiring trumpeter who meets and falls for Carole's character while visiting Panama. Next, David O. Selznick cast Lombard in her first and only color film. *Nothing Sacred* teamed the actress opposite Fredric March, who played New York newspaper reporter Wally Cook, a man sent to Vermont to interview Hazel Flagg, played by Lombard, who pretends to be dying of radium poisoning. Thinking the story will boost newspaper sales, the story is published, leading to Flagg receiving a parade in her honor, and the key to the city.

Next, the actress starred in her last film for Paramount, the offbeat *True Confession* alongside John Barrymore and Fred MacMurray. Lombard's character is a compulsive liar who confesses to a murder. She then made a movie for Warner Brothers called *Fools For Scandal*, which was regarded as the worst film of her career. It was the only movie she made in 1938, as she was taking time off to be with the new love interest in her life—Clark Gable.

**Her Man Gable**

An Ohio native, Gable was a day laborer turned Broadway actor turned Academy Award winning leading man. Several versions about where the two began their romance have been offered through the years, but the prevailing story is the pair's romance was sparked at a Valentine's Day "white-themed" party given by the Countess di Frasso in 1936. According to gossip columnist Louella Parsons, the couple "danced and looked very cozy." But they had a fight that night, and the next morning, two doves awakened Gable. Carole had paid the hotel clerks to release the birds in Gable's room as a peace offering.

Lombard knew of Gable's love for fast cars, so for Valentine's Day, she had a decrepit old Model-T Ford painted white with big red hearts all over it. Carole had it delivered to the MGM lot where Clark was working. A note on the steering wheel said, "You're driving me crazy." Being a good sport, he went along with the joke, and picked Carole up for a date that night in the car. They chugged down Hollywood Boulevard at ten miles per hour, laughing all the way.

Soon the free-spirited liberal and the blue-collar Republican were seen all over town at nightclubs, the horse track, skeet shoot ranges and movie premieres. Carole realized her new boyfriend was nothing more than a big kid who liked fast cars and gadgets—and she set out to fulfill the role as not only his lover but also surrogate mother.

While Gable was still married to second wife Ria Langham, the pair flaunted their romance. Carole appeared on the cover of countless movie magazines and received sacks full of fan mail. She landed the cover and lead story in *Life* magazine the week of October 17, 1938, largely due to her glittering romance with Gable. Writer Noel F. Busch summed up the box office sensation thusly:

"Salient quality of Carole Lombard is superfluity of nervous en-

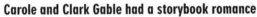

**Carole and Clark Gable had a storybook romance**

ergy. She gets up too early, plays tennis too hard, wastes time and feeling on trifles and drinks Coca-Colas the way Samuel Johnson used to drink tea. She is a scribbler on telephone pads, inhibited nail-nibbler, toe-scuffler, pillow-grabber, head-and-elbow scratcher, and chain cigaret [sic] smoker. When Carole Lombard talks, her conversation, often brilliant, is punctuated by screeches, laughs, growls, gesticulations and the expletives of a sailor's parrot."

But not every publication overlooked the fact that many Hollywood power couples were married to other people. Kirtley Baskette penned an article for *Photoplay* magazine in December 1938 called "Hollywood's Unmarried Husbands and Wives." Baskette criticized these couples, writing, "They build houses near each other, buy land in bunches, take up each other's hobbies, father or mother each other's children—even correct each other's clothes—each other's personalities!" Feeling the heat from the press, and Carole eager to become the next Mrs. Gable, the two got the green light to proceed with wedding plans after Gable's wife agreed to a divorce.

## The Marriage of the Century

On March 29, 1939 Clark and Carole drove to Kingman, Arizona to elope. Gable's publicist, Otto Winkler, phoned MGM publicity man Howard Strickling who was told to plan a press conference at Lombard's home for the following day. But Carole couldn't shake a building fear. The couple had announced their engagement to Louella Parson, promising the columnist exclusive coverage of their nuptials.

While driving back to Los Angeles, a panicky Lombard forced Gable to pull into the nearest gas station so she could phone the columnist. Unable to reach her, Lombard phoned Louella's best friend, and mistress of newspaper mogul William Randolph Hearst, Marion Davies. Davies was furious at Gable and Lombard's perceived betrayal and recommended they send Louella and Hearst a telegram, which they eagerly did, with the simple message, "Married this afternoon. Carole and Clark." Ms. Parsons was livid to find the telegram on her desk the next day. By then, the scoop about the marriage was old news.

Over the summer, Mr. and Mrs. Gable bought a modest 20-acre ranch in the San Fernando Valley. Preferring quiet evenings at home, the couple's lifestyle bordered on reclusive. Ma and Pa, as they referred to each other, tended their farm, went hunting and fishing and played tennis. Journalist Faith Baldwin even commented, "[Carole] can handle a shotgun as easily as a lipstick."

Carole's closest friends were tennis player Alice Marble, press agent Russell Birdwell and best pal Madalynne Field Lang.

More than anything, Carole longed for motherhood. The actress claimed only three days a month she did not bleed. "God has me built backwards," She said. "There's only a couple of days a month I'm not bleeding."

Despite seeking the opinion of specialists, Lombard was deemed unable to have children. When Carole learned David Selznick bought the movie rights to Margaret Mitchell's popular novel, she encouraged Clark to lobby for a role.

It was to be the first feature film in color, and entitled *Gone With the Wind*. A year in the works, a drawn-out talent search employed the

**Clark and Carole loved their rural home and gardens**

public to aid in the casting of Rhett Butler and Scarlett O'Hara. Gary Cooper, the first choice for Rhett said, "Gone With The Wind is going to be the biggest flop in Hollywood history. I'm glad it'll be Clark Gable who's falling flat on his nose, not me."

Clark had reservations about taking the role, saying, "There are going to be six million eyes on me, all daring me to fail." India-born British actress Vivien Leigh won the role of fiery Southern belle Scarlett O'Hara. Leslie Howard, and Olivia de Havilland co-starred. It ran nearly four hours, yet went on to sell more tickets than any other motion picture in history. With a budget of $4 million, it has made $400 million in profits and remains one of the most popular films ever made.

Deep down, Carole had coveted the role of Miss O'Hara, but kept any disappointment to herself, as she appeared on her husband's arm at the film's premiere—decked out in her finest furs and jewels. The couple greatly wanted to shoot another movie together. They never got the chance.

Carole made two films in 1939, gravitating towards dramatic roles. *Made For Each Other* opposite James Stewart showed the less glorious side of whirlwind marriage. The plot of *In Name Only*, co-starring Cary Grant, mirrored her real-life experience of being in love with a married man. Lombard hoped her performance in 1940s's *Vigil in the Night* would earn her an Oscar nomination, but the Academy overlooked her work. Moviegoers preferred Carole in screwball settings, not in tearjerker roles. *They Knew What They Wanted*, a flick directed by friend Garson Kanin, lost almost $300,000 at the box office.

In 1940, Clark underwent surgery on his shoulder in Baltimore. Carole traveled with him, and before they returned home, both were invited to personally speak with President Roosevelt.

Later that year, Lombard was offered the lead role in a melodrama, *Smiler with a Knife*, to be directed by newcomer Orson Welles, but the project never got off the ground. Welles turned his attention to his pet project *Citizen Kane*. Carole accepted the lead in the comedy, *Mr. and Mrs. Smith*, with Robert Montgomery and Gene Raymond.

Alfred Hitchcock directed the motion picture—one of the few comedies in his career, claiming it was done only as a favor to Lombard. Tensions were high on the set; nevertheless, Carole drove around the set on a motor scooter and played practical jokes.

When she learned Hitchcock considered all actors to be "cattle," she had a small corral built on the sound stage that housed three cows. They had on nameplates that read: Raymond, Montgomery, and

Lombard. Also, Hitchcock appeared on camera, and Carole decided to direct him in his scene. She teased him about his posture and told him to "give" more in his performance—all while sitting in his director's chair, of course.

In 1941, Lombard had secured a role in the Ernst Lubitsch dark comedy *To Be or Not to Be*. Despite her minor role, she received top billing over co-star Jack Benny. The motion picture satirized the Nazi takeover of Poland.

After the bombing of Pearl Harbor on December 7, 1941, pacifist Carole decided to join the war effort. Gable was named chairman of the Hollywood Victory Committee. The government got in touch with MGM, requesting that stars agree to make personal appearances selling war bonds. It was decided either Clark Gable or Mickey Rooney would be sent on the road for the fundraiser. Presidential adviser Harry Hopkins suggested the bond drive kick off in the Midwest and selected Ohio-born Gable over New Yorker Rooney to be the featured celebrity. Gable balked at the prospect of making the grueling sojourn.

Carole tried to persuade her husband to make the trip, but he cited a fear of crowds and lack of salesmanship. Lombard decided to go in his place, traveling to her home state of Indiana to sell war bonds. She invited her mother Elizabeth Peters and press agent Otto Winkler. The tour was set for January 1942 with the party set to arrive back home right before the premiere of *To Be or Not to Be*.

Biographer Robert Matzen claims Lombard angrily confronted Gable the night before her trip about rumors he was having an affair with his 21-year-old co-star Lana Turner on the set of their movie *Somewhere I'll Find You*. Despite life-long denials from Turner, several friends and one of Lombard's nephews confirmed the allegation.

### Heads or Tails

On January 12, 1942 the crew set out for Indianapolis, making stops in major cities such as Salt Lake City and Chicago. In Indianapolis, the movie star sold over $2 million worth of bonds in only one hour's time in the first statewide bond drive in the nation. The actress was warmly received by the crowd, gave a short speech and led a rendition of *The Star-Spangled Banner*. She concluded: "Before I say goodbye to you all—come on—join me in a big cheer—V for Victory!"

Despite her unprecedented success raising money for the war, her blow-up fight with Gable loomed heavily on her mind. Returning to California by rail would take three days, but the actress didn't want to wait until January 19th to arrive home. The morning of January

**Carole Lombard did not even like to fly, but she hurried home to be with Clark.**

16th she forced her change of plans onto her traveling companions.

Lombard told her mother and Winkler they would be flying home instead, despite their fear of airplanes. Winkler's wife later claimed he had a premonition of being killed in a plane crash. When Elizabeth Peters learned the party's intended flight was TWA Flight 3 leaving Indianapolis, she professed the unlucky quality of the number three. Winkler suggested he toss a coin. Tails, they would proceed home by train, heads they would fly. Otto and Elizabeth lost.

The flight faced weather delays and a refueling stop in St.

Louis. With cramped quarters, Carole and her companions struggled to sleep despite near exhaustion. When Flight 3 arrived in Albuquerque, New Mexico, Carole was informed she and her party had to be bumped to make room for mail and Army men. The movie star threw a fit, citing her status as an important actress who had just raised millions of dollars for the war effort. Four passengers gave up their seats to make room.

With the plane loaded with luggage and equipment, only a finite amount of fuel was added, requiring yet another stop before the flight could make it to Burbank, California. Refueling attempts in New Mexico and Arizona were thwarted because of a lack of landing lights.

The flight stopped at what is today known as Nellis Air Force Base in Las Vegas. Once fueled, the plane took off that evening at seven minutes after seven. Pilot Wayne Williams veered the aircraft off course, his vision obstructed by cockpit lights and the fact that many airway light beacons were switched off during the war. At 7:22 p.m., a mere 32 miles from Las Vegas, the plane collided with an almost vertical rock cliff, near the top of Potosi Mountain. The point of impact was at an elevation of 7,770 feet, about 80 feet below the top of the cliff, and about 730 feet below the crest of the mountain, which has an elevation of 8,500 feet.

The tail of the plane telescoped into the nose, broke in two, and cascaded down a ravine. Elizabeth Peter's fear of the number three proved to be prophetic. All onboard were killed instantly.

**Many pieces of the wreckage remain on the mountainside today**

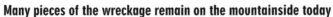

The number three had followed Carole all her life. She was the third of three children, she was Clark's third wife, married three years, and of course had perished on TWA Flight 3 at 33-years-old.

"All you could see was orange in the sky," Rex Bell Jr., the son of actors Rex Bell and Clara Bow, recalled. He was eight years old at the time of the crash and lived 65 miles away near Searchlight, N.V.

A search party formed to trek the icy conditions of the mountain and look for survivors. Gable flew to Las Vegas and waited for news. Carole was finally identified by a wisp of blonde hair, and "the contour of her face." Gable later had her recovered ruby and diamond brooch made into a locket he wore daily.

Carole Lombard's funeral was held January 21st at the Church of the Recessional at Forest Lawn Cemetery in Glendale, California. A poem, called *The Weaver*, by Grant Colfax was read at the service at her request:

*My life is but a weaving*
*Between my Lord and me;*
*I cannot choose the colors*
*He worketh steadily.*

*Oft times He weaveth sorrow*
*And I, in foolish pride,*
*Forget He sees the upper,*
*And I the under side.*

*Not til the loom is silent*
*And the shuttles cease to fly,*
*Shall God unroll the canvas*
*And explain the reason why.*

*The dark threads are as needful*
*In the Weaver's skillful hand,*
*As the threads of gold and silver*
*In the pattern He has planned.*

*He knows, He loves, He cares,*
*Nothing this truth can dim.*
*He gives His very best to those*
*Who chose to walk with Him.*

After the service, a devastated Gable sobbed, "Oh, God! I don't want to go back to an empty house."

Clark did return home, and was said to have aimlessly wandered the farm, alongside Carole's dachshund, Commissioner, who had never shown him any interest when Carole was alive. The dog and Gable now were each other's closest confidants.

Clark retreated from society, watched Carole's movies, and avoided most of his friends. The ones he did speak to said what a changed man he had become, and when he did speak, he only spoke of Carole.

**Carole Lombard was one of Hollywood's most beloved stars**

Soon after he joined the United States Army Air Force, flying on combat missions in B-17s out of Peterborough, England, functioning as both the head of an aerial film unit and as a turret gunner. On January 15, 1944, a Liberty ship was named SS Lombard in honor of Carole, and Gable attended its launch.

President Franklin Roosevelt, who admired her patriotism, declared Carole the first woman killed in the line of duty during the war and posthumously awarded her the prestigious Presidential Medal of Freedom.

Despite rumors of potential Nazi sabotage, the crash was ruled pilot error due to the pilot's use of an erroneous compass setting. It was later decided to cut the line in her final film, *To Be Or Not To Be* in which her character asks, "What can happen in a plane?" The movie was released two months after her death, to mixed reviews.

Friends were shell-shocked by her death, remembering Lombard as the firecracker who once served as honorary Mayor of Century City, California, when the first and only thing she did was declare a studio holiday and send all the workers home, much to the chagrin of studio boss David Selznick. Frederick Othman, who knew Lombard well said, "She was thoughtful, considerate, always joyous and bouncing, full of pranks and risqué stories. And she was frank to the point of treason in a land where frankness is not valued too highly."

Today, the curious can see items recovered from the crash, housed in the Lowden Veterans Center and Museum in Las Vegas. Aviation archaeologist Robb Hill recovered hair barrettes, belt buckles and even a newspaper from the scene of the accident.

Lombard's childhood home in Fort Wayne, located at 704 Rockhill Street, is now a bed & breakfast and has been made an historic site in honor of its most famous inhabitant.

Carole always planned on retiring from films in favor of becoming a housewife and mother. She asserted, "I want to live a natural life before I'm an old lady. I want to get off the pogo stick. Do you think I'd stick around this racket until they start feeling sorry for me? Not this dame. You've seen these poor devils hanging around, trying to get parts, trying to remain part of this tinseled life, trying to be 'somebody.' You won't see me there. I'm quitting at the top."

She told the press she hoped the company making her last film would advertise it as "Lombard's Farewell Appearance."

"It'll be the world's first real 'farewell appearance.' When they put that on the billboards it'll be true. When I'm set they can say good-by to Lombard. Boy, won't that be somethin.'"

# 3.

# JEAN HARLOW:
## *Kansas City Bombshell*

WITH HER PLATINUM BLONDE LOCKS, PAINTED EYE-brows, shapely hips and crimson lips, moviegoers had never experienced such a luscious figure as Jean Harlow. Her sexy and sassy movies succored the psyche of a public beaten down by the economic hardships of the Great Depression. Harlow played opportunistic vamps and social climbers who never had the luxury of education or good breeding.

Off screen, the actress was often in poor health and retreated to the watchful care of her mother "Mama Jean" or hobnobbed at swank nightclubs with her latest beau, usually men old enough to be her father. Friends recognized a child-like quality to Miss Harlow and her nickname until she died was "Baby."

A budding intellectual, Harlow was often seen with a book under her arm walking the MGM lot. When not wearing revealing dresses and négligées for film roles, she preferred wide-legged trousers and sweaters.

She was a budding novelist who longed to be taken seriously, appreciated for her kind heart and intellect and not merely for her striking alabaster beauty. The movie star loved entertaining friends. She played her records constantly, and was adept at cooking and sewing.

Harlow emerged as one of the first female stars of the talkies with her casting in Howard Hughes' multi million-dollar 1930 spectacle *Hell's Angels* in which she uttered the salacious line, "Would you be shocked if I put on something more comfortable?" Films such as *Red Dust, Dinner at Eight* and *Bombshell* solidified her standing as one of MGM's most popular and lucrative movie stars. She played opposite Clark Gable, Spencer Tracy and William Powell, the latter regarded as the love of Harlow's life.

Over eight decades after her sudden death in 1937, at the age of 26, controversy still engulfs Hollywood's first blonde bombshell. Did her much older second husband really commit suicide? Did she fraternize with dangerous mobsters? Through the ensuing decades her death has been blamed on everything from a botched abortion, sunburn, alcoholism and toxins from her hair dye.

She was born Harlean Carpenter on March 3, 1911 in Kansas City, Missouri, a bustling metropolis of around 250,000 people. She was the only child of Montclair Carpenter, a dentist, and Jean Harlow, an aspiring actress. Her parents' troubled marriage was over by 1922 and Mr. Carpenter faded from his daughter's life.

**Jean as a toddler**

The young girl whiled away summer vacations at her maternal grandparents' estate along the Missouri River. She was tenderhearted towards animals and would pull three pigs around in a red wagon. She had a pet pony, plus dogs, chickens, ducks and lambs as playmates. She and Mama Jean moved to Hollywood briefly, then settled permanently in Chicago for the girl to continue her education. At age 14, Harlean suffered her first round of lifelong health afflictions when she contracted scarlet fever while away at camp. She also suffered a year with spinal meningitis.

In 1926, Mama Jean married a crooked Sicilian businessman named Marino Bello. He lived the rest of his life off his stepdaughter's earnings, presenting himself to the press as a doting family man, who in reality was abusive to her and had ties to organized crime.

Harlean attended Ferry Hall, an all-girls school founded in 1869 in Lake Forest (a suburb of Chicago). The education was made possible by the girl's affluent grandfather.

According to "Illinois High School Glory Days," Ferry Hall was not regarded as a finishing school for wealthy society girls, as it offered a rigorous course of study, including preparatory, collegiate, and music. The prep courses offered were reading, writing, arithmetic, history, morals, and Latin.

The collegiate classes included advanced math, sciences, modern languages, philosophy, and government. Students could study science and had access to laboratories.

Mama Jean lived in nearby Waukegan, Illinois, which allowed for frequent mother/daughter visits.

By age 15, Harlean had blossomed into a beautiful young woman. Despite the attention, she preferred spending quiet evenings at home with her best friend—Mama Jean—instead of going to parties. Because Harlean was inexperienced with boys and had never had a boyfriend, fellow classmates eased up on their petty treatment of the attractive blonde.

The teen rebelled against wearing flats vowing, "I won't wear such hideous shoes; I'll go home first." Harlean kept wearing her high heels as well as lipstick, but was bullied by peers for being more sophisticated. She then became popular with classmates because of her willingness to listen to their "boy troubles" for hours on end.

She wasn't a particularly ambitious student and more often than not failed to complete her homework. But to the surprise of her instructors, Miss Carpenter aced her exams. Dramatics instructor Miss Brown cast Harlean in the annual spring play, a Shakespearian work called *The Winter's Tale* in which she played Princess Perdita.

By the time she turned 16, Harlean was no longer shy around men. A mutual friend introduced her to 19-year-old Charles F. McGrew, III, a member of a prominent Chicago family. "It was love at first sight," the actress said in a self-penned article in 1934. "From the beginning it was serious. All that summer Chuck and I were together constantly. Then we started talking of marriage. Like most youngsters who are infatuated we refused to listen to the advice of our elders."

They envisioned a Christmas wedding, but the young lovers couldn't wait. The couple wed on September 21, 1927. First the pair traveled to New York, and then took a ship through the Panama Canal to Los Angeles. Upon his 21st birthday, McGrew came into his inheritance and was able to buy a Spanish bungalow in Beverly Hills.

"There were no motion pictures, no work, no studios, in my life then...since he had inherited a comfortable income there was no necessity for him to work, so we had 24 hours in which to play. Our life was one continual party," the actress wrote in later years.

Mama Jean and Bello moved to Los Angeles and bought a house nearby the newlyweds. "Once again mother and I had the understanding, sister-like companionship of my school days," she added.

Harlean credited friend Lucille Lee with getting her in the

movie business. She offered to drive Lee to Fox Studio in order for her friend to not be late for work. It was then that Harlean was introduced to staff that gave her paperwork to fill out for work as a movie extra.

A few weeks later, she decided to return to the studio, expressing an interest in film work, but declined initial parts due to nerves. She registered at Central Casting under her mother's maiden name: Jean Harlow.

"I'll never forget the terrifying bewilderment of that first day's work. Fortunately there were dozens of other extras and my inexperience went unnoticed. It was a thrilling experience," the actress recalled.

The following week, she accepted work at Paramount and appeared in *Moran of the Marines* starring Richard Dix and Ruth Elder. In December 1928 she signed with Hal Roach Studios for $12 a day, receiving uncredited parts in early talkies. She got bit parts in Laurel and Hardy short films and made *The Saturday Night Kid* starring Clara Bow, then *The Love Parade*, a Maurice Chevalier and Jeanette Mac-Donald picture.

**Jean as a brunette**

The McGrews separated on June 11, 1929. Charles claimed his wife had posed for lewd photos and was not a proper wife; she claimed in the divorce hearing he was "profane and abusive." Looking back on the union years later Jean reflected, "Understand, I don't blame Chuck for what happened to our happiness. I blame our youth."

Jean may have gotten her heart broken by her first serious romantic relationship, but her striking looks and willingness to learn how to act provided steady employment.

The actress was released from her contract with Roach. She learned of a big-budget movie— which was garnering major publicity in the newspapers—was being re-worked. Originally filmed as a silent movie, the filmmaker felt in order for the piece to be in vogue, it needed to be re-shot with sound. Leading lady Greta Nissen had a heavy Norwegian accent, preventing her from portraying the British character, Helen. Harlow decided to test for the role, captivating the attention of an eccentric filmmaker named Howard Hughes.

## The Billionaire and the Bombshell

At just 18-years-old, Jean Harlow was cast in her first major motion picture, the most expensive film made up to that time—*Hell's Angels*. But the World War I film was a risky venture; it went obscenely over budget, was grandiose and considered the laughing stock of the movie colony. Directors quit. Millions of feet of unedited footage got scrapped. Sound was added over air footage and dialogue was re-filmed. Censors ultimately clipped an entire half hour of material from the final product.

Harlow was paid $100 a week for her work.

Hughes did some of his own flying scenes, one ending with a crash landing that resulted in broken bones. In addition, a mechanic and two stunt pilots were killed in the making of some stunt flying.

*Hell's Angels* told the story of British brothers, straight arrow Roy and cad Monte Rutledge, who decide to join the British Royal Flying Corps. Jean plays Roy's fiancée who then seduces the brother by asking, "Would you be shocked if I

**Jean with Howard Hughes**

put on something more comfortable," whereby she sheds her tight-fitting evening gown and slips into a robe. Throughout the film she wore alluring dresses with plunging necklines and went without undergarments.

The film was noted for its convincingly choreographed dog-fight skirmishes, German-led zeppelin raids over London and experimentation with a scene in Technicolor—the only known footage of

Jean with Ben Lyon in *Hell's Angels,* 1930

Jean Harlow in a color film. Sexually provocative with the inclusion of swear words, the flick was seen as risqué but moviegoers were impressed with the combat scenes and explosions, as well as the leading lady's shapely figure. Harlow received top billing on movie marquees, but in reality, her male co-stars Ben Lyon and James Hall received higher salaries.

Three years after Hughes began production on *Hell's Angels,* his first major film, the flick was released on May 24, 1930 at Grauman's Chinese Theater. Hughes, infamous for being a man who could make an entrance, brought in arc lighting to illuminate the street leading to the theater, had a fighter squadron fly overhead, and a crowd of 50,000 spectators and invited celebrities required the Los Angeles police force to bring in the National Guard.

A glamorous Harlow swept the red carpet, letting the adulation wash over her like an ocean tide. Inside the theater, however, the actress was a bundle of nerves waiting for the movie to start. "I sat through *Hell's Angels* in a cold perspiration trying to realize that the girl on the screen really was me," Harlow recalled. "I disliked the type of films in which I played that cold, hard type of girl and I didn't even see two or three of them."

While Jean's acting skills were not compared to those of Sarah

Bernhardt, the teenager's star quality was compared to that of "It" girl Clara Bow. While brunettes had been regarded as the glamour girls in film, with blondes seen as comedic relief, Harlow proved actresses with light locks could be multi-faceted entertainers and box office smashes.

Now signed to a five-year contract with Hughes at RKO, the director sent his new ingénue on the road for publicity appearances, not sure what to cast her in next. Hughes loaned Harlow out for a string of films—

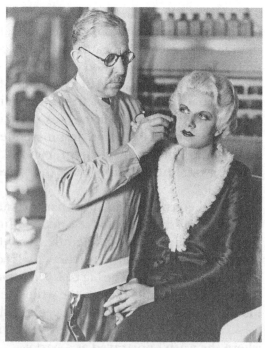

Max Factor lightened the shade of Jean's hair

seven in 1931 alone. Jean made an uncredited appearance in the film *City Lights* starring Charlie Chaplin, then had a role in the crime drama *The Secret Six* with newcomer Clark Gable, whom she would work with numerous times. The most prominent film the actress made in 1931 was the underworld saga *The Public Enemy* starring James Cagney.

The film *Iron Man* —a sports drama—and *Goldie*, a romantic drama followed. She also teamed with Spencer Tracy.

Next Harlow starred in the Loretta Young comedy *Platinum Blonde*. Originally entitled "Gallagher," Hughes convinced the producers to change the name in order to bank on the label Harlow now relished.

Women across the country went to their beauticians requesting to have their hair bleached to look like Harlow. Identifying the popularity his leading lady's image sparked, Hughes offered any hairstylist $10,000 for triumphantly matching Harlow's light hue.

But it wasn't just Jean's hair color that created her unique look. Granted, Hollywood beauty consultant Max Factor (and specifically his global creative director Pat McGrath) had lightened her hair to a platinum shade. But Factor, et al also created Jean's signature doll-like make-up style of fresh skin, fine brows, artfully emphasized Cupid's bow lips, and flirty elongated lashes. The look combined with Jean's strong screen presence to make her one of the greatest movie stars of all time and an eternal beauty icon. Harlow's look is repeatedly reinvented and referenced by today's make-up artists, designers, musicians and actresses, for the ultimate in coquettish glamour.

That summer, the actress gave an interview to a reporter who was surprised to learn Harlow was nothing like the image cultivated by Hughes and the studios. Jessie Henderson wrote, "What do you think of the European situation? You ask, just for fun. And, by gosh! She tells you. Lucidly. From there the conversation slides to books. She reads 'em."

When confronted about her unassuming manner compared to her sexpot persona, Harlow retorted, "...Just because I've been playing vamps with my clothes falling off? Darn it, that's the idea the public gets. You have no notion the letters I've received warning me as to the wickedness of my life. The big compensation is receiving other letters—chiefly from women—that say the writers feel sure I'm not like the roles I'm playing. If I were, I'd have been in jail long ago."

Harlow expressed interest in playing straight dramatic parts where she wasn't portrayed as a harlot.

"Why, I've never been mixed up with gangsters or gone smoldering around people's parlors in my life! I prefer tennis," she said in her defense.

Harlow's next picture was called *Three Wise Girls*, a drama released by Columbia. She was then loaned out for MGM's portrayal of vigilante justice in *The Beast of the City*. Impressed with the spitfire blonde's panache, MGM writer/producer Paul Bern took the actress under his guidance. Bern convinced studio executive Irving Thalberg to buy out Harlow's contract from Hughes and sign her on April 20, 1932.

Bern believed Jean a natural fit for the lead in a movie he was producing entitled *Red-Headed Woman*. Harlow donned a red wig and played the smooth criminal Lil Andrews. F. Scott Fitzgerald originally wrote the script but Thalberg recruited Anita Loos to add comedic elements to the piece, in turn completely rewriting the manuscript. The film co-starred Chester Morris, Una Merkel and Charles Boyer.

Stepfather Marino Bello acted as personal manager of Jean's career, taking credit for securing the role in *Red-Headed Woman*. Bello and Bern disliked each other, but remained cordial out of respect for the actress.

Marino Bello is reputed to have introduced Jean to mobster

Abner "Longie" Zwillman, a member of the Meyer Lansky mob, who wined and dined the starlet, buying her jewelry and a red Cadillac. It is believed Bello wanted to get in the good graces of the mobsters for protection from the feds to open a speakeasy in Manhattan and offered his sexy stepdaughter as collateral.

The flick was released in June and by then it was clear to cast and crew that Harlow and Bern had become an item. Marilyn Monroe and Arthur Miller's relationship nearly 33 years later would be reminiscent of this odd couple pairing.

Jean wed the German-born movie executive on July 2, 1932 in the home she shared with her parents. Jean was 21. Paul was 42. It was the first wedding for her MGM executive husband, but Jean wasn't his first wife.

### The First Movie Star To Survive A Scandal

The newlyweds settled into Paul's home in Benedict Canyon, located on 9820 Easton Drive in western Los Angeles. Upon marriage, Paul transferred ownership of the home to his young bride as a token of his affection. Modest by Hollywood standards, the home had a small pool and the couple had a few servants to attend to household duties.

**Jean with 2nd husband Paul Bern**

Their only documented marital quarrel centered around Jean's disdain for their house, feeling it was too secluded.

Studio chiefs and Jean's parents believed Paul was too old for the "Baby" but Jean insisted they were in love. "[Paul's] advice, wisdom and understanding were the greatest influences in my life," Jean later opined.

Harlow's over-attachment to Mama Jean made mother/daughter sleepovers a common occurrence. On the evening of September 4, 1932, two months into their marriage, Jean bid Paul farewell and left their home embarking on dinner and an overnight stay with her mother and stepfather.

As housekeeper Winifred Carmichael was leaving the Bern residence that night, on her way to meet up with Jean at the Bello home, she saw a car pull up to the house. Upon returning to the Bern home later that evening, she claimed to have heard Paul arguing with a woman at the pool saying, "get out of my life" followed by a female's scream. She discovered a wet yellow swimsuit abandoned on the patio title. A silhouette of a woman ran across the property and disappeared into a waiting car, her identity belonging to the night. Nonplussed, Winifred retired to her private quarters.

The following morning, Labor Day Monday, gardener Clifton Davis found a broken and bloodied champagne glass in the home. Worried someone had been injured, Winifred's husband John, who worked as a butler and chauffeur for Bern, went looking for the master and mistress of the house. Jean was still at her mother's home. John walked into the master bedroom and located Mr. Bern. John fainted at the sight.

Clifton then entered the room, discovering John and his employer both on the floor, and approached Bern's nude contorted body. The writer at the movie colony's most prestigious studio had sustained a fatal gunshot wound to the head.

MGM brass was called to the residence early that morning, hours before the Los Angeles Police Department was notified of the situation. Samuel Marx, an MGM producer and story editor received a phone call that morning alerting him of the discovery. When he arrived at the home he found studio head Louis. B. Mayer and producer Irving Thalberg already at the scene. Officers from MGM's private police force had also been brought in to investigate.

Head of MGM's publicity department, Howard Strickling, known as "The Fixer" along with Eddie Mannix, intercepted all personal correspondences sent out of MGM. These men made careers out of influencing public perception of MGM's stars. They withheld negative stories and released authorized material to the press. Marx considered Strickling a "press agent second, a suppress agent first."

In his 1990 book pertaining to Paul Bern's death, Marx wrote, "In an early hour of 1932's Labor Day, Strickling had to determine how Paul Bern's death would be presented to the press. It was imperative that the tragedy not cause harm to Jean Harlow—and if carried out successfully it might even enhance her career."

A handwritten letter was found on Bern's dresser, immediately labeled a suicide note. It reads:

"Dearest Dear,

"Unfortunately this is the only way to make good the frightful wrong I have done you and to wipe out my abject humiliation. I Love You. Paul." Added at the end is the haunting line, "You understand that last night was only a comedy."

While arousing, the note was not dated and not specifically addressed to Jean. Nevertheless, the press swarmed the Bello residence looking for the newly widowed Harlow. She refused to see them.

A white-washed coroner's inquest was held on September 8th in which studio executives, witnesses at the scene and Marino Bello testified, all pointing to the agreed upon scenario that Bern had killed himself and had spoken of his depression on numerous occasions. District Attorney Buron Fitts, a man who was later brought up on bribery and perjury charges, headed the inquest. Jean did not attend the hearing.

Her refusal to speak with the press and her cloistered existence caused fervor with reporters. The identity of the "veiled lady" heard and then seen leaving the premises that night also piqued the interest of the masses. Who was she?

Jean's first public appearance since Paul's death was at his funeral, held September 9th at the Grace Chapel of Inglewood Park Cemetery. Bern's remains were cremated and his ashes interred. MGM was content with burying the secrets Paul took with him to the grave, but a revelation to the media kicked the MGM "fixers" into high gear. In an interview, brother Henry Bern revealed, "Paul never married before he wedded the screen star Jean Harlow, but he lived with a woman once, a long time ago. He took care of her just the same as though she were his wife."

This damning statement could not have been forgotten no matter the amount of damage control enacted by MGM. Paul Bern had a common law wife named Dorothy Millette. She had been desperately trying to speak with Paul at the time of his death. He had been expecting her visit.

According to Samuel Marx, one afternoon Paul told him Dorothy had been in a coma for a staggering ten years. Unable to cope with her condition, Paul walked out and began a new life in California. Bern then told Marx one day Dorothy woke from her comatose state, and having no sense of time, still regarded Paul as her partner and began writing to him.

Marx believed the word coma was a euphemism for mental illness, namely schizophrenia. She and Paul had lived together in the Algonquin Hotel in New York City for five years—long enough to be regarded as a common law marriage. There is speculation that the pair may have even been married, perhaps in Canada. No records have surfaced.

In May 1932, Dorothy relocated to San Francisco and got in touch with Paul, writing to him frequently. Dorothy, a former stage actress in her late 40s, received monthly support checks from Paul. With the emergence of a common law wife, Jean Harlow now found herself embroiled in a love triangle that centered on bigamy.

Theories abounded as to what led up to the events at the home in Benedict Canyon. MGM decided to circulate the theory that Paul killed himself to spare Dorothy and Jean the shame of being attached to a bigamist. Indeed, in the early years, Samuel Marx believed the notion that Paul acted out of gallantry.

After Dorothy Millette left the Bern residence (records show in a hired car paid for by Paul), she headed for San Francisco. Upon arriving at a hotel, she put her belongings in a trunk and left it at the front desk, alerting the staff she would be back to fetch her belongings. On September 6th, she boarded the Delta King steamboat bound for Sacramento. But when the boat arrived at its destination, Dorothy was not aboard.

Police requested the Sacramento River be dredged, believing somewhere along the journey Millette went overboard, willingly or otherwise. On the morning of September 14th, a fisherman spotted a body floating facedown in the water in the area of Georgiana Slough. Local sheriff Don Cox decades later said that "As soon as the body was found, those MGM people rode into Sacramento like a thundering herd."

Dorothy's hotel room was later found ransacked with personal affects missing. Her death was quickly ruled a suicide by the coroner and she was buried in a small ceremony attended by only a handful of people, mainly reporters.

In a most peculiar turn of events, just four days before his death, Paul had applied for an $85,000 life insurance policy, to be awarded to Jean. Had he suspected the impending visit from his common law wife would bring trouble? A ruling of suicide voided the policy, and lawyers were brought in to sort through Bern's estate.

Rumors swelled. Had Jean been at the house that night, caught Paul and Dorothy in a compromising position (Paul had been found nude), and killed him in a jealous state? Had that sent Dorothy Millette running for her life, eager to get to Sacramento?

As for Millette's death, officially it was deemed suicide due to her history of mental instability, but had she killed herself out of guilt for shooting Paul? Or was Dorothy the victim of homicide, having been followed north by a hitman sent by MGM to finish the job?

Sheriff Cox had his doubts. "It's too late now, we'll never know, did she fall, did she jump, or was she pushed?" he said.

The genesis of the alleged suicide note remains turbid. Due to his involvement in the inquest and having been one of the first men at the scene of the crime, it was rumored Louis B. Mayer may have written the note. Another prevailing view is that Paul Bern had written the note weeks earlier as a way of apologizing to Jean after an argument.

Irene Mayer Selznick, daughter of mogul Louis B. Mayer and wife of producer David O. Selznick wrote in her memoirs that Paul was, "probably the single most beloved figure in Hollywood. He was special in many ways, the only person I ever knew who cherished people he loved as much for their frailties as for their virtues."

Uncertain as to how the public would react to the bigamy angle, Louis B. Mayer leaked a story to the press in a move he hoped would garner even more sympathy for his blonde starlet. He circulated the theory that Paul Bern was impotent and his inability to perform sexually led to his suicide.

Journalists wanting to appease the movie scion accepted his story as gospel truth, including columnist Adela Rogers St. John, who scored the first interview with Harlow following Bern's death.

Published in *Liberty* magazine November 26, 1932, St. John claimed, "It was the medical men who revealed the fact that Jean Harlow could have been a wife in name only. It was the autopsy—the coroner's inquest—which dragged forth the fact that Paul Bern could never have consummated their marriage."

St. John, acting on orders from the publicity department at MGM, offered an alleged first-hand story as to why Paul Bern would have followed through with killing himself. "I remembered long ago, when Paul Bern wanted to marry [actress] Barbara La Marr. I remembered that Barbara said to me. "If I married Paul, he'd kill himself in six months."

The journalist wrote of how Bern had dated other famous leading ladies, such as Joan Crawford and Mabel Normand, insinuating that he sought the company of glamorous, desirable women like Jean Harlow, even though he was sexually inadequate.

Jean spoke of her shock upon learning of her husband's death, saying she "had no warning, no reason to think of such a thing. We were so happy." When asked about the suicide note, Harlow said she knew of its contents but had not seen it. Whether or not Jean could truly attest to Paul's impotence, or had been pressured into going along with the story, Adela quoted her as saying, "Paul knew that didn't make any difference. He knew I loved him. I made him know it didn't matter."

### The Comeback Kid

At the time of Paul's death, Jean was filming a movie now regarded as one of her defining roles. In *Red Dust*, she plays a prostitute on the run in French Indochina. She has a tumultuous relationship

Jean Harlow in *Dinner At Eight* in 1933

with a rubber plantation owner, played by Clark Gable, who is also romancing a colleague's wife, played by Mary Astor. The film was released that October and turned a profit for MGM. Jean told the press that throwing herself into her work helped ease her grief.

Her next movie paired her once again with Gable, with their 1933 romantic drama *Hold Your Man*. Then Harlow was cast in the all star "comedy of manners" flick *Dinner at Eight*, working opposite old guard Hollywood greats such as Marie Dressler, John and Lionel Barrymore and Wallace Beery. Harlow played a brassy social climber.

Her white satin gown, designed by Adrian, was so form fitting she had to be sewn into it. In between takes she was unable to sit in a chair, so a special "leaning board" was brought in for the actress to recline and read a book or magazine until she was needed on the set.

In a role that reflected some of her own struggles with fame and the press, Harlow was then cast in *Bombshell*, as movie star Lola Burns, a woman fed up with moochers and publicity hounds who contemplates giving up the business.

Boxer/actor Max Baer, in the process of a difficult divorce from wife Dorothy Dunbar, became infatuated with Harlow. Jean told the press the two were merely friends and any socializing she did with the boxer was due to his link to Marino Bello, who was interested in managing his career.

Harlow told gossip columnist Louella Parsons, "I've been over on the set of *The Prizefighter and the Lady* several times, watching the big fight scenes between Max and Primo Carnera—but so has every other star on the lot. And Max has been at the house several times to see Bello, but I bet I haven't seen him five times in my life—and never once alone!"

She began dating the cinematographer for *Bombshell*, Harold Rosson, a man 16 years her senior. Jean told the press she and Harold had become good friends after the death of her husband, and their relationship grew into a romance. The couple wed on September 17, 1933 but the marriage only lasted through the spring.

Harlow explained to the press, "Although the romance ended, our friendship remained. Hal did not fail me. I like him and I respect him as much as I did when we were married. It is hard to explain the failure of our match other than to say it simply did not work out as we expected."

The year 1934 started out with the actress playing a husband-hunting showgirl. Censorship required all films to be vetted upon release and the original title "Born to be Kissed" was regarded as too titillating so the flick was re-titled *The Girl From Missouri*. She paired with frequent co-star Franchot Tone.

At first, Jean was hesitant to sign on for the role of Mona Leslie, a musical stage star accused of killing her husband, because of the controversy that surrounded her behavior after Bern's death. But Jean agreed to the role and was cast alongside Franchot Tone and her latest flame, William Powell, for the motion picture *Reckless*.

Her character decides to not let the rumor mill dictate her life, and instead of fading into obscurity after her husband's death (ruled suicide), she returns to the stage in order to support their young son.

Jean Harlow was always elegant

Upon facing hecklers, Harlow's passionate speech as Mona Leslie may have echoed her real-life feelings when she refuted the audience's scorn with, "How dare you? How do you dare? I tell you I had nothing to do with that awful thing that happened. All I did was to marry a sweet unhappy boy. Loving him. Hoping somehow to make him happy. I didn't [kill him]. I couldn't. His unhappiness was too deep in him. So deep he died of it ... and if this is the last song I'm ever to sing for you, please have the decency to let me finish."

Thrice married Harlow fell hard for the sophisticated William Powell. Nineteen years her senior, Powell found fame playing villains in his early roles until he found his niche playing worldly characters such as Nick Charles in *The Thin Man* series, opposite his favorite leading lady, Myrna Loy. Powell had been married twice before, to Eileen Wilson, then to movie star Carole Lombard.

Harlow and Powell were the new "It" couple, frequenting nightclubs and hobnobbing at parties thrown at the homes of the rich and powerful. Jean appeared on the cover of countless movie magazines. She posed for glamour portrait photographer George Hurrell whose dramatic black and white images were used for promotion campaigns for Hollywood's major stars. The most famous Hurrell shot of Harlow features her positioned on a bear skin rug, wearing a billowing white dress and looking provocatively off in the distance.

According to Hurrell, "I always positioned my key light at a low angle, because her eyes were deep set and you had to get the light under them or her eyes would just get too dark."

With a work schedule that lasted 20 hours a day Monday through Saturday, the actress spent her day off at a beauty parlor having her roots bleached. When not on the set, Harlow ditched her tight revealing gowns for pants, sweaters and tennis shoes and kept her makeup to a minimum.

"Personally, I dislike a made-up look," Harlow revealed to an interviewer. "I never wear mascara unless my screen work demands it. I only use powder and lipstick. I believe too much make-up [sic] is bad for women who prefer a healthy, natural complexion. Every woman should know what make-up [sic] she desires, and she should deal with it judiciously."

At first, news that blonde bombshell Jean Harlow was working on her first novel was met with indifference; the public figured it was merely a stunt to drum up publicity for her next movie. Jean shared her excitement at this new creative outlet. "Writing the story has been the hardest work I ever did, but I want to keep on doing fiction. Wouldn't it be swell too, if I did my own novel in the movies?" She explained none of her characters were inspired from real-life people.

Her romance novel entitled *Today is Tonight* is set in the 1920s and follows the lives of socialites Judy and Peter Lansdowne. Jean described her heroine as "a girl with an abundance of love who weakens now and then, but who clings to an ideal that finally emerges triumphant through her great love of her husband." Harlow worked on her manuscript over the course of several years.

After *Reckless*, Harlow teamed again with Gable for *China Seas*, a story of a steamer between Singapore and Hong Kong that is targeted by pirates. Rosalind Russell and Wallace Beery co-starred.

Next, Harlow played a tuna cannery worker who along with her fisherman love interest, played by Spencer Tracy, goes on strike against the owners of the cannery in a film entitled *Riffraff*. Mickey Rooney and Una Merkel also appeared in the flick.

In February 1936, MGM released their smash hit *Wife vs. Sec-*

*retary* wherein Harlow plays the sexy secretary opposite a magazine publisher, played by Clark Gable, and his wife, portrayed by Myrna Loy. Loy's character grows suspicious of all the time her husband spends with the blonde secretary. Jimmy Stewart pursues Jean's character in this romantic comedy.

Harlow was beloved by MGM's cadre ranging from producers, directors and film crew, who all called her Baby. Many felt the movie star was unpretentious and generous with her money. She was known for her love of gambling, placing bets and playing craps with the guys. She en-

Ms. Harlow was down-to-earth

joyed socializing but preferred evenings with Powell or Mama Jean.

Jean also spent time bedridden, suffering from one ailment after another. In her final years, the actress endured a severe sunburn covering most of her body. She had high blood pressure as well as undiagnosed nephritis—inflammation of the kidneys.

### A Ticking Time Bomb

Jean's relationship with William Powell was passionate, yet troubled. Jean wanted to marry and have children, while Powell shied away from settling into domestic bliss. He presented her with a massive 98-carat star sapphire ring and a diamond bracelet at Christmas in 1936. However, the two claimed it was not to mark an engagement.

Harlow again teamed with Franchot Tone, playing his wife in the World War I drama *Suzy*, co-starring Cary Grant. The film received a lukewarm response at the box office.

Her next movie, the screwball comedy *Libeled Lady*, saw Jean playing an impatient bride-to-be whose fiancé, played by Spencer Tracy, is too caught up fending off a reader, played by Myrna Loy, who brings up a libel case against his newspaper. Tracy recruits a character played by William Powell to seduce Loy to get her to drop the suit.

Still regarded as one of MGM's most lucrative actresses, Harlow was then cast in *Personal Property* opposite Robert Taylor. The romantic comedy was the last film role Harlow was to complete.

Taylor and Harlow made a personal appearance trip to Washington, D.C. and attended the Inaugural Ball. First Lady Eleanor Roosevelt took the movie star on a personal tour of the White House. On the train ride back to California, Jean came down with a persistent case of influenza.

Jean's next film, *Saratoga*—a comedy centered on horseracing—was shot on location in Saratoga, New York with scenes filmed in Lexington and Louisville, Kentucky. In the movie, Jean's father, played by Lionel Barrymore, loses his horse farm due to his gambling habit and the property falls into the hands of a roguish bookie, played by Clark Gable. Walter Pidgeon signed on as Harlow's wealthy and respectable beau.

During filming, the actress needed to have three impacted wisdom teeth extracted, complications of which landed her in the hospital for a month. Jean's spirits were lifted at the prospect of completing her film and celebrating her third anniversary of dating William Powell.

Jean was bloated, ashen-faced and she perspired profusely during filming. She became out of breath easily and it was clear to those on the set that Harlow was ill. On May 29, 1937, Jean collapsed while rehearsing a scene with Pidgeon.

Inexplicably, instead of being transported to a hospital, she was taken to her home. William Powell rushed to her side. Over the next several days she was examined by a doctor, and visited by two nurses, and on June 2nd it was announced she was merely suffering from "influenza." Ernest Fishbaugh, who had been called to Harlow's home to treat her, diagnosed her with an inflamed gallbladder but did not arrange hospitalization. Harlow felt better on June 3rd and co-workers expected her back on the set by Monday, June 7, 1937.

However, Clark Gable, who had visited her, said he smelled urine on her breath when he kissed her—an ominous sign of kidney failure. On the evening of June 6th, William Powell had her transferred to Good Samaritan Hospital in Los Angeles. She was put in an oxygen tent and received two blood transfusions.

On the morning of June 7th, Harlow sustained brain swelling and slipped into a coma. After a half hour of resuscitation measures, she was pronounced dead at 11:37 a.m. from cerebral edema and acute uremic poisoning.

Her funeral was attended by invitation only with thousands of fans thronged outside, necessitating police protection. A brief 20-

minute service was held for Jean at the Wee Kirk o'the Heather church at Forest Lawn cemetery.

For her funeral, Harlow was dressed in the gown she wore in *Libeled Lady*, and in her hands she held a white gardenia and a note that Powell had written: "Goodnight, my dearest darling." The simple inscription on Harlow's crypt is, "Our Baby."

She left an estate estimated to be worth $100,000 to her mother Jean Bello, who had been divorced from Marino Bello since 1935.

At first MGM felt it best to shelve *Saratoga*, but Jean's fans wanted to see her final film. The movie was mainly finished, but a body double was brought in to complete Harlow's remaining scenes. The movie was released a month later.

Newspapers across the country speculated as to what triggered the 26-year-old's sudden kidney failure. Had she died from a botched abortion? Did she have a drinking problem? Was she poisoned from her hair dye?

Makeup artist and friend of the late actress Violet Denoyer told the press that while applying cosmetics to Jean's face for the final time, the actress said, "You know, Violet, I have a feeling I'm going away from here and [will] never come back." Two hours later, Harlow became ill on the set.

Contrary to rumor, Jean's mother had not denied the actress medical care due to her Christian Science beliefs.

Louella Parsons composed a 34-page biographical magazine supplement about the late actress. She wrote, "So many things happened in those last few weeks of the little girl's life that will be indelibly stamped on the hearts of those who loved her."

After Harlow's death, her mother sold the film rights of her daughter's unpublished novel to MGM, but no movie was ever made. She retained the publishing rights until her death in 1958, at the age of 67.

Interest in Harlow's legacy was renewed in 1965 when *Today is Tonight* was released, having been completed with the help of screenwriter Carey Wilson.

Also in 1965, two fictionalized accounts of Jean's life—both highly dramatized—were put on film. *Harlow*, released by Paramount, cast Carroll Baker as Jean with a cast that included Peter Lawford, Leslie Nielsen and Angela Lansbury as Mama Jean. The script was based on the book *Harlow: An Intimate Biography*, penned by screenwriter Irving Shulman.

But five weeks before the Technicolor melodrama of the bombshell's life was released, Magna released a low budget black and white film (with the same title) with Carol Lynley in the lead. It co-starred Efrem Zimbalist, Jr., Hurd Hatfied and Ginger Rogers—in her last film performance before retirement—as Mama Jean.

Jean's elderly father, Dr. Montclair Carpenter, filed a $3 million lawsuit against Shulman claiming the book was suffused with tales erroneously provided by Arthur Landau, a former agent of Jean's. Carpenter died in 1974, at the age of 96.

William Powell defended his former flame. "Arthur Landau knew very little about Jean's private life. He was her agent for a short while only. I understand he was broke and some years ago he had an operation on his throat for cancer, but nothing would justify such a depraved contribution."

She was leered at by some of Hollywood's most famous producers—and hounded continually for her morals by anti-indecency campaigners, who dubbed her "the filthiest woman ever to have set foot in Hollywood." With Harlow's image tarnished by the salacious book and films, former colleagues, such as MGM executive Ralph Wheelright, gave their views on what Harlow had been like. "She didn't have a mean bone in her body," he reflected. "Money meant nothing to her and, while she didn't like her stepfather, she put up with him for her mother's sake. She had class."

Jeanette MacDonald, an actress and prolific opera singer who sang at Jean's funeral, surmised, "Harlow always played such sluts on the screen. At heart, she was really a naïve, nice girl who was being exploited—and wanted just to be somebody's wife. She was a very unhappy young girl."

Tony Rennell wrote that "Her mother was controlling to the point of madness and her stepfather a gun-toting pervert who climbed up ladders to spy on his naked, sleeping stepdaughter. She herself was ...drawn to middle-aged men who let her down...instead of giving her the love she craved."

"She was the antithesis of the hard-boiled characters she played on the screen," William Powell remembered of his lover. "She was shy and gentle. Perhaps the reason she was so excellent in her films was because, being so nice in real life, she was able to get rid of her frustrations in her work."

MGM writer Harry Ruskin recalled the doleful atmosphere hanging over the studio after Harlow's passing. "The day 'the baby' died there wasn't one sound in the commissary for three hours...not one goddamn sound."

# 4.

# SPENCER TRACY:
## *A Life On the Rocks*

SPENCER TRACY IS A NAME SYNONYMOUS WITH NATURAL, UNDER-stated acting. Audiences instantly bonded with and rooted for him, even when he played the villain. He made movie-goers believe they weren't watching a scripted scene shot on a soundstage, but rather were in the presence of Spencer Tracy just being Spencer Tracy. He was an actor's actor revered by his colleagues who tripped over themselves singing his praises. Tracy was nominated for a dazzling nine Academy Awards, and was the first actor to win the statuette two years in a row, for *Captains Courageous* and *Boys Town*.

Moviemaking seemed to come easy to the self-effacing actor whose public persona painted him as just a regular guy devoted to Catholicism and his family. Actor David Niven dubbed Tracy "The Pope" and the nickname stuck. But to his closest friends and lovers the real man remained submerged inside a bottle of booze. Tracy suffered from crippling depression, insomnia, bellicosity, pathological insecurity and abuse of alcohol and pills that blended into a Molotov cocktail, served on the rocks. He was the walking definition of a man grappling with "Catholic guilt."

For over 25 years he took up with a woman not his wife, a Bo-hemian with feminist and liberal views who was a self-proclaimed athe-ist and regarded as the greatest actress in movie history—Katharine Hepburn. The pair made nine movies together but their personal re-lationship was not publically acknowledged until after the deaths of both Tracy and his wife. While the decades have allowed for a Romeo and Juliet-esque rendering of their romance to be written, in actuality, their dynamic was more akin to that of a deep-seated friendship with mutual understanding—and devotion on the part of Hepburn.

Tracy was not the long-suffering husband whose wife would

not grant him a divorce as film folklore has proclaimed as fact in an attempt to romanticize the Tracy-Hepburn saga. He clung to his marriage out of moral obligation and loyalty to the mother of his children but retreated into the doting arms of Hepburn, a woman who had no interest in ever marrying him.

He was born Spencer Bonaventure Tracy on April 5, 1900 in Milwaukee, Wisconsin with a face full of freckles and a head of sandy red hair.

Spencer's father John was a hard-drinking Irish-Catholic who worked as a truck salesman. He had married up the social ranks to Caroline Brown, a Presbyterian whose descendants had founded Brown University. The Tracys proved the saying opposites attract and they provided the children a middle-class lifestyle. Alongside older brother Carroll, Spencer had a strict religious upbringing, attending Catholic schools and serving as an altar boy. Mr. Tracy had hopes that one of his sons would enter the priesthood. Spencer was a raucous youth who failed his classes—when he bothered to show up at all—and was a perpetual fighter who was often expelled. "I attended maybe 15 to 18 grammar schools before I finally graduated," Tracy confessed.

Due to financial difficulties, the Tracys moved into a poorer Milwaukee neighborhood and Spencer continued to fail his classes seeing just one merit of getting an education. "The only reason I went was so I could [learn how to] read the subtitles in the silent movies."

Spencer soon met a more serious, grounded young man who had his life planned out. His name was Bill O'Brien and he was determined to become an actor. A student at Marquette Academy, a private Catholic high school, Spencer wanted to emulate his new friend and asked his parents if he too could attend.

**At the Navy Academy, 1919**

The Tracys were so pleased that their son had a renewed interest in learning, they promptly enrolled him in the academy. Tracy excelled in theological studies and spoke seriously of entering the priesthood. But "itching for a chance to go and see some excitement" upon turning 18, Tracy dropped out of school and he and O'Brien enlisted in the United States Navy together. They were sent to the

Naval Training Station in North Chicago, where they were students when World War I came to an end. Spencer was discharged a year later, having never stepped foot on a boat.

He then moved back home and got his diploma. In 1921, Tracy was accepted to Ripon College where he decided to study medicine. He joined the debate team and tried out for several plays, finding his calling in public speaking and entertaining audiences. Wanting to now pursue a career in dramatics, he auditioned and was accepted to the American Academy of Dramatic Arts in New York City, where his old pal Bill—who now called himself Pat O'Brien—was also a student. They roomed together, sustaining themselves on rice and pretzels and sharing one decent suit between them.

After graduating from the academy, Spencer joined a stock company headquartered in West Plains, New York trying to find his niche. On the train bound for his next acting location–Grand Rapids, Michigan—he met a refined and far more established actress by the name of Louise Treadwell.

He and the actress, four years his senior, struck up a rapport that blossomed into a romance. Within six weeks, the couple was engaged. They wed in Cincinnati, marrying between the matinee and night shows of their play. Louise was an Episcopalian, but the couple

**With Louise Treadwell**

believed that their religious differences could be overcome—after all, Spencer's father had also married a Protestant. Their son John was born on June 26, 1924 in Milwaukee.

Louise pressed the pause bottom on her career, staying home with her son and had help from Spencer's mother. John was a happy, quiet baby who provided the couple with much happiness, but the financial burden fell on Spencer's shoulders. Unfortunately the man loved to act, but hated to work, and money was hard to come by in the Tracy home. Spencer lived on 35 cents a day when in between plays.

But hope was renewed when he was offered a role in *Yellow* by the Broadway icon George M. Cohan who would become his mentor. It was at this stage in his career that Tracy believed that if this play proved a flop, he would give up acting and find a typical nine to five job. Cohan liked what he saw proclaiming Tracy "the best goddamned actor I've ever seen." While it garnered mixed reviews, *Yellow* ran for 135 shows and was followed up by the successful *The Baby Cyclone*.

When John was only ten months old, Louise was attending to household tasks and accidentally let a door slam while the baby was napping. Worried that her child would surely cry out in anguish, she ran to him. But when she got to the boy, he lay motionless in his crib. Alarmed, she took the boy to see doctors, demanding answers as to why her son was so unresponsive. The verdict was grim. John Tracy was deaf, and had been so since birth. She was told the boy would never speak or learn to communicate. Almost as much as she despaired at the thought of her son being disabled she was beside herself in how and when she would tell Spencer the news.

Louise confided in some of her husband's friends and co-stars. She and the baby traveled to Brooklyn to stay with Spencer. One day while father and son played, the actor noticed that the boy did not respond to his voice. Addressing Louise he said, "Hey, this kid acts like he isn't hearing me!" It was then she revealed their son's prognosis. Spencer was inconsolable, having burst into tears saying, "He'll never be able to say 'Daddy.'"

Louise recalled, "My husband was thinking, of course, that being deaf meant being dumb; in those days, the two were thought to go together like salt and pepper."

Longtime friend Pat O'Brien remembered, "What happened next was typical of both Louise and Spence. Louise suffered, and took her boy to doctors to find out what could be done. Spence suffered and went out and got drunk. It was the first big drunk of his life, as far as I know. He was gone for days and finally was found holed up in the St. George Hotel there in Brooklyn." Spencer blamed his womanizing for the baby's condition, believing that venereal disease passed on to his wife during her pregnancy had somehow caused their child to be born deaf.

In truth, John suffered from Usher Syndrome, a rare genetic condition that can develop only if both parents are carriers of the gene. It is characterized by deafness and poor vision that eventually leads to blindness. By the time the child was six, he had also developed polio, which disfigured his right leg. His eyesight worsened over time and he became blind as an adult. Doctors told the Tracys it would be best to institutionalize their son. They refused. True, specialists and hospitals cost money, but Louise was steadfast in her beliefs. She was committed to teaching her son to speak but refused to allow her husband to give up acting for a more lucrative profession.

As the 1920s came to a close, Spencer moved from one play to the next in an effort to keep his family clothed and fed. To add to the stress, his father John was dying of cancer. Spencer then got a part in Cohan's play *Whispering Friends*. One night between acts Tracy got the news that his father had died. But he did what any other professional would have done; he went back out on stage and finished the play.

Tracy next took over the lead role in *Conflict* after its star Clark Gable could no longer complete the project. It was the start of a life-long rivalry between the two men who eventually worked together in the movies and later became pals. The next play, *Dread*, debuted to critical acclaim, but within the week of its opening, the stock market crashed and the show lost its funding. Tracy decided it was time to return home to Milwaukee.

But providence intervened and the following January the actor was offered a chance to star in an edgy play called *The Last Mile* about a serial killer on death row. It ran for almost 300 performances and revitalized his fledgling career. Realizing there was money to be made by going out West to make a film or two, the Tracys packed their bags for Hollywood. Spencer was hired to appear in two Vitaphone short movies called *Taxi Talks* and *The Hard Guy* but like many stage actors he believed his stint in Tinseltown would be brief and that the legitimate stage was his home.

Yet director John Ford was so impressed by the actor's performance in *The Last Mile* that he wanted the actor to star in the feature film *Up the River* alongside newcomer Humphrey Bogart. Fox Film Corporation agreed that Tracy, while not classically handsome, was talented enough to be on the payroll. The studio proposed a five-year contract with a guaranteed $70,000 yearly salary. Spencer Tracy accepted the offer and never looked back.

## He Made It Look So Easy

Tracy sent for his mother Caroline and brother Carroll (whom he wisely chose as his financial manager). He provided his wife and son a modest but comfortable home and got to work on one comedy after the next, playing criminals and con men, mainly. With worry lines on his forehead, stubble on his cheeks and an intense gaze, Tracy looked the part of the bad boy, but 1932's *Disorderly Conduct* broke the pattern when he played a policeman. *Me and My Gal* opposite Joan Bennett did poorly at the box office and the pair wouldn't work together again until 1950's *Father of the Bride*.

He gave strong performances in *20,000 Years in Sing Sing* and *The Power and the Glory*, but his star failed to rise.

In June of 1932, Louise gave birth to a daughter who was given her namesake, but the girl went by Susie. The children were raised Episcopalian, a decision to which devout Catholic Tracy apparently voiced no objection. They tried to settle into domestic bliss but in a year's time, it was clear that the marriage was over. He separated from his wife on April 29, 1933, informing the press that the split was amicable and the couple had no desire of filing divorce papers. Louise seemed unfazed by her husband's playboy reputation and dalliances with younger leading ladies. She even encouraged her husband to see other women.

While on the set of 1933's *Man's Castle*, Spencer began an affair with his 21-year-old co-star, Loretta Young. The movie slogan mirrored the drama encircling their whirlwind romance: "Theirs was a love as sweeping as a thundering torrent—as mighty as life itself." Spencer seriously considered divorcing Louise but he was guilt-ridden, "What could I say to Johnny? How could I make a nine-year-old little boy understand that I'm leaving his mother?" Biographer James Curtis hypothesizes that Young, not Hepburn, was the love of Tracy's life, "I think they were drawn together because of the shared bond of faith," Curtis wrote.

Young's Catholicism bordered on fanatical. She and Spencer went to Confession on Saturday afternoons and Mass on Sundays at the Church of the Good Shepherd in Beverly Hills. During one Confession the priest denied Loretta's request of absolution. Distressed, the actress told the clergyman the details of her affair with Tracy in a lame attempt to win his sympathies. Taking pity, the priest granted absolution under the condition that she return every Friday henceforth for counseling. No such provision was made for Tracy, who had declined to disclose to Loretta whether or not he had been granted absolution. Even though Loretta attended these sessions, it was no use; the relationship had been doomed from the start.

On the evening of June 14th, the couple ended their relationship. At the time, Tracy tried to downplay their fling by telling reporters, "Aw, it was all platonic anyway." In actuality, Spencer wouldn't leave his wife and even if he had wanted to, he and Loretta couldn't get married in the Church because Catholicism does not recognize divorce. Loretta issued a press statement saying that the two agreed to stop seeing each other out of obligation to their religion.

In her old age, the actress claimed to have been in the dark about Tracy's marital status, reasoning that by the time she learned the truth, she had already fallen in love with him. Despite intense feelings for each other, Spencer would go on to have numerous affairs. In 1935 Loretta had a tryst with her married co-star Clark Gable, which resulted in the birth of a child she passed off as her adopted daughter.

While Tracy made no attempt at being faithful to Louise, the couple reconciled after the Loretta Young fiasco, at least for show. Tracy tried to bond with his children, doting on Susie and teaching John how to play polo and giving him scripts to read. While his drinking had become infamous at the studio, Tracy appeared in a staggering 22 films between 1930 and 1934. While the actor was filming 1935's *It's a Small World*, his drinking intensified. He missed rehearsals causing production to go over budget. On March 11th, just as shooting was wrapping up, Spencer didn't report to the set.

He turned up in a hotel in Yuma, Arizona. Due to commotion coming from his room, the manager called the authorities who soon

**Spencer with his wife and children**

arrived, charging the actor with being drunk and disorderly, resisting arrest and destroying public property. The story exploded in the papers.

Spencer's refusal to appear in *The Farmer Takes a Wife* was the final straw. He was fired from Fox on April 8th. That same day he signed a contract with MGM on the urging of producer Irving Thalberg. Head of the studio Louis B. Mayer recoiled at signing an actor who went on disruptive drinking binges, but Tracy's acting ability assuaged any doubts.

MGM micromanaged its actors and Tracy thrived on structure, knowing that his lucrative deal with the most prestigious studio in the business was worth showing up on time and curbing his booze intake. In fact, the actor's sobriety was known to stretch into years. He drank gallons of coffee and tea to keep off the bottle. The combination of consuming caffeine during the day and nagging depression turned him into a chronic insomniac. He took barbiturates to sleep and Dexedrine to stay awake.

Tracy's first picture for MGM was *The Murder Man* with Virginia Bruce and Jimmy Stewart in his first film role, followed by Fritz Lang's drama *Fury*—a popular draw at the theaters. The actor had proven his star potential and was given a supporting role in the Clark Gable/Jeanette MacDonald vehicle *San Francisco*. Tracy played a priest, and while he only appeared on the screen for 17 minutes, he had gotten the attention of the Academy of Motion Pictures, receiving his first Oscar nomination.

Tracy then starred in the screwball comedy *Libeled Lady* alongside Jean Harlow, William Powell and Myrna Loy—actors at the top of MGM's roster.

The year 1936 had proved financially successful and Tracy bought a 12-acre Mexican style ranch in Encino, California. The family enjoyed horseback riding, swimming and attending to the plethora of farm animals and Irish Setters. It was Tracy's sanctuary away from the hurried and glamorous backdrop of Hollywood. Regrettably, Spencer spent less and less time with his family, living mainly in hotels.

But Louise Treadwell Tracy was far from the little woman waiting at the window for her husband to return. She took a $100 correspondence course through the Wright Oral School and learned their method for teaching deaf children. Louise read countless books and articles on the subject and sought the opinion of every doctor in the field. Her patience knew no bounds; she would repeat a word as many as 3,000 times to John in an effort to teach him how to read lips. By

**Spencer admiring his Encino, CA house but he spent little time there**

age 11 he could verbally speak and carry on conversations.

When not working with her son, Louise enjoyed playing polo. She founded the first women's polo league on the West coast. Well educated and intellectual, she also wrote poetry and submitted articles to *The New York Times*. Without a doubt, the honeymoon was over in the Tracy household, their romance now replaced with a friendship. But Louise read all of her husband's scripts, viewed his performances and offered feedback. James Curtis suspects that Spencer "had a tremendous emotional attachment to Louise. If you want to call that love, if you want to call that devotion, if you want to call that a need, I can't put a label on it necessarily. But that was an important relationship for him and it was important 'til the day he died."

Tracy's colleague, the famed director Joseph L. Mankiewicz theorized, "Tracy didn't leave Louise. He left the scene of his guilt."

Busying himself with moviemaking, the actor went to work on four films in 1937, the biggest one being Rudyard Kipling's coming of age novel *Captains Courageous*. Tracy plays Portuguese-American fisherman Manuel Fidello. He struggled with formulating an accent and wasn't pleased with the final result. He hated curling his hair for the part and upon viewing his reflection declared, "If my father had lived to see it, this would have killed him!"

He dismissed his performance in the film, saying the success of the project was thanks to co-stars child actor Freddie Bartholomew, and old guard actors Lionel Barrymore and Melvyn Douglas. Ironically, it was Tracy who was nominated for an Oscar for Best Actor. Believing he had no chance of winning and holding the pageantry of the function in disdain, he opted not to attend. Instead, he went into the hospital for hernia surgery. Louise attended the ceremony solo just in case her husband won. When Spencer Tracy was named the winner, she was there to accept the statuette.

More memorable film roles followed, including *Mannequin* with Joan Crawford and *Test Pilot* with Clark Gable and Myrna Loy. MGM believed that Tracy was right for the role of Father Flanagan, the priest who founded the Village of Boys Town, a place at-risk youth could find stability, hope and compassion in their lives. Tracy was overwhelmed at the thought of portraying a man he so revered, and in his usual fashion attempted to pull out of production at the last minute. His insecurity was so infamous that when other actors tried to wiggle their way out of doing a movie it was said they had come down with "Spencer Tracy Syndrome." The actor reconsidered, figuring that taking the part would have made his father proud.

The crew set up shop in Omaha, Nebraska on the grounds of the actual Boys Town. Spencer followed Father Flanagan around for a week to emulate the priest's speech and demeanor. It was one of the

**In costume as Father Flanagan, with director Norman Taroug**

few instances Tracy studied another individual for an acting role. The flick premiered in Omaha to massive fanfare. It was believed that Tracy was a shoe-in for the Oscar and indeed he won the award saying, "I don't feel that I can accept this as a tribute to my performance in *Boy's Town*, but I do accept it as a tribute to the man who inspired the picture, Father Flannigan."

It was erroneously reported to the press that

Tracy co-starred with Ingrid Bergman and Lana Turner in *Dr. Jekyll and Mr. Hyde*

the actor was donating his Oscar to Father Flanagan. Tracy refused to relinquish his statuette, so MGM sent Boy's Town a duplicate Oscar that remains on display there to this day. Unfortunately. the success of the motion picture led the public to assume that Boy's Town was flush with cash; donations evaporated. MGM donated $250,000 to keep the establishment from closing its doors.

    *Boom Town*, Spencer's last pairing with Clark Gable, was one of the most popular flicks of 1940. In April 1941 Tracy signed a new contract with MGM upping his salary and reducing his workload. He resumed his role as Father Flanagan in *Men of Boys Town*. Then he performed to mixed reviews in the horror flick, *Dr. Jekyll and Mr. Hyde*.

    In 1942 the actor was signed to star in *The Yearling* but pulled out due to production and weather related setbacks. He was now free to pursue a film project that had piqued his interest. It would be one of the most peculiar pairings in filmdom—the paternal, Average Joe from the Midwest and the devil-may-care New Englander with progressive ideals. They say opposites attract and if the adage is true, Spencer Tracy and Katharine Hepburn collided like a thunderbolt, setting the silver screen aglow with inimitable chemistry.

### Spencer Met His Match With Kate

    Katharine Hepburn had been labeled "box office poison" in

1938 and left Hollywood for the stage. She was the antithesis of a glamour girl or classic beauty—she was a modern woman who valued her mind over her looks. She had dirt under her fingernails and liked to wear trousers and suit coats. Kate played characters that were merely extensions of her own personality.Hepburn returned to movies in 1939 with her comeback smash *The Philadelphia Story* and was eager to sink her teeth into an equally meaty role. She convinced MGM to buy the movie rights to a story written with her in mind called *Woman of the Year*. But there was a catch. She wanted Spencer Tracy as her leading man, an actor she regarded as the best in the business and she was willing to give him top billing. Spencer Tracy accepted Hepburn's offer.

While Kate had seen all of Spencer's movies—some of them dozens of times—he was less familiar with her acting. They met for the first time on the set and as the story goes, the statuesque Hepburn approached her new co-star and said, "I'm afraid I'm a bit tall for you, Mr. Tracy." Joseph L. Mankiewicz quipped, "Don't worry, Kate, he'll cut you down to size."

The film was the first of nine pairings in which the duo fought the battle of the sexes, to the amusement of audiences. By the time the motion picture wrapped, the two were living together, embarking on a reticent romance kept hidden from the press—and Louise Tracy. Fellow actors observed the couple from afar. As Gene Kelly commented, "At lunchtime they'd just meet and sit on a bench on the lot. They'd hold hands and talk—and everybody left them alone in their little private world."

Although there can be no doubt the two were genuinely close, William J. Mann, the author of *Kate: The Woman Who Was Hepburn*, details what he says was Hepburn's lesbianism and Tracy's bisexuality. Scotty Bowers, a procurer to the stars, writes in his memoirs, *Full Service*, that the Tracy/Hepburn connection was more of a tabloid love affair that was used as a smoke screen for their homosexual pursuits. ("I fixed her up with every bit of 150 girls" over 39 years, he wagers). The late columnist Liz Smith confirmed Hepburn was gay. Former *Vanity Fair* writer Matt Tyrnauer, who has extensively researched the subject, commented recently "people are in willful suspension of belief about this supposed golden couple."

Meanwhile, Spencer's wife Louise had successfully created a normal existence for son John, but she wanted to share her breadth of knowledge and establish a facility with cutting edge treatments available. In 1942 her dream came to fruition. Starting out in a cottage on the University of Southern California campus, she opened the John

Tracy Clinic. "Our purpose was to train and guide the parents of young deaf children. Thirteen mothers. That is where it all began," she said. The clinic was the first of its kind and its services were rendered free of charge. In the early years the facility was funded solely by her husband's film career.

Tracy was re-teamed with Hepburn in *Keeper of the Flame* and made a series of war movies as the decade progressed. In 1945 he made his first play in 15 years. "I'm coming back to Broadway to see if I can still act," he told a reporter. *The Rugged Path* had potential, but the actor quit the show six weeks later due to depression and health problems. He failed to make any films in 1946. The only people he would see were Katharine and his brother Carroll.

Finally Tracy went back to the studio and made several movies including 1948's *State of the Union*, in which he portrays a Republican candidate for President whose sponsor is a corrupt newspaper magnate (Angela Lansbury) who plans to be the power behind the throne. She convinces him to pursue the nomination and, for the sake of appearances, reunite with his estranged wife (Katharine Hepburn). His spouse agrees to support him because of what she perceives as his idealism, though she is unaware of the publisher's nefarious plans.

The storyline was a morality play about political corruption and

**Spencer with Katharine Hepburn, Van Johnson and Angela Lansbury**

how the candidate finally sees the light, rebukes his backers on national radio, and does the right thing. Shortly after completion, *State of the Union* was screened exclusively for President Harry Truman and reportedly helped convince him to run for office again.

Spencer then made *Cass Timberlane* with Lana Turner, culminating with the popular *Adam's Rib*, alongside Kate wherein they play husband and wife lawyers on opposite sides of the courtroom.

The year 1950 marked a career comeback when he was cast as a man coming to emotional and financial terms with the marriage of his daughter in *Father of the Bride.* Joan Bennett and Elizabeth Taylor made a believable mother-daughter pairing, but Tracy stole the show.

In the last scene he uttered a line that still resonates with a generation of fathers, "My son's my son 'til he gets him a wife, but my daughter's my daughter all of her life." Tracy was nominated for an Oscar and a sequel was in the works. It was his most profitable movie to date.

*Father's Little Dividend* was released ten months later, debuting in April of 1951 at

**Spencer with Elizabeth Taylor in *Father of the Bride***

Grauman's Egyptian Theater. The event served as a fundraiser for a new, larger facility for the John Tracy Clinic. A year later construction was complete and the Tracys attended the opening ceremony. Spencer addressed the crowd, declaring, "You honor me because I am a movie actor, a star in Hollywood terms. Well, there's nothing I've ever done that can match what Louise has done for deaf children and their parents."

In 1952, Tracy and Hepburn joined forces in *Pat and Mike*. He then took on a fatherly role in *The Actress*, winning a Golden Globe Award. 1955's *Bad Day at Black Rock* is a Western meets film noir motion picture wherein the actor appears as a one-armed stranger—a part that earned him an Oscar nomination. That year he did not renew his MGM contract, and instead became a free agent.

Tracy starred in *The Old Man and the Sea* and while he got another Oscar nomination with that part, Ernest Hemingway panned the actor's performance. *The Last Hurrah* had Tracy playing an Irish-American mayor seeking re-election.

His career stalled until late 1960 when he teamed with director Stanley Kramer with *Inherit the Wind,* a fictionalized account of the Scopes "Monkey" Trial. Tracy's character was based on Clarence Darrow. Once again, the actor received an Oscar nomination.

The disaster movie *The Devil at 4 O'Clock* cast Tracy as a priest, with box office revenue surpassing the success of *Father of the Bride*.

Friend Stanley Kramer was to direct Spencer's final three films. *Judgment at Nuremberg* was a favorite of Tracy's and he plays Chief Trial Judge Dan Haywood. At the end of the movie, he gave a 13-minute speech in one take. This role earned him his eighth Oscar nomination.

Novelist Hemingway disliked Tracy's performance

Hepburn biographer Karen Karbo wrote of the measures the couple resorted to in keeping their romance under the radar. "For decades hence not much was known about what went on between Tracy and Hepburn. It was said to be an open secret in Hollywood, but they remained as discreet and disciplined as a pair of top-notch father confessors."

While in Berlin filming *Judgment at Nuremberg*, Spencer and Kate feared being seen together, even though they had been a couple for 18 years.

Colleagues couldn't understand why Tracy never left his wife and married Kate. The press agreed not to publish stories hinting that the two were anything more than friends. It was wrongly assumed that

Louise was the holdout for the divorce, but from the start it had been Spencer who balked at the idea. Louise didn't object; the Tracy name helped propel her clinic and his financial support gave her a comfortable lifestyle.

Miss Hepburn also seemed fine with the arrangement. "I was not in the business of capturing anyone into a marriage…we never really thought about or discussed marriage. He was married and I wasn't interested," she wrote in later years. However prominent Hepburn became as a feminist icon, her dynamic with Tracy was far from egalitarian. In her 1991 memoir, *Me* the actress revealed, "We did what he liked. We lived a life which he liked. I struggled to change all the qualities I felt he didn't like. Some of them which I thought were my best I thought he found irksome. I removed them, squelched them as far as I was able."

Because his body was failing due to years of hard living, Tracy had to turn down a role in the all-star cast of *How the West Was Won*, serving instead as the film's narrator. He regarded himself as "gray and fat" and at one point tipped the scales at 210 pounds. Kate encouraged him to quit smoking, exercise and eat better. She had always been trim and athletic, but her advice failed to make an impact. In 1963, Kramer gave Tracy a minor yet memorable role in the classic comedy *It's a Mad, Mad, Mad, Mad World*.

It featured an impressive, all-star cast including Edie Adams,

**Spencer gave a hilarious performance in *It's A Mad, Mad, Mad, Mad World***

Milton Berle, Sid Caesar, Buddy Hackett, Ethel Merman, Mickey Rooney, Phil Silvers, Terry-Thomas, Dorothy Provine, Jonathan Winters, and Dick Shawn—with cameo appearances by Jack Benny, Joe E. Brown, Peter Falk, Jimmy Durante, Paul Ford, Jim Backus, William Demarest, Eddie "Rochester" Anderson, Norman Fell, Buster Keaton, Don Knots, Jerry Lewis, ZaSu Pitts, Carl Reiner, Madlyn Rhue, and The Three Stooges, among others. The storyline concerns the hilarious pursuit by a diverse and colorful group of strangers of a buried treasure worth $350,000 in stolen cash. Spencer Tracy played the police chief, Captain T.G. Culpaper, who in the end tries to steal the money for himself to escape his harping wife and irksome teenage daughter. The ensemble comedy premiered on November 7, 1963.

Spencer Tracy would give his final performance in a motion picture that challenged society's bigotry against interracial marriage in *Guess Who's Coming to Dinner*. He and Hepburn star as a couple whose daughter (played by Hepburn's niece, Katharine Houghton), announces her plans to marry a black man, played by Sidney Poitier. Tracy's performance was hauntingly moving, as the affection he showed for Hepburn's character mirrored his real-life feelings. The tears glistening in Katharine's eyes were sincere.

Due to his frail health, he was deemed a liability at the studio, making him uninsurable. Hepburn and Kramer put up their own salaries as collateral. Filming wrapped in May of 1967. Tracy had barely sustained through production, although his performance never once hints that the actor was nearing the end of his life.

Katharine Houghton recalled in an interview with TCM that during the shooting of the motion picture, due to Spencer Tracy's fragile health, "There was a lot of tiptoeing around and praying for him—if he's going to wake up tomorrow. Stanley and my aunt, their primary task was to get him through. I'd never known [Katharine] to be so stressed out. It was just terrible on her. When [Spencer] finished the last monologue—which was done over a period of days because he couldn't work for more than a couple of hours at a time—he went up to Stanley, put his hand on his shoulder and said, 'Well, Stanley, now if I drop dead, you've got it.' And he was so pleased, so glad, so relieved. Spencer was just ebullient—brimming over with joy. Stanley was, too. They both wept."

On June 10, 1967, Spencer Tracy died of a heart attack at the residence he shared with Hepburn. On the morning of his funeral, his long-time partner arrived at the mortuary and helped load Tracy's body into the hearse. She followed the car headed for the service. But at the last minute she decided not to attend the funeral.

A few days later, Hepburn dialed Louise offering an olive branch. Mrs. Tracy was amenable to forging a friendship with the other woman but shockingly said, "But you see, I thought you were only a rumor." Katharine would later remark, "After nearly 30 years, a rumor?...It was a deep and fundamental wound, deeply set, never to be budged. Almost 30 years Spence and I had known each other,

**A rare candid photo of Kate and Spence at the home they shared**

through good and bad times. Some rumor. Spencer, the guilty one. She, the sufferer. I had not broken up their marriage. That happened long before I arrived on the scene."

Gossip columnist Louella Parsons had been critical of Kate due to the actress's snubbing of the press. She is quoted as referring to the Tracy/Hepburn union as "the greatest love story never told."

*Guess Who's Coming to Dinner* was released six months after Tracy's death, grossing more revenue than any of his other films. Spencer received his ninth and final Oscar nomination, posthumously. But it was Katharine who took home the statuette; she won the award for Best Actress, a feat she would accomplish four times in her long career.

Louise Tracy continued her philanthropy, going on to receive five honorary degrees and countless humanitarian awards. Fittingly, in 1975 she was given the Father Flanagan Award for Service to Youth. She passed away on November 13, 1983. Today, the John Tracy Clinic helps more than 25,000 families yearly.

It was only after Mrs. Tracy's death that Miss Hepburn spoke publically about her life with Spencer. She had been devoted and madly in love with him, although confessed that Tracy never told her he loved her. "But he wouldn't have stuck around if he hadn't, would he?" the actress reasoned. Katharine died on June 29, 2003, at the age of 96. The American Film Institute named her the greatest female star in Hollywood history. Tracy clocked in at number nine on the list of male stars.

John Tracy had overcome handicaps to lead a productive and humble life away from the public eye. "I'm an artist, writer, photographer...I got married and had a family. I'm also profoundly deaf, going blind, had polio. What can you do?" he said. John died on June 15, 2007, of an undisclosed illness.

Little can be said about Spencer Tracy the actor that could be deemed unflattering. So skilled in his approach, so fine-tuned was his craft that one had to wonder if in his off-screen life he had been just as triumphant. More than five decades after his passing, he still seems so fortunate to have had a lucrative film career, a charming family, women who adored him, and legions of fans.

When Burt Reynolds was getting his start in the business, he befriended Tracy while the two were working at the same studio. One day Burt turned to his idol and said, "Mr. Tracy, you're so good at everything. Is there anything you're not good at?"

To which Tracy replied, "Life."

# 5.
# ANNE BAXTER:
## *Curtain Call*

ANNE BAXTER ADDED A TOUCH OF CLASS AND REFINEMENT TO every movie she made. Profoundly witty and elegant, on and off screen, she led her life with self-effacing humor, treasuring her friends and family, and devoting herself to her career.

Anne is best remembered for her Academy Award-nominated role as the conniving Eve Harrington in the 1950 classic *All About Eve*. Baxter's other noteworthy films include *Follow the Sun*, *The Magnificent Ambersons*, *The Ten Commandments*, *The Razor's Edge* (for which she won the Oscar), and nearly 50 other movies. She also has a star on the Hollywood Walk of Fame.

Anne was born on May 7, 1923 in Michigan City, Indiana, a tourist-driven city about an hour's drive from downtown Chicago. Anne's father Kenneth Stuart Baxter was an executive with Seagrams Distillery Company, providing the family with an affluent lifestyle. Mother Catherine Wright Baxter worked as a schoolteacher, estranged from her famous father—legendary architect Frank Lloyd Wright.

In her 1976 autobiography, *Intermission*, Anne wrote, "[Mother] was his favorite as a child and he used to call her 'Taffy.' She was beautiful and saucy and thoroughly individualistic, all of which he loved. But when the family broke apart (a divorce granted in 1922) she'd understandably sided with her mother and there had been many painful scenes."

She went on to say of her famous grandfather, "He and I had no such ravines between us and had discovered deep affection easily."

Anne's daughter Melissa Galt told this author that Catherine held a life-long grudge against her father Frank Lloyd Wright for abandoning the family: "Very bitter. Very whiny. Very complainy her whole life. I never knew her when she wasn't. And very hard on mom."

Despite the family's dysfunction, several heirs followed in Wright's artistic footsteps. Frank Lloyd Wright, Jr. became an architect, as did grandson Eric Lloyd Wright. John Lloyd Wright invented Lincoln Logs in 1916, stating that his creation was inspired by the construction of his father's design of the Imperial Hotel. Granddaughter Elizabeth Ingraham worked as an architect, and the family includes numerous interior designers, including Anne's daughter.

Anne was a beautiful baby

The Baxters moved to New York City when Anne was a preteen, and she was raised amidst luxury and sophistication. Her parents enrolled her at the elite all-girl Brearley School. At age ten, Baxter attended a Broadway play starring theater legend Helen Hayes, and was so impressed with the actress that the young girl declared to her family that she wanted to become an actress. By the age of 13 Anne had appeared on Broadway in the play *Seen But Not Heard*.

The aspiring young girl studied under actress Maria Ouspenskaya, founder of the School of Dramatic Art. There, Baxter learned "method acting," a technique that originated in Russia and in which actors do not manufacture emotions and expressions, but rather, they draw upon personal experiences. Another student of Ouspenskaya formed his own acting school. His name was Lee Strasberg.

In her teens, Baxter moved to Hollywood to try her hand at movie acting. She tested for the role of Laurence Olivier's wife in the film *Rebecca*, but director Alfred Hitchcock wanted a slightly older actress for the part. Joan Fontaine, six years Anne's senior, won the role instead.

Not long after, Baxter would make her first film entitled, *20 Mule Team*. Two years later, she would be cast in the critically acclaimed *The Magnificent Ambersons*, a book adapted for the screen by Orson Welles. He insisted that the young actress be cast in the film. The movie follows the lives and secret past of an Indiana family. Joseph Cotten and Agnes Moorehead co-starred.

Anne's follow-up film was *Five Graves to Cairo*, directed and co-written by Billy Wilder. Tyrone Power plays a British corporal with whom Anne's character falls in love. The picture was nominated for three Academy Awards, further exposing moviegoers to the fresh young actress.

Next Anne appeared in 1943's *The North Star*, the first film where she received top billing. The movie was a critical and financial success and Anne came in for her share of plaudits.

In 1946 Anne made another film with Tyrone Power entitled *The Razor's Edge* wherein Power portrays Larry Darrell, a former World War I pilot in search of the meaning of life. His decadent acquaintances are in stark contrast with his mission to find inner fulfillment. Baxter plays Sophie Nelson, a close friend whose life is nothing short of pitiful. Clifton Webb, Herbert Marshall and Gene Tierney also appeared.

At first, producer Darryl Zanuck felt Anne was all wrong for the part. "[He] thought all women were either broads or librarians. He thought I was a librarian. He thought I was smart…Darryl said 'she has no sex. She's a cold potato,'" Anne later recalled.

Yet Baxter's performance of the alcoholic Sophie won her the Academy Award for Best Supporting Actress as well as a Golden Globe.

"*The Razor's Edge* contained my only great performance," Anne said. "When we shot that hospital scene in which Sophie loses her husband, child and everything else, I relived the death of my brother, [Toby] whom I adored and who died at three. It gives me chills right now to think of it."

Husband #1 John Hodiak

Soon after garnering her film accolades, Anne married fellow actor John Hodiak on July 7, 1946. A man of Ukrainian and Polish descent, he spent his youth in Hamtramck, Michigan. He was nine years her senior. His most notable film role was opposite Tallulah Bankhead in 1944's *Lifeboat*. In 1948, husband and wife teamed up for the Clark Gable/Lana Turner vehicle *Homecoming*. Baxter played Gable's wife who witnesses an illicit affair between him and Turner.

Hodiak and Baxter welcomed their only child, Katrina, into the world on July 9, 1951.

However, the couple grew apart, and Anne blamed herself for the failure of the marriage. They divorced when their child was only 15 months old. A little over a year later, at the age of 41, Hodiak suffered a fatal heart attack while shaving, at the home of his parents. His film, *On The Threshold of Space*, was in post-production at the time. Anne was his first and only wife, and although they had divorced, she considered herself a widow.

## Fasten Your Seatbelts

Anne appeared in a string of films, but 1950 would bring her most well-known and iconic role as Eve Harrington, in writer/director Joseph L. Mankiewicz's masterpiece *All About Eve*. Jeanne Crain was originally cast as Eve, but pregnancy prevented her from appearing.

Eve closely follows the career of her idol, aging stage star Margo Channing (portrayed by Bette Davis). Margo's best friend, Karen Richards (played by Celeste Holm) pities Eve's sob story and agrees to let her meet Margo after a performance. Eve smoothly integrates herself into Margo's circle. She becomes her right-hand-woman, a starstruck young girl who is a long way from the farm in Wisconsin. But Eve sets her sights on Karen's husband, producer Lloyd Richards, played by Hugh Marlowe. She also flirts with Bill Sampson, Margo's director/boyfriend.

John Garfield and Ronald Reagan were considered for the Sampson role, but Gary Merrill was cast instead. George Sanders played the role of cynical theater critic Addison DeWitt, who sees through Eve's facade.

The movie speaks of broader human fears, desires, and behaviors, having been inspired by a short story that ran in *Cosmopolitan* magazine in 1947 entitled, "The Wisdom of Eve."

Claudette Colbert was signed to portray Margo. Anne was favored to play Eve because Mankiewicz and producer Darryl Zanuck felt Baxter bore a striking physical resemblance to Colbert. But a debilitating back injury forced Colbert to back out of the role last minute, so Bette Davis was chosen as her replacement. Marilyn Monroe also made one of her early film appearances, playing a young budding actress. This movie features the Davis character line, "Fasten your seat belts, it's going to be a bumpy night."

The film was nominated for a stunning 14 Academy Awards, an achievement not matched until 1997's blockbuster *Titanic*. *All About Eve* is the only movie in history to garner four actress Oscar nominations: Davis was nominated for best leading actress, Thelma Ritter (who played Margo's maid) and Celeste Holm were acknowledged in the best supporting actress category. Anne Baxter allegedly was first nominated in the supporting actress category, but she lobbied to get nominated alongside Davis.

Ultimately both women were nominated in the lead actress category, a first time occurrence in movie academy history.

Anne's daughter Melissa reflected, "My bet is that she didn't do it with an ulterior motive, as much as she did it with a logic: 'Look at this. I'm in every scene here. I'm on the screen just as much as Bette Davis is. I'm a lead actress in a title role'...That sort of thing. I don't think it would have been out of maliciousness...Mom was not a backstabber. Absolutely not...I don't buy into it. If it happened and she was behind it, it would have been...people pushing her to do it. Because mother was easily swayed."

The film won six Oscars, including best picture of the year. Davis and Baxter were up against Gloria Swanson for *Sunset Boulevard*, and 29-year-old starlet Judy Holliday for *Born Yesterday*. Holliday

**Anne Baxter and Bette Davis in *All About Eve***

won—to everyone's surprise. Swanson and Davis were devastated, both being women over 40 with few leading roles in their futures. Fans and critics alike have blamed Baxter for the upset. Melissa defended her mother, stating, "She was very ambitious, but...I don't think my mother ever could have been an Eve in real-life."

The motion picture ranks 16th on the American Film Institute (AFI) list of the 100 greatest movies ever made. Eve Harrington was voted 23rd on the AFI list of the 50 greatest villains of all time.

*All About Eve* was adapted for Broadway and re-titled, *Applause*, starring Lauren Bacall. When Bacall left the show, Baxter took over her part, not as Eve, but as Margo Channing. Baxter rose to the occasion despite playing the opposite role.

Following the success as playing the vindictive Eve, Baxter was cast in *Follow the Sun*, which depicts the life of golf hero Ben Hogan, portrayed by Glenn Ford.

In 1953, Baxter made the Hitchcock thriller, *I Confess* with Montgomery Clift and Karl Malden. Clift took top billing playing a Catholic priest who learns of a murder during confession and in turn, is accused of the crime. Anne plays his childhood friend and former lover Ruth who helps aid the priest on his quest to be exonerated.

Swedish actress Anita Bjork was originally cast, but after Jack Warner learned she had a child out of wedlock, he gave Baxter the part. Hitchcock wasn't pleased with the switch and was already at his wit's end with Clift's "method acting" and heavy drinking. Baxter met the famed director one week before production began, on location in Quebec. "He was very particular about wardrobe and hair," Anne later recalled. "I felt I wasn't as pretty as he wanted a woman to be in his films, and as he wanted me to be. There was a lot of Pygmalion in him, and he was proud of how he transformed actresses. When I arrived, everything happened so fast that they didn't design a new wardrobe for me; they altered Anita Bjork's clothes. Naturally, I was a little overwrought about the haste, but he simply said, 'Anne, it's only a movie!'"

Anne appeared on Broadway in 1953 opposite Tyrone Power in Charles Laughton's *John Brown's Body*. Her next film, *The Blue Gardenia*, centers on Baxter's character Norah Larkin who awaits the return of her fiancé from the Army, only to discover he has sent her a reverse "Dear John" letter. Distraught, she decides to go out with lothario Harry Prebble—a character that had been courting her roommate, played by Ann Sothern.

Prebble, played by Raymond Burr, wines and dines the lonely young woman with plans to later take advantage of her after dinner.

**Anne with famed crooner Nat Cole in 1953's *Blue Gardenia***

The incomparable Nat King Cole serenades them at the swanky dinner club with his latest song *Blue Gardenia*. Arranged by Nelson Riddle, Nat sings:

> *"I lived for an hour.*
> *What more can I tell?*
> *Love bloomed like a flower,*
> *Then the petals fell.*
> *Blue Gardenia—*
> *Thrown to a passing breeze,*
> *But pressed in my book of memories."*

Back at Prebble's apartment, and in a drunken stupor, Norah resists his forceful advances by striking him with a fireplace poker before fleeing the scene, leaving behind the blue gardenia he bought for her. The next morning, she awakens in her apartment with only a vague memory of what happened. Then she discovers Prebble was killed and assumes she committed the crime. The suspense thriller has a surprise ending that exonerates the young woman.

In 1955 Anne appeared in the period picture *The Spoilers*, this version being the fifth run of the film. It starred Jeff Chandler and Rory Calhoun.

The year 1956 saw the release of Cecil B. DeMille's *The Ten Commandments*, showcasing an all-star cast including Edward G. Robinson, Yul Brynner, Vincent Price, Yvonne De Carlo, and Charlton Heston, as Moses. Baxter traded in her usually elegant accessories for the exotic attire befitting Egyptian queen Nefertari. The film is the fifth-highest grossing movie of all time in the U.S. and Canada. It won the Academy Award for Best Visual Effects, having been nominated for six other Oscars. Long-time friend and costume designer Edith Head worked with Anne for this movie.

**With Yul Brynner in *Ten Commandments***

Ms. Head was the foremost costume designer in her heyday. She was nominated for 35 Academy Awards, winning eight, more Oscars than any other woman has won. She dressed Mae West in *She Done Him Wrong*, Gloria Swanson in *Sunset Boulevard*, Bette Davis for *All About Eve*, the Hitchcock women and Natalie Wood, among others.

Edith also served as godmother to Anne's daughter Melissa, who observed of the famous costume designer, "She was working all the time. She was basically a workaholic. I think that is one of the reasons why mother and she got along so famously. They both were completely devoted to their craft. And my mother would be the first to tell you that. Her career was way before her family. Aunt Edie didn't have family beyond Uncle Bill.

"At the studio she had the persona. The bun in the back of her head, and the bangs and the glasses, the little gray suits. And very business-like. And the stars in front of her were the stars there. At home, she relaxed, she cut up, she laughed. She liked to [joke] that she dressed like a Spanish omelet. She was very Bohemian in her dress at home. Nothing like what you saw at the studio...She didn't even know how to draw when she dove into costume design!"

## Out Front in the Outback

Douglas Fairbanks, Jr. produced the underrated suspense *Chase a Crooked Shadow* in which Anne was cast as South African heiress Kimberly Prescott. She grapples with whom to trust when a stranger, played by Richard Todd, arrives claiming to be her deceased brother. Friends and relations back up the man's claims—yet she knows better.

In 1959 Anne filmed *Summer of the Seventeenth Doll* on location in Australia. While there, she stayed with friends Peter and Edwina Baillieu who tried to set their widowed friend up on a blind date with rancher Randolph Galt. Baxter, on her way back to the States, declined to meet her mystery man. She and her family were meeting up in Arizona to spend Easter with Frank Lloyd Wright at his home "Taliesin West." It was the last time she would see her grandfather. Wright passed away on April 9, 1959 at the age of 91.

**With Frank Lloyd Wright**

Anne reflected, "Like many famous men, my grandfather had been too busy to be a good father. But he was a charming grandfather. He designed plans for me for a doll-house."

Shortly after he died, Anne appeared on a San Francisco television show commemorating Wright. After the broadcast, Anne received a call at the station from Peter Baillieu. But when she went to the phone it was not her friend, but rather her mystery man— Randolph Galt. She agreed to meet him at the Clift Hotel. They hit it off immediately, even though Galt had to leave for Australia ten days later to look into buying a cattle station in the bush.

The two would meet again in September and Ran proposed to Anne on New Year's Eve. However, she was concerned about the age difference, being six-and-a-half years older. "I had become one of the billions of women who'd dropped their lives and followed for love. Very old-fashioned, and very real," she reflected.

But before the two were married, a deranged male fan of Baxter's, distraught at the news of her engagement, threatened to sabotage the wedding by murdering her fiancé. He contacted famed columnists

Louella Parsons and Hedda Hopper with his plans, which of course, exploded in the newspapers. The stalker got as far as threatening Baxter's agent at gunpoint. The wedding proceeded in Honolulu, amidst the press and with police protection. It was held at the Galt family church, St. Andrews Episcopal Cathedral. Anne, close to her parents, was saddened by the fact that they declined to attend the services. "They did not dislike Ran. It was the idea of Australia they hated," the actress later wrote.

Baxter agreed to move into the residence called Giro, sight-unseen. The broken down farmhouse was 180 miles north of Sydney—

**Anne Baxter was a favorite pin-up girl**

and a million miles from anything Anne had ever known or loved. Cattle branding, long muddy trips into the nearest town, limited electricity and resources and frequent flights in small planes became the norm for the movie star. Ran adopted Anne's daughter Katrina—however, in her early 20s, she took her original last name back.

Anne's next role came in the form of Dixie Lee in the Glenn Ford flick *Cimarron*. The lavishly produced movie failed to draw large audiences, but it did receive two Oscar nods for Best Art Direction and Best Sound. The world premier of the movie was held in Oklahoma City. Anne also appeared in *Dance Man* opposite Dean Stockwell, and then *Goodbye, My Love* directed by Ida Lupino and costarring Ronald Reagan. Baxter reflected, "Ronnie was sweet, although I hoped he wouldn't bring his soapbox. Conservative politics were his consuming passion. I was an apolitical preservative."

But there was trouble in paradise, or rather, the desolate bush where a movie star was an oddity, and a woman who valued the finer things in life was all the more obscure. Anne documented her stay in her memoir: "Loneliness was a prescription at Giro. You took it every morning, like vitamins." Anne continued, "My love for Ran was enormous. But it was suicide to live in his pocket. He had a right to his world. I just wished he'd share a bit more of it with me."

Anne compared her lifestyle to that of early pioneer women on the frontier. "Most people asked about my Adjustment, that chimera. What could I say? Tell them my plates were too big for the sink? Or never to wash sheets when the river is up? Or that I missed being coddled like an egg by American anything? Or that I was horror-stricken at maggoty garbage? Or that I was singularly inept at floor mopping? Or that I was often desperate for a dial phone with a friend at the other end. That I wasn't up for much of any of it and secretly despaired at all my professional training going to waste."

She suffered a miscarriage early on in the marriage, a blow she wrote about in her memoir. Anne then learned she was once again with child.

The actress next appeared in the risqué 1961 movie *Walk on the Wild Side*, set in a brothel and featuring an early film appearance by Jane Fonda. Laurence Harvey, Capucine, and Barbara Stanwyck were fellow costars. Tensions were high on the set, egos clashed, and Baxter tried desperately to hide her growing pregnancy. She wore full-skirts and loose-fitting dresses and followed a strict diet. Anne was seven months pregnant when production wrapped up.

The baby arrived almost a month overdue, and was born on

October 4, 1962. She and Ran named their child Melissa. A younger sister, Maginel, would be born March 11, 1964, on Anne's parents' 44th wedding anniversary. The baby was named after a sibling of Frank Lloyd Wright's. When the girls were young, Anne and Ran separated and then divorced.

Melissa speculated, "My guess is that it started to unravel when she took me back for the year and was pregnant again, with Maginel. There were four miscarriages in between, so it was a very scary pregnancy. And she really needed to be in the States, for a lot of different reasons. And so they came back. I think they spent about six months in Hawaii, and then they went to New Mexico for two or three years. And then they went up on the West Coast. And that's when they split up (in 1969)."

Melissa laughed about her home life in those days, "What the hell was [mother] doing in New Mexico for three years...where she's out walking the wilds of the dry riverbeds, the aronias, doing lines? How bizarre is that?

"Ran—and yes, I do call [my father] Ran—didn't remarry until his mother died, and my mother died. And they died in like six months of each other. And he also became 'Born Again'...Ran was never really cut out for marriage. He just wasn't. He could do anything he wanted, and pretty much did. And that's what tanked the marriage as far as I can see. He was not responsible, he was not reliable. He was great as an escort...great as a boyfriend, but sucked as a husband or a father. And I wouldn't have any problem telling that to his face. Near as I know, my younger sister might speak to him once or twice a year. I haven't spoken with him in probably 13 to 15 years.

"He was charming, and handsome, and swept [my mother] off her feet, and somehow—what was she thinking? He convinced her to run off to Australia! And she did. And then she found out that he was not all that."

Melissa observed, "My father's one of those guys that wanted to keep her away from everything. And it was manipulative, and it was not smart. And it's not how mother chose to live. Mother liked to live what I call, 'Engaged. Connected. Tuned in. And turned on. Each and every day.' That's my mother. My father's not. My father's the antithesis of that! They were like oil and water. It was a mess!"

After the divorce, Anne took her daughters to live in the States year-round. Despite her movie star status, Melissa insists her mother was a down-to-earth woman. "There was no glamour, there was no glitz. There were no limousines. I didn't see the point in celebrity status. To us it was an annoyance. Don't misunderstand me, we didn't lack for anything...But it's not like it is today where a person makes one movie and they're suddenly a multi-millionaire person. Mom wasn't like that. Mom was a celebrity in the days when celebrities were real people."

Melissa explained that Hollywood was not a welcoming place for an over-40 actress.

"She had me when she was 38-years-old. She'd been out of Hollywood for about four years at that point. And they were none too keen when she tried to come back. They basically said, 'We're sorry; you left at your height. You're done.' So she reinvented herself for television. But television doesn't pay the way that movie stuff pays."

Baxter did make a comeback appearing on television. She went on the game show *What's My Line?*, appearing as the mystery celebrity guest. She played villain "Zelda the Great" in two episodes of *Batman*, and "Olga, Queen of the Cossacks," in three episodes, making her the only actress to play two distinct characters on that show.

Baxter teamed up with *Blue Gardenia* co-star Raymond Burr on his popular show *Ironside*. Anne appeared frequently as a guest and stand-in host of *The Mike Douglas Show*, and was featured in an episode of *Columbo* called "Requiem for a Fallen Star." Baxter also made the television films *Sherlock Holmes* and *The Masks of Death*.

Anne valued her private life and tried to keep herself and her children out of the Hollywood limelight. Melissa did not grow up with the impression that

With TV host Mike Douglas

what her family was involved with was anything significant.

"I didn't think they were famous. We never had a swimming pool. We didn't have a butler. We didn't have a maid. Mother was into Jell-O before Bill Cosby discovered it. If you wanted soft towels, you better do the laundry, because if mom did it, she hung it out on the line in the backyard, thinking it smelled good, and you got sandpaper for towels. She was not big on modern conveniences. We had them, but she didn't use the dishwasher. She believed in washing dishes by hand," Melissa explained.

Despite having a famous grandfather, Anne did not use that as a way to propel her career. Melissa emphatically recalled, "I wasn't raised with the idea that I had a famous great-grandfather. I honest to goodness did not know of his significance in American culture until I went back to design school at age 30. When he was showing up in my textbooks, I suddenly thought, 'Oh my! He was big.' So understand, that's how grounded my mother was.

"They were human. They weren't grand. Their legacy has become grand, and I think there's a part of that they would each fight. Great-grandfather might not fight it as much because his ego was grand. But I don't think that as a person he was necessarily grand. He

**Anne's career came first, motherhood second**

put on his pants one leg at a time.

"In other ways he was very lonely, which is why he always had a woman on his arm. From the way I understand it, Mamah (Mamah Borthwick Cheney, Wright's mistress) was barely dead from the massacre when he had somebody else there. That was quick! He didn't like being alone. So he always had somebody there to cater to his needs."

## The Curtain Falls

When asked if she felt her mother's career was more important than the role as mother, Melissa emphatically states, "Oh, it was more important! It's not a feel, it's a know! She sat me down at 17 and said 'I never should have been a mother.' And I didn't take that to mean anything bad, but when I ran that by my aunt in the last couple of years she said, 'Oh yes! She meant that!' (Laughs.) So it's not that she didn't love us, she did! But my aunt said, 'she took an intermission, just like the name of her book. Everybody else was having babies, so your mom wanted to take that time out and have babies, too.'"

Melissa explained, "We were definitely secondary to her. She never felt that she had been enough of a mother. She really hadn't been. She made a choice. Her career was first. It's why we had such a bizarre series of caregivers. I can't call them nannies or housekeepers because they really didn't do that. There's a whole other book in that scenario!

"She missed so many things when we were growing up. She was never available for the parents' nights, or when she showed up, she was the 'Belle of the Ball,' not us. Imagine how that feels when you're ten or 12-years-old. That's hard. No I don't still resent it, I'm over it, but I can definitely see that it was very hard at the time. I went through four years of college, and I didn't tell anybody who my mother was. Why should I? She's her. She's my mother. She shows up at graduation, which was intended. I had friends look at me like, 'Why didn't you tell us?' I'm like, 'Why does it matter? Who's your mother?' (Laughs.) That's hard. That's hard to grow up with...You get eclipsed by your parent's fame. It's not by your parent, but it's by your parent's fame."

Despite the hassles of celebrity, Anne made time to interact with her public. "Mother was always incredibly gracious with her fans," Melissa recalled. "Even when they botched things up like when we were on the Circle Line in New York in fifth grade. It's a big boat and it was packed. And they announced that Anne Bancroft was onboard and then they had to correct themselves. Mom handled it all extremely well. She was an incredibly gracious person."

Anne married for a third and final time in 1977. She and stock-broker David Klee were regarded as a solid romantic match, and Melissa observed that he treated Anne like a queen—the way her previous husbands had not. While working on renovations on their Connecticut home, he died unexpectedly in October of 1977, after only nine months of marriage. The house itself was architecturally reminiscent of Frank Lloyd Wright's flat-roofed structures. Baxter remodeled the living room fireplace to resemble the fireplace in her grandfather's masterpiece, Fallingwater.

Melissa and her mother grew apart for several years as the girl entered adulthood. However, Ms. Galt warmly recalled a Christmas break in college when she went home to visit her mother and sisters. Anne had wanted a "Flexible Flyer" wooden sled, despite being a woman in her mid-50s. Melissa recalled that her mother never lost her child-like sense of wonderment, and was over the moon when her daughters finally got her what she had been asking for, for years.

In 1983, Bette Davis starred in the pilot of the nighttime drama *Hotel*, costarring James Brolin and Connie Sellecca. Due to suffering a stroke, broken hip and having undergone a mastectomy, Ms. Davis was not able complete her contractual obligations. With just 72 hours notice, Anne Baxter stepped in to fill Davis' role as the owner of the hotel. Contrary to the bad blood from their time filming *All About Eve*, the two women got along in later years. That summer, Baxter invited Davis over to her home "to dinner and to dish."

Baxter told *People* magazine, "My initial reaction was concern that Bette might be distressed [over taking over the role]. I was told she knew perfectly well what was happening and wanted me." Davis disapproved of the show's controversial material and always referred to *Hotel* as "Brothel" instead. Indeed, for its time, the show pushed the envelope of propriety with episodes dealing with abortion, rape, suicide, same-sex relationships and abuse.

The 61-one-year-old actress disclosed her daily routine of staying fit and active. "I have to rest at noon when I'm working. I take a 40-minute catnap in my dressing room after I eat my rabbit food and take my vitamins." She began her day at 3:45 a.m. then would power walk before her 7:30 a.m. call on the set. She went on to star in 75 episodes of Hotel.

While the rifts between mother and daughters were on the mend, and Anne's career was going strong, her life was cut short. While hailing a cab in New York City, the actress collapsed due to suffering a stroke. She never regained consciousness. Eight days later on December 12, 1985, she passed away at the age of 62. Baxter was cremated and interred in the family plot at Wright's beloved Taliesin, located in Spring Green, Wisconsin.

"Mom never lost her excitement for life," Melissa reflects. "She had an enthusiasm that powered her out of bed in the morning, and made her not want to go to sleep at night. And she had it about her work, she had it about travel, she had it about her writing. She was definitely a perfectionist. She really struggled with that. And we all three got that one from her. But that also came from her mother, who told her she wasn't good enough. And so she told herself she wasn't good enough. And then she told us we weren't good enough. It all comes around full-circle."

Today Melissa Galt is a successful interior designer out of Atlanta, as well as a motivational speaker and author. She remains estranged from her father and older sister but says she speaks occasionally with her younger sister Maginel. "Mother was the glue that held this family together. She held the three of us girls together. And without my mother, there is absolutely no glue. None. We each have intensely different recollections in terms of our over-all emotional feeling about my mother, and I'm really great about where I am with it. I miss her like crazy. I think about her all the time.

"[Maginel] turned to religion and became Catholic…We just have different values…I think mother would be extremely unhappy that the three of us are so far apart, because she was an only child, and she valued family a great deal."

But Melissa says she is at peace with Anne's flaws as a parent. She cherishes the memories of her mother who was an elegant, talented, and beautiful woman who left a lasting mark on movie history.

Anne Baxter had a saying she carried with her through the years, "See into life, don't just look at it."

"It is just absolutely my mother," Melissa stated. "See it. Taste it. Touch it. Feel it. [Life] is not to be gone through as a robot. This is not to be viewed from the perimeter. It's not a game and you're sitting in the stands. You're on the field."

# 6.
## JEAN SEBERG:
### *Living On the Edge*

JEAN SEBERG HAD AN OLD-FASHIONED, SMALL-TOWN UPBRINGING. Despite having no formal acting training, at age 18, she beat out 18,000 other contestants for the role of Joan of Arc in the film *Saint Joan*, directed by Otto Preminger. After a series of failed movies, the actress was regarded as too green (and politically too red), to spark much interest at the studios, so she took her career abroad. She became the darling of French New Wave cinema, dined with the Kennedys and Charles de Gaulle, married Frenchmen and wore the latest Yves Saint Laurent fashions. But her support of leftist groups—particularly the Black Panther Party—caught the attention of FBI director J. Edgar Hoover who wanted to "neutralize" Seberg at any expense.

Jean Dorothy Seberg was born on November 13, 1938, to Dorothy and Ed Seberg in Marshalltown, Iowa, then a city with a population of roughly 20,000 inhabitants (around 27,000 today). The Central Iowa town remains a hub of manufacturing and has a thriving arts and culture community. The city is also the hometown of gay rights activist and presidential biographer Merle Miller and major league baseball player Cap Anson.

Jean's father was the town's pharmacist, her mother a schoolteacher and "Twilight Sweetheart" on radio station KFJB during the 1930s. The family helped out at the Seberg Pharmacy where all the kids learned how to craft ice cream sodas. Eldest child Mary Ann arrived two years before Jean, and brothers Kurt and David followed in 1941 and 1949, respectively.

The young girl became interested in the arts at an early age. In the fourth grade, she wrote a play called *Be Kind to Animals*, which won first place in an Animal Rescue League contest. She developed an interest in poetry, especially the works of Emily Dickinson and Edna

St. Vincent Millay. Her childhood friend Hannah Heyle remembered how they used to go down and rest on the banks of the Iowa River and read poetry. "Jean was supersensitive, and she enjoyed poetry, but I think she enjoyed the idea of reading it even more. It was the sort of thing no one in Marshalltown did," Heyle said. At 12 years of age, Jean wrote this introspective poem:

*"You Laugh*
*And say I'm too naïve.*
*Not really — I just prefer to believe."*

After watching Marlon Brando in the *The Men*, wherein he plays a wounded veteran readjusting to life in a wheelchair, Jean resolved to become an actress. She would often say, "I'm going to become a very famous actress, you know." Most believed she would, or at least they found her to be a highly theatrical child. Jean would also cryptically say, "I'm going to die young. I won't live past 40."

Ed and Dorothy were good-natured, hard-working and tolerant people. They preached equality, compassion towards the marginalized, and regularly attended a Lutheran church. After Jean's confirmation ceremony in 1952, she served as a Sunday school and Bible studies teacher.

Dorothy Seberg described her husband as a man who "resembled Jimmy Stewart because he was tall, quiet and kind." While an educated man, he was at a loss for understanding his middle child's political and social interests. Ed's sister Velma Odeggaard reminisced, "She was always reading. I remember asking Ed about [the books] and he'd say 'they're beyond me.'"

At age 14 Jean applied by mail to the Des Moines chapter of the NAACP. Asked to comment on this years later, Seberg stated, "I can think of a thousand reasons for my joining the NAACP that make me sound terrific, but the only valid reason I can think of is a kind of alienation. I was raised in a rather strict atmosphere, and I thought that other people who were alienated in other ways must feel much more deeply." Her father was worried people would think she was a Communist. "Papa," Jean replied, "I don't care what people think."

Carol Hollingsworth, née Houghton, was the Marshalltown High School speech instructor and acting coach. Under Carol's guidance, Jean won an American Legion oratorical contest, earned a Division I rating in the Iowa High School Speech Association, and won the outstanding player award at the Drake University Play Festival for her work in *Happy Journey*. Her high school newspaper declared Jean the future Helen Hayes, but speculated that she would still work for her father as a soda jerk at the pharmacy in her spare time.

In December of 1955 Governor Leo Hoegh named her the first teenage chairwoman of the Iowa March of Dimes campaign. The two even made a short promo film in which a very articulate and mature Jean spoke of the need for young adults to help in eradicating Polio.

During her senior year, Jean played the lead in the play *Sabrina Fair*, a role made famous by Audrey Hepburn in the 1954 film version. Seberg was voted Most Likely to Succeed, and graduated 11th out of 195 students in her class. For a time she even considered a career in politics. The local newspaper, the *Times-Republican*, followed the activities of their popular citizen. Its editor, Warren Robeson, stayed in regular contact with the actress—even after she reached international stardom. Robeson wrote of Jean's early acting ability, "Few folks other than parents and other close relatives often attend high school plays, but Jean's abilities attracted others. How often I remember my wife saying, 'That girl will be a movie star' after watching her in the high school's production of '*Sabrina Fair*.'"

Carol secured a scholarship for Jean to work in summer stock in Massachusetts and New Jersey. The aspiring actress jumped at the chance. While on the East Coast, Jean and some friends attended a movie at the Cape May theater and saw a trailer about director Otto Preminger's talent search in casting the lead role for his forthcoming film on the life of Joan of Arc. Jean found the contest contrived and put it out of her mind. However, her friends and colleagues weren't so dismissive.

J. William Fisher, who owned one of Marshalltown's major manufacturing companies, Fisher Controls, believed Jean would be perfect for the role. He and Ms. Seberg's speech teacher submitted Jean's name for the contest. According to Carol Hollingsworth, "I was the fourth person to recommend Jean. Her summer stock group in the East also submitted her name, and she knew it. But I get either the 'credit' or the 'blame,' when actually I was low on the totem pole."

Within a matter of weeks, Seberg received a letter that she was a finalist in the search and was asked to audition at the Sherman Hotel in Chicago. Her parents were hesitant. They insisted she register for college at the University of Iowa where older sister Mary Ann was attending. "I took my suitcases into the University and met my roommate, and then left immediately for Chicago," Jean reflected. She never returned for class.

Mary Ann told this author, "My first thought was that she had gone through 'rush' at the University of Iowa and she was going to be my sorority sister. I was rather disappointed."

When it was her turn to appear before the board, Jean went into the casting room and met the crusty Otto Preminger. She told the director she was 17 years and 11 months old. When asked if she wanted to be an actress, Jean replied, "very badly."

She agreed to chop off her long blonde hair for the part, which sparked a short hairstyle craze that would soon sweep the world. Mia Farrow would later receive credit for starting the pixie cut, but it was Jean who pioneered the look—ten years before Farrow. In October, Jean was presented to 60 million television viewers on the *Ed Sullivan Show* as the winner of the talent search. Sullivan referred to his guest as "The girl who caught lightning in a bottle."

On November 13th, Jean's 18th birthday, the young girl from Iowa was on a plane to London to begin filming. The tyrannical Preminger ruled his set with an iron fist. He physically intimidated Jean, yelled and threatened to replace her. He recklessly allowed Jean to sustain injuries when her character was burned at the stake. Seberg briefly caught on fire, enduring lifelong scars as a result. Preminger kept the cameras rolling and the scenes were used in the final film.

*Saint Joan* was a box office disaster. *Time* magazine felt Seberg had been "drastically miscast."

**Jean as Joan of Arc**

One film critic berated Preminger and suggested Jean go "back to the Iowa high school where he found her."

Surrounded by massive amounts of publicity, albeit some negative, Jean granted an interview with bigwig gossip columnist Louella Parsons. The brash reporter asked Jean if she planned to wed Preminger, a man 33 years her senior. "Certainly not!" the actress replied. "He's much older than I am, and he has been like a father to me."

*Confidential* magazine, a precursor to today's checkout line tabloids, ran a scathing article entitled "Svengali and the Druggist's Daughter." The piece had so embarrassed Ed Seberg, that he bought all the copies in Marshalltown and burned them. Jean addressed the failure of her first movie to *Photoplay* magazine in August of 1957, reflecting "I think, more than anything else, I want to develop as a human being."

Perhaps surprisingly, Preminger cast Jean for the lead in his next film *Bonjour Tristesse*, which translates as "hello sadness." It co-starred David Niven, who played her father, and Deborah Kerr as the new love interest who upsets the close father/daughter bond.

Jean admitted to *Coronet* magazine that she worried about the success of her latest film, declaring, "Otherwise I might wind up as one of the youngest has-beens in movie history." Jean then appeared on the *Mike Wallace Show*, answering his questions—some impertinent—about acting, fame, and her life.

*Bonjour Tristesse* was not a success despite the big-name actors, prompting Seberg to comment wryly "all the publicity in the world will not make you a movie star, if you are not also an actress." So she took an apartment in New York, and applied for admission to the Actor's Studio. Lee Strasberg dismissively told her to go home and write to him for formal permission to be an "auditor."

"And I did write," Jean confirmed. "Three times—and they never even bothered to answer me." She later recalled, with some bitterness, "What really hurt me then is that I had to learn to act in front of the whole world."

A picture she made with Peter Sellers, *The Mouse That Roared*, was yet another failure at the box office. "I was dejected and downhearted, naturally," Jean wrote in a self-penned article for *Modern Screen* magazine. She had shifted focus away from her career and onto her love life. The actress met a 23-year-old French lawyer and relative of film director William Wyler, named François Moreuil. His companionship was the salve that soothed Jean's wounds. Meeting the handsome bon vivant "was like coming upon a creek in a dry field, an oasis in the barren Sahara of my heart…we went strolling, hand in hand, through the snowy lanes of Central Park on wintry afternoons or we ambled along Broadway's neon-glittering sidewalks and talked about love and courage and death, about Ella Fitzgerald and Frank Sinatra, about beatniks and sex and college life," Jean wrote.

"Somehow I was comforted and relieved of the pain of my failure. When François asked me to marry him, I wanted to run down the street and shout to the world that somebody cared, somebody in the outside world wanted me to be his," she explained.

On October 5, 1958 Seberg and François were married at Trinity Lutheran Church in Marshalltown, a building that today serves as a homeless shelter and soup kitchen called the House of Compassion, and is supported by area churches.

Strong physical attraction and a warm friendship may have fused Jean and François together like two magnets, but their

Jean and 1st husband François Moreuil

polar opposite upbringings, lifestyles and priorities acted as repellent.

Seberg was a fish out of water in their fancy Parisian apartment and unaccustomed to catered affairs—which were nightly events at the homes of her husband's friends. Jean agreed to star in a film directed by François called *La Recreation* (*Playtime*). But she was miserable.

The young starlet wrote her parents and grandmother Frances Benson a letter informing them she felt her marriage was in shambles and perhaps the two should divorce. Wanting to extend her support, Frances flew to Paris and witnessed the dysfunction between Jean and François on and off the set.

"He would scream at me and then I would cry and Grandmother would try to patch things up," Jean remarked. Unbeknownst to François, Jean had filed for divorce at the Marshall County, Iowa courthouse. "We both learned all too soon and sadly that you don't marry to fight the world. You marry to be a part of it," she opined.

During the summer of 1959, Jean met a young director named Jean-Luc Godard who was interested in using her in a new film. Jean agreed to meet with the director, mainly because she did not have any pictures lined up with Columbia. The eccentric director explained to Jean that his approach to filmmaking was far less structured than that of Hollywood. He offered her a leading role in *À bout de soufflé*, translated as *Breathless*.

According to some, Seberg's entry into French films was a shrewd, calculated move, because she knew these flicks would also play in U.S. art houses, where they would be accorded more respect by critics enamored with foreign films. But it was hard work. "I remember it amazed me when I first came to France and discovered how seriously the French took the cinema. Where I come from, the cinema was an entertaining way of passing the time," Jean later remarked.

As Jean was under contract and thus not able to freelance, Godard placed all his cards on the table. He sent Columbia a 12-page telegram asking them to loan out Jean. He offered the studio $12,000 (which he didn't have), or half of the worldwide profits of the movie. Columbia had never heard of him, and had no immediate plans for casting Jean in a picture, so they accepted the money. Had they taken the latter option, Columbia would have made $3 million. But no one would have guessed the success of the movie— especially Ms. Seberg.

"So I did *Breathless*—no salary, no script. Godard worked from day to day and would come in with these crumpled sheets of yellow paper. We literally thought we were making home movies that would never be seen," she said in a 1974 interview with *Films Illustrated*. "Then after about two weeks we saw the first batch of rushes, with Godard

**Jean with Jean-Paul Belmondo in the avant-garde *Breathless***

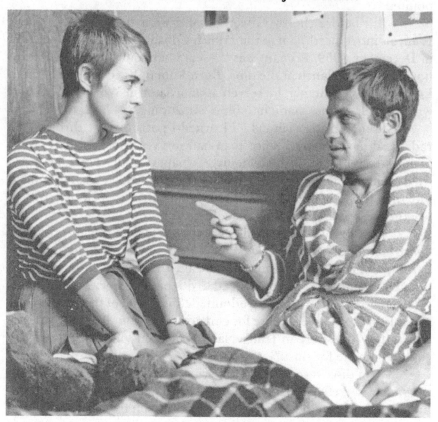

*Going Hollywood: Midwesterners in Movieland* **109**

and François Truffaut, whose idea the film was. We sat and looked at it and we said, 'well, it may never get out, but it sure is different to what any of us had ever seen.'"

## Riding a New Wave

Indeed, the world hadn't seen anything quite like *Breathless*. It featured jump cut scenes, 25 minutes of straight dialogue and took viewers on a tour of Bohemian Paris. Jean and co-star Jean-Paul Belmondo gave raw, natural performances. Jean played an American in Paris by the name of Patricia Franchini whose ill-fated romance with a Parisian thug builds to a dramatic climax.

"I still don't know why I should have meant anything to the French," Seberg confided to *Cosmopolitan* in 1969. "This strange, awkward creature with rather bad teenage skin and extremely short hair— what could she possibly have symbolized? I don't know. I only know that even today, if I autograph a picture in France and I'm not wearing my hair in the, you know, the Buchenwald cut, they're terribly disappointed."

But before the two divorced and went their separate ways, Francois introduced Jean to the French Consul General Romain Gary in December 1959. Romain was 24 years her senior and married to novelist Lesley Blanch at the time. Born Roman Kacew in the Russian Empire, now Lithuania, he served as an aviator in World War II and wrote novels—some made into films—including *The Roots of Heaven*.

François later claimed, "I learned I got a divorce through the radio and newspapers." Since Jean had not yet informed him of her plans, he was able to file his own divorce papers under French law. He cited Jean's infidelity with Romain Gary as the cause. Jean and Romain hid their relationship and awaited Lesley Branch's decision as to whether or not to grant Romain a divorce.

Jean flew to Leopoldville, Congo to film the Italian-produced *Congo Vivo*. She wrote Louella Parsons a letter, which was published in her September 1961 column. "I'm afraid I've let myself in for more than I bargained for, when I agreed to do this love story set in the current Congo situation," Seberg admitted. She spoke of the political unrest due to the people's desire for emancipation from Belgium. Louella responded, "If I were in Jean's place, I'd get out of there so fast, you couldn't see me for dust."

Jean discovered she was carrying Romain's child but kept her pregnancy secretive. Alexandre Diego was born on July 17, 1962. She hid the existence of her child for two years—even from her family. According to sister Mary Ann, "My parents went to visit Jean and Romain in Majorca and Jean said, 'I have someone I want you to meet.' Of course they were surprised, but also thrilled to have a grandson." However, Mary Ann doesn't want to speculate on what her sister's motives were in keeping her pregnancy under wraps. Most likely the movie star wanted to wait until she and Romain could

Jean and husband #2 Romain Gary dined with JFK

legally marry. "It's very difficult for me to talk about what she might have been thinking," her sister reflected.

Jean won the lead in the romantic film *In the French Style* and began filming immediately after giving birth. Her contract with Columbia was renewed, and the flick was hailed as the first successful picture she made in the States.

Seberg also appeared in the rarely mentioned sequel to *Breathless* called *Le Grand Escroc* (*The Big Swindler*) wherein her character is in Morocco working as a reporter.

With her career on fire, she graced the cover of *Life* magazine the week of March 8, 1963. On June 20th, Jean and Romain were invited to a private dinner with President John Kennedy and his wife Jacqueline, an occasion Jean always regarded fondly. That autumn, Jean and Romain wed after Lesley finally agreed to a divorce.

"After a hazardous trek that has included nine movies, one shattered marriage and some of the worst reviews of our time, a modern Cinderella has arrived," wrote *The Saturday Evening Post* contributor Peter Hamill. In the interview Jean reflected upon her lackluster start and difficulty in becoming an established actress.

Screenwriter Thomas Ryan defended Seberg to the *Post*, "Every time I read about poor little Jean Seberg I have to laugh. This was a tough little dame, very resilient, who knew exactly what she wanted. And Otto [Preminger] despite the stories, did try to make it up to her. That's why he put her in a second movie, *Bonjour Tristesse*."

But then Preminger "dropped me like a used Kleenex," Seberg bemoaned.

Jean was suggested for the lead in the edgy 1964 classic story *Lilith*. She cited this role as the first one she really fought to secure. Her character Lilith Arthur, a schizophrenic in a mental asylum, seduces an occupational therapist played by Warren Beatty. Peter Fonda and Gene Hackman also starred. Director Richard Rossen had the film shot on location in a real mental asylum. Jean even befriended a patient whom she maintained a correspondence with for several years.

"Warren Beatty still hates it," Jean laughed. "I told him that in Europe it is a cult picture which is screened in the art houses every three months or so."

Sister Mary Ann told this author, "It was the first film when I didn't look at her as my sister on the screen."

Jean enjoyed her life as the wife of a French diplomat and her film career slowed. On February 18, 1964, she and her husband lunched with French president Charles de Gaulle, who told Jean he was a fan of her movies. She made the war drama *Line of Demarcation* in 1966, followed by her first Hollywood movie in several years in the Lana Turner-esque—*Moment to Moment*.

The title of Jean's next film, which she made with Sean Connery, was a preview of what was to come in her life. It was called *A Fine Madness*.

That summer, Jean flew to South America to shoot *Estouffade à la Caraïbe* (*Revolt in the Caribbean*), where she portrayed the daughter of a mobster. After the experience, Jean told friends, "If I had lived in South America, I would have fought with Che [Guevara, the Marxist revolutionary]."

Seberg agreed to star in 1968's *Birds in Peru*, written and directed by her husband. After viewing the finished product, Jean was aghast. The movie was pornographic. She felt sexually objectified by her spouse and embarrassed for people—particularly in Marshalltown—to see the movie, in which she plays a depraved nymphomaniac. This was the first film to receive an X rating by the Motion Picture Association of America and was banned throughout Europe.

Robert Ebert gave the movie a searing one star review, writing, "Oh yes, she has a lovely face...We see it for minutes on end...Gary holds his close-ups much too long...The beach photography, by the way, was apparently meant to be surrealistic...as if, this were a Salvador Dali retrospective. But none of it works. The movie doesn't grow. The characters drift through their vacuum. Rarely has so much pretension created so much waste."

Despite appearing in risqué pictures, Jean refused to ever be filmed naked. Any film in which she appeared "in the nude," was actually the work of a body double.

Jean had a small role in the George Peppard movie *Pendulum*. Ten days into filming, Jean learned her 18-year-old brother David had been killed in a car accident. The loss of the youngest child was the first in a series of blows to the Seberg family.

In 1969, Alan Jay Lerner asked Jean to play the female lead in the musical comedy meets western, *Paint Your Wagon* with Clint Eastwood and Lee Marvin. It was the big-budget spectacle her film career needed. Jean and Eastwood began a torrid love affair during filming. When Romain found out, he challenged Eastwood to a duel, yelled, then left the movie set in a huff. Jean admitted to have developed a crush on Clint, whom she liked because "he was the absolute opposite of Romain, an outdoor type, a kickback to my days in Iowa." Jean and her husband agreed filing for divorce was best, but their friendship remained intact.

Jean with Clint Eastwood in *Paint Your Wagon*

Jean was given a small role in the block-buster disaster film *Airport*. It co-starred Burt Lancaster, George Kennedy, Jacqueline Bissett, Van Heflin, Dean Martin and her childhood idol Helen Hayes. The film was nominated for ten Academy Awards, and led to three sequels, none of which Jean was ever invited to appear in. It was Seberg's final United States film project.

The actress devoted herself to various civil rights causes, organizations and individuals. In Iowa, she gave the Meskwaki Bucks at the Tama Indian settlement near Marshalltown $500 to buy basketball uniforms. In the 1970s, she bought a boardinghouse for black students attending Marshalltown Community College to live in due to segregated conditions. She gave money to Jim Brown's Negro Industrial Economic Union, attended Southern Christian Leadership Conference rallies, opposed the Vietnam War and even spoke politics with Robert

Kennedy at various Hollywood events.

Through her travels, Jean made the acquaintance of the charismatic black leader Hakim Jamal (born Alan Donaldson). He was married to Dorothy Durham, a distant relative of Malcolm X. Hakim always played up the relation, referring to the slain activist as "Cousin Malcolm." His founding of a Malcolm X Foundation and Montessori School in the Compton/Watts area of Los Angeles, appealed to Jean. She supported Jamal's plan to provide ghetto children with free breakfast, bought them a school bus, and helped provide funding. She also volunteered there.

In turn, Jean endured verbal, physical, mental and sexual abuse from Jamal and his minions. She supported the group's platform that black and impoverished people deserved decent housing, free health care, an education, as well as self-defense against the racist and often violent police. Jean gave the group a total of $10,500—over $64,000 by modern day standards. The pharmacist's daughter from Iowa was now a card-carrying member of the Black Panther Party.

### One Step Closer to the Edge

In June of 1969, G.C. Moore, the FBI official in charge of monitoring extremist groups, proposed "an active discreet investigation be instituted on American actress Jean Seberg who is providing funds and assistance to black extremists, including leaders of the Black Panther Party." With that, the Immigration and Naturalization Service was instructed to search Seberg's luggage at Customs. Her photo and personal info were sent to FBI field offices across the country. The bureau wanted Jean to cut ties with the Panthers—or suffer the consequences.

Seberg began receiving anonymous, threatening phone calls. She believed her phones were tapped and she was being followed. One day she discovered a pistol lying on a table in her house. Her cats were poisoned. Jean fled back to the States in a whirl of panic.

It is rumored that the place in which she took sanctuary was the residence of acting coach Paton Price. Seberg told him and his wife Tilly that she was shaken up over being shot at by the police. She asked to stay the night, and gave Tilly a box wrapped in brown paper, telling her to dispose of it. The next day the Prices had plans to take a short trip out of town, although were reluctant to leave Jean. But the mania from the night before had passed, so the Prices decided to proceed with their plans.

Upon returning home they found a note from Seberg informing the couple she was doing well and on her way to Rome. The Prices' relief was short-lived. Tilly had thrown out the package as per Jean's request, but retrieved it from the garbage out of sheer curiosity. In the box she found a man's pink shirt that was covered with blood.

The FBI contacted Rome and Paris, informing them Seberg would soon be arriving and to keep a watchful eye on her and her activities. The agency was closely following her movements, her marriage and the fact she was expecting a baby.

In February 1970 newspapers including *The Cedar Rapids Gazette* featured Jean in their Celebrity Cookbook section. She shared two recipes: Midwestern Lemon Meringue Pie and Cucumber Soup.

Emphasizing her Heartland roots, Seberg told the newspaper (located in a city about 70 miles east of Marshalltown), "I love that country and only Middle-westerners can know how beautiful that country is. Other people can drive through and think 'oh, another zillion miles of cornfields.' But it was all the different kinds of birds, crabapple trees and tulips in bloom. And the sight of that rich black soil. When you see the loam when it's just been tilled, you realize there's no nation on Earth that wouldn't like to have that kind of soil. Remember Khrushchev even visited an Iowa pork farm when he came to the U.S. It's that, wow, kind of nature that's so extraordinary."

J. Edgar Hoover, who headed the FBI from 1924 until his

**Jean telling children about her career, but the FBI said she was a threat to national security**

death in 1972 didn't find the Midwestern actress quite so wholesome and kind-hearted. He was reputed to have said he was going to "take care of those two bitches"—referring to Jean and Jane Fonda. He believed the only way to calm racial tension was through "vigorous law enforcement." When asked by a reporter, "How about justice?" Hoover replied, "Justice is merely an incidental to law and order."

On April 21, 1970, the actress received a middle of the night phone call in Paris from Panthers Elaine Brown and Raymond Hewitt. Jean jokingly called Hewitt Johnny Appleseed, for "planting your little

**The FBI plots a smear campaign to destroy Jean Seberg**

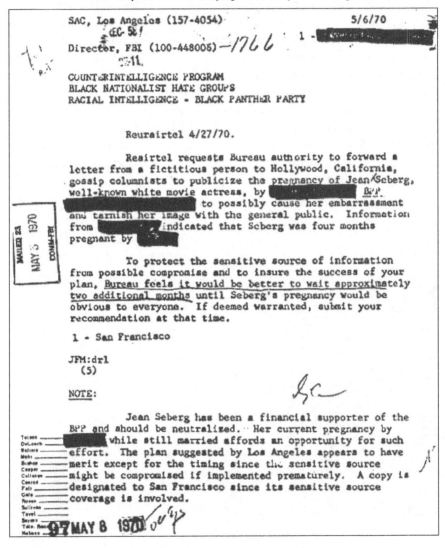

SAC, Los Angeles (157-4054)        5/6/70
EC-58

Director, FBI (100-448006) —/76 6   1 -

COUNTERINTELLIGENCE PROGRAM
BLACK NATIONALIST HATE GROUPS
RACIAL INTELLIGENCE - BLACK PANTHER PARTY

      Reurairtel 4/27/70.

      Reairtel requests Bureau authority to forward a letter from a fictitious person to Hollywood, California, gossip columnists to publicize the pregnancy of Jean Seberg, well-known white movie actress, by _____ BPP _____ to possibly cause her embarrassment and tarnish her image with the general public. Information from _____ indicated that Seberg was four months pregnant by _____

      To protect the sensitive source of information from possible compromise and to insure the success of your plan, Bureau feels it would be better to wait approximately two additional months until Seberg's pregnancy would be obvious to everyone. If deemed warranted, submit your recommendation at that time.

1 - San Francisco

JFM:drl
(5)

NOTE:

      Jean Seberg has been a financial supporter of the BPP and should be neutralized. Her current pregnancy by _____ while still married affords an opportunity for such effort. The plan suggested by Los Angeles appears to have merit except for the timing since the sensitive source might be compromised if implemented prematurely. A copy is designated to San Francisco since its sensitive source coverage is involved.

MAILED 21 MAY 1970 COMM-FBI

Tolson
DeLoach
Walters
Mohr
Bishop
Casper
Callahan
Conrad
Felt
Gale
Rosen
Sullivan
Tavel
Soyars
Tele. Room
Holmes

97 MAY 8 1970

seeds around"—a reference to him recently impregnating two women, a shock because Hewitt believed himself to be sterile. The FBI had been eavesdropping and believed they had struck blackmail gold.

Six days later, R.W. Held of the Los Angeles branch of the FBI sent a memo to Hoover with the supposition that Ms. Seberg was carrying Hewitt's child. Held wanted to plant the hearsay with the press. "It is felt that the possible publication of Seberg's plight could cause her embarrassment and serve to cheapen her image with the general public," the agent wrote.

Just nine days later, Hoover replied to the proposal. "It would be better to wait approximately two additional months until Seberg's pregnancy would be more obvious." The director added, "Jean Seberg has been a financial supporter of the BPP and should be neutralized."

Only one month later Held sent Hoover a newspaper clipping of an article written by *Los Angeles Times* gossip columnist Joyce Haber—touted as the successor of the loathsome Hedda Hopper. Haber had taken the bait. "According to really 'in' international sources...Miss A is expecting and... Papa's said to be a rather prominent Black Panther," she wrote.

Although estranged from Romain Gary, he publicly denounced the article and claimed paternity. It was never confirmed whether or not Jean intentionally overdosed, but on the night of August 7th, she was rushed to the hospital where she was living in Majorca, to have her stomach pumped. Gary then moved her into a hotel in Geneva to relax. But on the 19th, Jean acquired the latest issue of *Newsweek* magazine, the first publication to refer to her by name in reference to carrying a Black Panther's child. In a matter of days, over 100 news outlets picked up the story. The next day, overwrought, Jean began experiencing contractions and the baby was delivered prematurely on August 23, 1970. Nina Hart Gary died two days later.

After giving birth, several European Black Panther "friends" came to Seberg's hospital room demanding her credit cards, money, car keys and typewriter. One member also waved around a gun. He said to her, "Here Jean, look. This is the best gun in Europe."

Seberg later recounted, "I took it and turned it over in my hands. Stupidly. Without thinking. My fingerprints were on it. He could kill anyone with that gun and furnish proof against me."

Bodyguard Guy-Pierre Geneuil even claimed Jean's son Diego was the victim of a kidnapping attempt days later at a hotel outside Geneva. Jean was summoned on the phone, spoke to the caller for only a few seconds, then called out to Guy-Pierre that she was told her son was about to be abducted. Asked by whom, she replied "The FBI." The bodyguard ran to Jean's child, who was playing across the street in the park. A car pulled up to the boy, a woman got out and grabbed him. Diego bit her arm and was able to escape. The kidnappers were never apprehended.

Jean wanted her daughter to be buried in Riverside Cemetery in Marshalltown. On her way to Chicago from Zurich, she drank and carried on loudly during the flight. The O'Hare Airport is one of the busiest in the world so security was highly visible. Jean spotted a black man in uniform. She wailed, "Traitor! You're black. How can you be a cop?" Jean's bodyguard Guy-Pierre, finally managed to get her on the connecting flight to Des Moines, where the Sebergs awaited them.

Jean's son Diego was almost kidnapped

At the viewing and again at the funeral, Jean insisted on an open casket and took a multitude of pictures. Roger Maxwell, a childhood friend, attended the ceremony. He told this author he felt upon seeing the child's remains the baby looked Caucasian based on the hair texture and nails. Nina was buried in the Seberg family plot mere feet from Jean's brother David.

Mark Adams-Westin, a teenager who worked at the Seberg pharmacy, performed two songs at the funeral service: *Jesus Was a Carpenter* and *What's This World Coming To*. Adams-Westin told this author, "When her daughter died, they were looking for someone to sing at the funeral. Ed approached me and asked if I would sing at the funeral service. It was a rather surreal experience. It was very dream-like for me...a lot of stuff a 19-year-old boy didn't understand."

After the funeral service, Adams-Westin recalled how "Six or eight of us sat around [the Seberg] home and played music. I brought my mother." He said the service had been recorded at least partially. "I think she took the music with her when she had a breakdown."

Jean confided her concerns and thoughts about Black Nationalism with her Marshalltown confidant, Rabbi Sol Serber.

Romain Gary however, didn't attend the service, citing sudden illness, but speculation led to the belief he was not Nina's father. He may not have been; after all, he and Jean were separated for a time, and no paternity test was done. In the end, French courts ordered *Newsweek* to pay $11,000 in damages and print the court's decision in their publication. Ultimately, the matter was settled out of court.

Doctors were also heavily medicating Jean, and at one point she was on Lithium. Jean most likely suffered postpartum depression, or even the more severe form postpartum psychosis. She was clearly unstable, even claiming to hear messages coming from the refrigerator, or seeing them in crumbled pieces of aluminum foil. Friends speculated Jean Seberg suffered from bipolar disorder or schizophrenia.

On December 29, 1970, the FBI put the actress on its Security Index-Priority 3 list, reserved for someone "because of background is potentially dangerous; or has been identified as a member or participant in communist movement, or has been under active investigation as member of other group or organization inimical to the U.S."

If there was a terrorist attack, assassination, or other national emergency, Jean would be arrested and taken into police custody "for the safety of the American people."

A few months later, Romain published the socially conscious book *White Dog*. It told the story of how he and Jean had taken in a shepherd dog that had been trained to attack black people and the couple's quest to "deprogram it." Her estranged husband remained a lifelong cynic of America's handling of race relations.

With Jean and Romain's divorce finalized, the two agreed Diego should remain in Paris for schooling, so their apartment was re-configured to allow separate living quarters for Jean and Romain. Jean was offered a part in the film *L'attentat* (*The French Conspiracy*) that was a success. She began dating aspiring director Dennis Charles Berry, son of John Berry, a Hollywood director blacklisted in the 1950s. After a mere three weeks of dating, the couple flew to Las Vegas and got hitched on March 12, 1972.

Seberg's professional endeavors were successful, at least overseas. She filmed *Kill! Kill! Kill!* with James Mason. In 1973 she directed her first movie, *Ballad for the Kid*. She told England's *Films Illustrated*, "Until I began directing, I never realized how little I had absorbed about film making. I have been acting for half my life and suddenly I am making 20 decisions a second and my mind is click, click, clicking... The one thing of which I am absolutely certain is that I adore acting and I want to go on doing it until I am a little old lady of 90."

She spent the next few years writing and making movies in Europe that were only released overseas. The film *Mousey* was a flick done in the cat and mouse style, and Seberg played opposite Kirk Douglas. Once again, the actress agreed to star in a film directed by a husband. Berry's *Le Grand Délire* (*The Big Delirium*) did not receive much praise.

While Jean devoted most of her free time to writing, she did agree to make the *The Wild Duck*, a German-language version of the Henrik Ibsen play, in 1976. She also began work on an autobiography.

Her marriage to Berry was shaky, and friends claimed Berry was physically abusive. That summer, Jean received a letter from the U.S. Department of Justice, informing her that it was the FBI who had planted the story about Nina's paternity in the press. Seberg's paranoiac fears were finally vindicated by the Bureau's confession she had been targeted by COINTELPRO (the Counter-Intelligence Program). It was an illegal agency within the FBI whose authority spanned the offices of the CIA, U.S. Army intelligence, White House, Attorney General, and even local and state law enforcement agencies. The mission, in the words of Hoover, was "to expose, disrupt, misdirect, discredit and otherwise neutralize specific groups and individuals." Victims included the Native American Rights Movement, anti-war, anti-racist, environmental groups, gender and class equality groups, and the Black Panther Party. Even Martin Luther King, Jr. was brutally harassed by COINTELPRO days before he was killed.

While the Feds claimed to no longer be monitoring her activities, Jean spent the rest of her life embittered and certain government agents still followed her. She made her last visit to Marshalltown in April 1977. That August, her grandmother Frances Benson passed away. Then in October, the home for black students got shut down due to Seberg's poor financial state as well as noise complaints.

Early in 1978, Jean made an uncredited appearance in the film *Le bleu des origines*, or *The Blue of the Beginning*. The once glamorous, bright-eyed actress now suffered the physical affects of years of heavy smoking, drinking and pill use. She wrote inarticulate letters to the French press and told the *International Herald Tribune*: "[The FBI] got my daughter and they're going to pay for it."

Mary Ann recalled pleasant encounters with Jean's husbands, but admitted her visits with them were few and far between. She told this author, "We had very little contact with any of them. They're all different from what we're used to. They were unique individuals. She was happy and that's what made us happy."

Jean went in and out of hospitals for mental evaluation, allegedly receiving the barbaric electroshock therapy. Upon her release that summer, she filed for divorce from Dennis Berry, and then wrote her parents a letter declining their invitation to visit Iowa. They did not know about her health, nor the letter from the U.S. government.

By the late 1970s, Jean had taken up civil rights causes in France, namely the mistreatment of Algerians. In early 1979, Jean told friends she was dating Abdul Aziz Bouteflika, Algeria's Minister of Foreign Affairs. She flew to Algeria, but Bouteflika refused to see her. Guy-Pierre Geneuil claimed the actress told him, "I will soon be the first lady of Algeria."

While dining at La Médina, Jean was introduced to the owner's nephew Ahmed Hasni. He charmed the older Jean, claiming to be a professional athlete, actor, and Algerian general. He told her he was 29-years old—he was only 19. A month later, the two took part in a church blessing that Hasni later claimed was a wedding. However, Jean was still legally Dennis Berry's wife.

Despite suffering mental and physical pain, Jean volunteered as an SOS Friendship listener for a Paris suicide help line. Raymonde Waintraub, one of the few friends the actress kept in touch with at this point in her life, described the situation, "It was really an instance of the drowning trying to save the drowning."

But Jean's writing proved a saving grace. She contemplated selling her memoirs and began the long road to sobriety. She flew to Guyana to begin work on *La légion saute sur Kolwezi*, or *The Legion Parachutes into Kolwezi*. Jean's friends perceived Hasni as possessive, manipulative and a con artist. She told Guy-Pierre how Hasni was involved with drug trafficking between France and Algeria, "She knew too much. She was afraid," he said.

According to Hasni, Jean attempted suicide over the course of several weeks and then vanished on the morning of August 30th.

**Jean had many looks**

John Berry, the father of Jean's legal husband, insists he was the one who initially phoned the authorities. On September 7th, the police officially announced they regarded Seberg a missing person. At dusk the next day, her white Renault car was found just three blocks from her home.

Stories vary as to when and who first discovered the car. But one thing was certain: on the floor of the backseat rested an object wrapped in a blue blanket. There were several empty pill bottles and a bottle of water. Upon unwrapping the bundle the authorities discovered it contained Jean's nude dead body, decomposed almost beyond recognition. It is believed she had been deceased since the day she disappeared. A note addressed to her teenaged son Diego was found in her hand. It was written in French and translates to:

"Forgive me. I can no longer live with my nerves. Understand me. I know that you can, and you know that I love you. Be strong. Your loving mother, Jean."

Her prediction had come true. She didn't live much past 40. Upon removal of her body, the car was cleaned (potentially destroying any fingerprints or evidence of foul play). She died as the result of a barbiturate overdose, officially ruled a probable suicide.

Seberg was buried in the Cimetière du Montparnasse, Paris. A memorial service was held for Jean in Marshalltown, because Romain Gary did not feel it best to have the Sebergs attend the funeral (even though son Diego had wanted them there).

Warren Robeson, the Marshalltown *Times-Republican* newspaper's editor, wrote a tribute article to Jean, which was circulated across the country by the Associated Press. He wrote, "Time and again she bounced back. That characteristic is what makes her death by suicide so incredible to me. It seems impossible that I will not again sit in the living room of her gracious parents, the Ed Sebergs, during one of her visits home and ask, 'Well, what's next Jean?' and hear her enthusiastic reply outlining a forthcoming film…The FBI admitted Friday that it planted the false story because she was supporting black causes. If they had only known Jean as we knew her."

The day after the funeral, *The London Daily Telegraph* gave a passing mention to the FBI's smear campaign against Seberg. The story consisted of brief coverage on page 19. The November 20th edition of *The London Times* published a slightly longer story on page nine. *The Los Angeles Times* gave the story front page and above the fold coverage. Its columnist who had first reported the story about Seberg's pregnancy, Joyce Haber, maintained the information published in her column was acquired from an editor, whom she did not name, and that she had not been aware of any FBI involvement in planting the rumor.

Romain Gary and several friends insisted Jean had been murdered. The police strangely had found a suitcase at Seberg's home that contained her driver's license (which had been reported stolen months before). Also found was money and her driving glasses, which she needed due to her increasingly poor vision. The alcohol level in Jean's bloodstream was at a level greatly above legal intoxication—so high in fact, it warranted a comatose state. Yet, there were no liquor bottles found in her car, only bottled

A shocking admission by the FBI

water. That would have meant that in a heavy state of intoxication and sedation she got in her car naked, wrapped in a blanket, unable to see well, and safely drove her car. Then she parked her car, swallowed pills, climbed in the back seat, and waited to die.

Had Jean overdosed, then was dumped in the back seat of her car and left for dead? Were drug dealers involved? Had the suicide note been planted (maybe even one she had written on another occasion, during one of her numerous hospital stays)? The note only specifically spoke of her nervous condition and her desire for Diego to show her compassion.

The Parisian police questioned Hasni, and he admitted to stealing money from Jean and selling some of her jewelry and artwork. On March 4, 1981, he was sentenced to two years in prison for his theft, serving eight months.

Tragically, Diego was made an orphan on December 2, 1980 when Romain Gary put a revolver in his mouth and pulled the trigger. In his suicide note he specifically said that his death had no relation with Seberg's demise.

## Dreams That Might Have Been

Mourners remembered Jean Seberg as the girl who at age ten gave her vacation money to a stranger she had met on the bus. At a movie premier in New York City she handed out twenty-dollar bills to hungry children. She befriended hippies. She nursed sick animals. She supported free breakfast programs and gave to Jesse Jackson's "Operation Breadbasket." In France she was an advocate of raising working conditions of low-income Arabs.

Plainspoken Ed Seberg said after his daughter's death, "Jean attempted all of her life to be help and comfort to any who were in need. The dogs and cats she would bring home when she was a child, saying, 'They followed me home.' The Indians, the Blacks, the friends, the relatives and others, any who thought she would help them. And she did. She lived her convictions until the people in our world showed they did not understand her convictions. Then she gave up."

But with Jean living so much of her life in Europe and keeping her struggles to herself, the Sebergs were never fully aware of the FBI's smear campaign or the trouble in her marriages. Mary Ann told this author, "There are quite a few things about which I wish I knew the whole story...I know she supported a lot more than the Black Panther Party."

David Keller, a long-time friend of Seberg's is certain she killed herself. However, he also had this to say: "Jean knew her phone was tapped. Everyone's phone was tapped...Once, in New York, she called to say that someone had been in her hotel room while she'd been out. She had put Scotch tape on the closet doors, and it was ripped when she came in. She was a little paranoid, but with good reason. It was very real. They were out to get her."

Robert Evans, who was at the helm of Paramount, and who produced Jean's movie *Paint Your Wagon*, had

**Jean with father Ed Seberg in happier times**

also been under surveillance by the FBI. He commented, "I hope what they've heard has made their faces as red as their necks."

Jean's FBI file totals 320 pages which includes heavily censored phone conversations, travel information, and memoranda from several FBI field offices, including the Omaha, Nebraska branch. One-fifth of it remains unreleased and may have been destroyed after J. Edgar Hoover's death in 1972.

Mark Adams-Westin told this author, "She reached out to me and made me feel a worth I had never felt in my life...I was more saddened than anything else [after learning of Seberg's death] because a person I cared about was ruined by people who had no ethics."

Interest in Jean Seberg has not waned through the years. She is often featured in fashion magazines such as *Elle, Marie Claire* and *Glamour* as a style icon of great élan. Numerous books have been published on the actress and a documentary called *Movie Star: The Secret Lives of Jean Seberg* was released in 2015. In her native Marshalltown, the Jean Seberg International Film Festival has become a regular event, celebrated around her birthday in November, and held at the Orpheum Theater—where Jean's first film was screened.

Even a few songs have even been written about Ms. Seberg. An Irish band called Divine Comedy performs a number called *Absent Friends*. It contains verses about several deceased celebrities including Jean: "Little Jean Seberg seemed so full of life, but in those eyes such troubled dreams. Poor little Jean, the singer croons."

Cedar Rapids, Iowa native Harvey Sollberger composed a song on the cello and violin entitled *The Entry of Jean Seberg into Heaven*.

Actress Kristen Stewart of the *Twilight* movies fame, will portray Seberg in the 2019 political thriller *Against All Enemies*. It focuses on the FBI's surveillance of the actress.

"My first thought in how I'd like Jean to be remembered is as a loving, caring daughter, sister, aunt and mother," sister Mary Ann told this author. "I always think of Jean as someone who was way ahead of her time in not only her thoughts, but her actions as well. I miss not having a sister with whom to visit and share special occasions. Jean was always very thoughtful about remembering birthdays and other family occasions, as well as keeping in touch with family no matter where she was. I continue to be overwhelmed by all the fans worldwide who follow her in films, books, on TV and in photographs, and show their love for and appreciation of her in so many ways."

A reviewer of her film *Playtime* summed up the complex actress simply, but astutely: "Jean Seberg has found her best role: herself."

# 7.

# JANE RUSSELL:
## *Gentlemen Prefer Brunettes*

EW MOVIE STARS OF THE 1950S WERE AS SPUNKY AS JANE RUS-sell. She was discovered by Hollywood billionaire Howard Hughes, a man who shaped her image and launched her career with the salacious film *The Outlaw*. Russell represented liberated and feisty women, playing opposite Robert Mitchum, Bob Hope and Clark Gable. She made 25 movies, appeared on Broadway, was used and abused by the men in her life, yet credits her faith in God for getting her through the "detours" in her life.

Underneath the sexpot image, there was a church-going wife and mother with solid Midwestern roots, who co-founded the Hollywood Christian Group and helped organize the World Adoption International Fund (WAIF) that forever changed the way overseas adoptions are conducted.

She was born Ernestine Jane Geraldine Russell on June 21, 1921, in the Northern lake town of Bemidji, Minnesota. Her mother, Geraldine Jacobi Russell, raised the five children in a strict Episcopalian home. Geraldine and her husband Roy Russell both came from frontier families who settled in North Dakota. They spent the early years of their marriage living in Canada while Roy served in the U.S. Army. They temporarily moved back to the States so Jane could be born in America. She and her younger brothers Thomas, Kenneth, James, and Wallace spent summers at Lake Bemidji and winters in Grand Forks, North Dakota with their grandparents. The family fostered a balance of fun, adventure and responsibility, while regularly entertaining friends and attending church together.

During the Depression, Roy Russell got promoted to general manager of the Andrew Jergens West Coast factory. The Russells got the chance to move to Glendale, California. They made frequent trips back home to the Midwest to see relatives. It was in the Heartland where Jane Russell felt most at home.

A tightly-knit family, the Russells spent time riding horses on their ranch and lived an affluent lifestyle with many modern luxuries, while still maintaining a strong sense of family and tradition. Jane's mother attended Emerson College and was a stage actress in her youth, and she wanted her only daughter to follow in her footsteps. A striking beauty in her youth, Mrs. Russell had posed for a portrait done by artist Mary B. Titacomb. It was originally entitled "A Portrait of Geraldine J." President Woodrow Wilson later purchased the painting. It hangs in the President's restored former home and is now entitled "The Girl in the Blue Hat."

In 1937, when Jane was 16 years old, her father died of a stroke. Not wanting to give up the ranch, her family came together to get the work done. To do her share of the chores, Jane washed the whole family's clothes by hand in a scrub tub.

The following year, Jane began a passionate and long-term affair with a moody and temperamental football player named Robert Waterfield with whom she had gone to high school. While the young girl was clearly enamored with the college athlete, their life together was turbulent and dramatic. "It was a game with him. Life was a constant contest or it was boring. If I objected to something he was doing, he'd pull the car over to the side of the road and say 'you don't like it, get out and walk.' He was terribly spoiled. It was impossible to discuss a difference of opinion. He just wouldn't, or I should say, he couldn't," the actress wrote in her memoir.

Russell described herself as "born married," feeling it was the most important aspect of her life, and that being a married woman would only lead to happiness and fulfillment.

Jane, 19, with mom Geraldine in 1940

She would soon learn that wouldn't be the case.

Jane graduated from Van Nuys High School in 1939. The following autumn, Robert went back to UCLA, and Jane was sent to a drama school run by Max Reinhardt. Her mother hoped this would "polish" her tomboy daughter. Soon after, a photographer by the name of Tom Kelley approached Jane's childhood friend, Pat Alexander and asked her if she was interested in modeling. He said she could bring a friend along if she wished. Pat immediately thought of her pal Jane Russell. After taking some pictures of Jane, Tom suggested she go to the 20th Century-Fox studio for a screen test. Word later came back that the young girl was classified as "unphotogenic."

With modeling not working out as planned, Jane took a job folding boxes at a factory, and then got employment as a doctor's assistant. Unhappy with her current state, she spent the summer of 1940 visiting family in Fontana, California, waiting for that "something good just around the corner to happen." By the time she returned home, her mother was waiting with the news that was about to change her daughter's life forever.

### The Gal in the Haystacks

Levis Green, a Hollywood agent, had tried to contact the young girl several times to tell her that casting agent Freddy Schussler wanted to see her for an upcoming motion picture. A Hollywood producer had seen Jane's 8x10s and was eager to meet her. The next day Jane drove to 700 Romaine Street, a large gray building—the Howard Hughes studio. There, Russell met Howard Hawks, the man who was to direct Jane in the up-and-coming Western entitled *The Outlaw*.

After her meeting with Hawks, Jane was observed by Hughes for the first time. He was standing outside Hawks' office waiting to catch a glimpse of his new star, but was too shy to meet her, so he only gazed at her from a distance. Despite no acting experience, the 19-year-old girl soon had a new wardrobe, a 1940 Ford coupe, and a movie contract.

*The Outlaw* was shot on location in Arizona. The movie co-starred Jack Beutel as Billy the Kid, Walter Huston as Doc Holliday, Thomas Mitchell as Pat Garrett, and Jane as Rio. Every fan magazine came to shoot pictures of Ms. Russell, but many pics were exploitive, and set into motion the Jane Russell sexpot image. Hawks and Hughes fought constantly about the direction of the picture until Hawks quit altogether. The movie crew was sent back to Hollywood where filming resumed at the MGM lot.

Though Hughes was no movie director, Jane was a novice, and whatever Hughes wanted from a scene, she willingly gave. Hughes was obsessed with every hand gesture, eye movement, and always wanted more takes than were needed. "Howard knew what he wanted, but he couldn't explain it from a motivation viewpoint. So he just did it over and over until he had one he liked out of 30 or 40 takes," Jane recalled. One simple shot in the movie required 103 takes. Jane believed Hughes ended up using the third shot.

"Everything about *The Outlaw* is different," Jane wrote. "It was probably the first western ever to focus on five characters at close range, instead of huge scenes of cowboys and Indians."

Howard Hughes, not oblivious to his young star's "assets," set out to design an innovative underwire push-up bra for Jane to wear in the movie. Russell described the bra as "uncomfortable and ridiculous." Instead, she covered the seams of another bra with tissue. "I never

Jane in a scene from *The Outlaw*

wore his bra, and believe me, he could design planes, but a Mr. Playtex he wasn't."

It took nine months instead of the usual six to eight weeks to film the movie. But despite the attention from the press and the sensation Jane was making in the picture world, the Hays censor office wouldn't allow the movie to be released in its current risqué state. This did nothing but make filmgoers more anxious to see the "forbidden film."

Gossip columnist Louella Parsons chastised Hughes for his portrayal of Russell as a sexpot. "The time has passed when any actress needs to appear indecently clad to win success," she snapped in her January 1941 column.

By 1942, Jane and Robert Waterfield were once again an item, and their reunion resulted in pregnancy. Despite her strict Protestant upbringing, Jane opted for an abortion, which was unsuccessful on the first try. Russell became very ill and nearly died from the experience. She would learn years later, that the abortion had rendered her unable to have children.

On February 5, 1943, *The Outlaw* was released in San Francisco. Russell did not see the picture at the premier. Instead Hughes took the cast out on the town. Jane and her costar Jack Beutel finally decided it was time to view the movie that was causing such a sensation among the public. One night the two decided to sneak into a showing of the film where an over-zealous usher tried to throw them out. While they had no tickets, they explained they were the stars of the movie—making the usher reconsider.

Russell's family was not exactly happy with Jane's newfound persona. As she remembered, her Aunt Ernie demanded to speak with Howard Hughes about her niece's public image. "You're selling my niece as though she were some cheap stripper, and I don't think that's right," she complained. Hughes, in his usual way, responded, "I can't very well sell her like Shirley Temple."

But the problems with Russell's image didn't stop there. As popular as the Western was becoming, not everyone hailed it as a box office triumph. The Catholic Church spoke out against the picture, going as far as excommunicating any parishioners who saw it. Jane always felt she fell prey to Hollywood typecasting because of that role.

To escape some of the troubles the film had produced, Jane decided she and Waterfield should officially tie the knot. They drove to Las Vegas with two of Robert's friends as witnesses. It was Easter 1943 when the couple married. Early on, it became clear that Robert and his football buddies took priority over Jane. Nevertheless, she devoted herself to her husband and his sports career.

Jane adjusted to married life and made a string of pictures including *The Young Widow* with Louis Hayward, *The Paleface* with Bob Hope and *Double Dynamite* with Groucho Marx and Frank Sinatra. At this time, Robert was traveling with the Rams, having been named Most Valuable Player and the country's number one quarterback.

*His Kind of Woman* was made in 1951 with Robert Mitchum and Vincent Price who described working with

Jane and hubby #1 Bob Waterfield

the sexy screen couple as, "Jane was a lovely, funny girl, with a great attitude and Bob was just hilarious."

Their next picture was completed the following year and named *Macao*. It solidified the pairing of one of the most beloved movie couples and the two were to remain lifelong friends. Mitchum biographer Lee Server explains, "He would tease her about her God-fearing ways, but he understood she was no Loretta Young, wallowing in piety. He loved to tell the one about the pestering reporter who couldn't believe a girl with her 'image' read the Bible and went to

Jane with Robert Mitchum in 1951

church each Sunday." Jane confronted the reporter by quipping, "Hey buddy! Christians have big breasts, too."

*The Las Vegas Story* was released in 1952, but Russell, who should have relished the success of the film, had a violent fight with her husband the night before the release, garnering her a black eye. This was to be one of many feuds and clashes within their marriage.

Hoping to strengthen their relationship, the two decided to start a family. They adopted a baby girl they named Tracy, who was born on Jane's 30th birthday. Jane wanted to adopt a slightly older boy next, and thought a trip to England where she was to perform for the Royal Court would be a good opportunity to look into adopting a foreign child.

A poor Irish woman who had read about Jane's adoption plans in the London papers informed the star that she had a little boy whom she couldn't take care of and wondered if she would consider adopting him. After the baby was cleared to leave the country, the boy, who was named Thomas, went to live with his new family. Russell was thrilled, but the press was intrusive and obsessed with reporting on her adopted children.

Back in England, Parliament was astir, demanding the child be returned to Great Britain. While Thomas's birth mother was Irish, he had actually been born in England. After a nine-month trial, Jane was granted permission to legally adopt the child. But Russell, who had visited a number of orphanages while in Europe, felt there was something very wrong with the adoption system. Russell traveled to Washington D.C. to speak with the State Department to find out how many

Marilyn Monroe and Jane Russell in *Gentlemen Prefer Blondes*

parentless children there were overseas who needed to be adopted.

She was told no children were available, but the Children's Bureau, apparently located just across the street from the State Department, begged to differ. However, they had no exact figures. Jane described the situation, saying, "At any rate, immigration laws had to be changed before any child could come into the country off the quota, so I was off to see the lawmakers, the Congress and the Senate."

While Congress debated the issue, Howard Hawks offered Jane a movie role. He bought the movie rights to a novel he thought would be a sure moneymaker. The year was 1953, and the picture was *Gentlemen Prefer Blondes* co-starring Marilyn Monroe. Russell remembered Monroe with fond memories, but also recalled the blonde's paralyzing insecurities, her overbearing acting coach Natascha Lytess and her chronic lateness to the set.

Despite the tension, the romantic comedy thrilled audiences across the nation with Russell and Monroe's tricky dance numbers, elaborate costumes and the debut of the now iconic song *Diamonds Are a Girl's Best Friend*. This box office success allowed Russell and Monroe the opportunity to cement their footprints at a joint ceremony at Grauman's Chinese Theater.

Robert Waterfield, who had been playing pro football for eight years, decided to retire, but took a job as assistant coach for the Rams. He was traveling more at this time, which allowed conflict at home to cease. With the publicity of the movie dying down, Jane decided to resume her work with the adoption system. As she described it, "I got the bright idea of trying my luck with the United Nations. Off I went to see Eleanor Roosevelt (who was a member of the U.S. delegation to the U.N.)."

But the former First Lady told the actress that she would be better off leading the fight independently, because the U.N. had enough on its plate at the moment and couldn't address this problem right away.

Triumph came with the passage of the Federal Orphan Adoption Amendment of the Special Migration Act of 1953. The act allowed children of American soldiers born overseas to be eligible for American adoption. In the years since then, the law has been changed to allow single parents to adopt and for children to be moved across state lines for "adoptive placement."

Jane Russell joined forces with the International Social Service organization and formed WAIF (the World Adoption International Fund). She and her friends raised money and hosted fundraisers, which were attended by the who's who of Hollywood elite. WAIF chapters sprang up all over the country. Joan Crawford, the mother of adopted children herself, was named an honorary chairperson of the organization.

At that time, Russell co-founded the Hollywood Christian Group that held monthly meetings at various stars' homes. Jane was always reaching out to her fellow actors. She even claimed to have received a message from God to give to Judy Garland, who was then going through a troubled

Jane with children Tracy and Thomas

period in her life. It was soon after giving Garland the message that Judy staged a comeback. Russell always believed in the power of prayer and she sought guidance from God on a regular basis.

Howard Hughes, always worried about appearances, wasn't thrilled that his leading lady was a family-oriented churchgoer who now headed an adoption agency. However, the two remained close friends throughout the years. While Jane fell out of touch with Hughes towards the end of his life, she maintained her belief that he was nothing but a quiet, shy, smart man who supported Jane's projects and always recognized special events in her life. Leonardo DiCaprio sought Jane's advice in preparation to play Hughes in the 2004 blockbuster *The Aviator*.

In 1955, Russell made her last film for RKO entitled *Underwater!* The movie premiered in a theater built at the bottom of a lake, where moviegoers, including Russell, were equipped with scuba gear. The picture turned out to be a huge success for RKO. Hughes, who sold the company at about this time, helped his star get a better contract with MCA. It was for $1 million, the first of its kind.

Russell teamed up with her husband to form Russ-Field productions. The first movie they made was the sequel to *Gentlemen Prefer Blondes*. Originally entitled *But Gentlemen Marry Brunettes*, the "but" was dropped for the movie's title. It enjoyed minor success. It lost money in the production, and lacked the star power of a Monroe vehicle. The sequel co-stared Jeanne Crain, who played Jane's sister. Russell was also making the film *The Tall Men* with Clark Gable at this time.

Early the following year, Russell became interested in adopting a third child. She named her son Robert Waterfield, Jr., or "Bucky" as he was later known. Now a mother of three, Jane never slowed down. She still actively oversaw WAIF, as well as made the movie *Hot Blood* for Columbia pictures. By this time in her career, she was known as the "Haystack Brunette" due to the sexy photos George Hurrell took of Russell for *The Outlaw*.

But many people speculated her relationship with Hughes was not platonic. Those "in the know," knew Jane and Hughes were just friends. Harry Cohn, the head of Columbia pictures, greeted Russell for the first time saying, "Well, I'm glad to meet you. You're the only girl around Howard Hughes who doesn't sleep with him, I hear." Jane replied, "Oh, there are quite a few of us, but it's nice to know the word's out."

## Always Fighting Buxom Babe Label

Russell then left Columbia and headed to 20th Century-Fox to make *The Revolt of Mamie Stover*. Some of Jane's most glamorous photographs come from this role. In the movie, Jane plays a red haired prostitute with a blonde Agnes Moorehead in the role of her Madame. Ironically, Moorehead was known throughout Hollywood as a devout Presbyterian even though she played wild characters in the movies. She is probably best known for her role as the flamboyant Endora on the television show *Bewitched*.

Jane and her husband were now immersed in the movie business as producers. The next two flicks did not feature Russell, but *The King and Four Queens* starred Clark Gable and Raoul Walsh. *Run For The Sun* was to follow. Russell starred in the next film they produced entitled *The Fuzzy Pink Nightgown* with Ralph Meeker and Keenan Wynn.

In the light comedy, Russell plays a fading star looking for a boost in publicity and decides to stage her own kidnapping. Jane, who donned a long blonde wig for the part, instead finds her character in the midst of a real heist. The film's tagline was "The hottest bundle ever hijacked." While a humorous vehicle for Russell, it suffered at the

Jane in *The Revolt of Mamie Stover*

box office, possibly due to competition from a "real" blonde bombshell, Jayne Mansfield, who had just premiered her film *Will Success Spoil Rock Hunter?* Russell blamed herself for the movie's failure, as she felt she should have insisted it be made in color.

In October of 1957, Russell pursued her dream to sing onstage by appearing in a solo nightclub act at the Sands Hotel. It was then her vocal talents became appreciated. She was also part of a girl group with her long-time friends Connie Haines and Beryl Davis, who all appeared on the Coral record label. Known mainly for pop music, the trio stood out for their gospel style. Their single *Do Lord* reached Number 27 on the *Billboard* singles chart. Bing Crosby, a prominent figure at Coral, felt the trio had potential.

In 1960, Russell and Waterfield ceased making movies together, and Robert got promoted as head coach of the Rams. Russell took a hiatus from movies, and appeared on Broadway in the summer of 1961 in the play *Janus*. Jane worried that she didn't have the skills required to perform a whole show live. She was accustomed to learning parts of a script at a time, and got used to the luxury of multiple takes. However, Russell proved herself capable as a Broadway star and more roles came her way. Three years later, Russell appeared in *Fate Is the Hunter*.

Problems at home were hard for the popular star to ignore. Jane drowned her sorrows in alcohol and had a series of affairs that put a strain on her already damaged marriage. Robert, also unfaithful, was growing more violent in his outbursts. But Jane didn't believe in divorce, and didn't want to disgrace her family. She and Robert were high school sweethearts and married life was all she knew. "Between the fights and the hangovers I wasn't much good at rehearsals," she quipped.

Jane finally filed for divorce after threatening to do so for several years. However volatile Robert was, Jane was quick to point out, "I'm no dainty violet either, in temperament or mouth. Believe me, I can be a bitch." Their divorce was finalized in July of 1968. Russell was now freed from the 25-year roller coaster ride.

With husband #2 Roger Barrett

She starred in the play *Catch Me If You Can*, and then made a film entitled *The Born Losers*. With her career on the upswing, she fell in love with her co-star Roger Barrett while appearing in the play *Here Today*. After a whirlwind romance, the two wed on August 25th of the same year. They were united in marriage at the Beverly Hills Presbyterian Church in a Spanish-themed wedding. With her usual dose of self-deprecating humor, Jane confessed that the wedding got off to a bumpy start when she was running late for it and found herself locked out of the church. After pounding on the doors, she was finally let in.

While the marriage seemed to have potential, it was short-lived.

On November 18, 1968 Barrett collapsed in the couple's bedroom right in front of Jane. He died from a massive blood clot at age 47. Russell still had obligations to appear in plays and tried to get through them as best she could.

She starred in *Mame*, *Pal Joey*, and *Company*. Rehearsals for *Pal Joey* were brief and intense, and Russell only had a week to learn her part, as she was a last-minute fill-in. Despite her insecurities onstage, her run turned out to be successful and her name filled seats.

Some nights were better than others. But when Jane flubbed lines or forgot song lyrics, she took it in stride and persevered. *Mame* was a happy experience for the actress, who opined that, "I think every actress in town had done *Mame* at one time or another." Russell, who began *Company* with injured ribs, had doubts about the show and had her manager Kevin Pines attend every rehearsal. She described him as being like her "Jewish mother."

Jane had problems being fitted for her costume—a phenomenon she was used to at this point in her career. Russell candidly described her finished outfit as making her look like "Ernest Borgnine in drag." She ended up buying her own clothing and accessories for the show. Despite the bumpy start, the show was a huge success and Jane was on cloud nine.

Around this time, Jane got a contract with Playtex bras to appear in television commercials promoting their undergarment line. This kept the now 50-something actress fresh and current with her "18 hour comfort bra." Russell made a picture in 1970 entitled *Darker Than Amber*.

She then met real estate broker John Peoples, with whom she fell in love and early on in their courtship, proposed to him. The two wed on January 31, 1974. They made their home in Sedona, Arizona and also spent time in California.

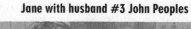

**Jane with husband #3 John Peoples**

Russell had found long-lasting love the third time around. Her children were grown and independent and she achieved contentment in her life. However, alcoholism was never far behind, and in the late

*Going Hollywood: Midwesterners in Movieland* **139**

1970s Jane found herself in a lawsuit pertaining to a car accident she caused while driving intoxicated. In criminal proceedings, Russell was sentenced to four days in jail. She served her time and decided that bad circumstances tended to follow alcohol abuse, so she stopped drinking.

She reflected upon her career in 1975, "I never got to do what I wanted to do. What that would have been, I don't know. But I kind of got stuck in an either-or situation. Either it was a western or a musical. There were no in-betweens."

In 1983 she made her last film called *The Yellow Rose*, a made-for-television movie. Her first husband Robert Waterfield passed away the same year.

Although Russell never won an Oscar, she was awarded the Women's International Center Living Legacy Award, the Golden Apple Award and the Humanitarian Award from the Motion Picture Society for her involvement in WAIF. At last count, WAIF has placed over 50,000 children into permanent homes.

She moved to Santa Maria, California after the death of Peoples in 1999. The actress stayed politically active and teamed with Elizabeth Ridenour (the National Council on Bible Curriculum in Public Schools) to put the Bible into the hands of school children. Russell was proud to say that Ridenour placed religion into 117 schools in 38 states. "And as a result of this effort 60,000 children have now been able to read the Bible," the actress stated.

Russell also sparked controversy as a pro-life supporter and was a self-professed "narrow-minded right-wing conservative Christian."

In 2006, Russell formed a show called "The Swinging Forties" that played twice a month at the Radisson Hotel. She was in her mid-80s. That April, Turner Classic Movies (TCM) asked Russell and Robert Mitchum to sit for an interview with host Robert Osborne for an episode of *Private Screenings*.

The pair flew to Atlanta to film the show. By this time, Mitchum was dying of lung cancer, looked emaciated and required oxygen. The night before the interview Mitchum, Russell and the production crew hit the bars and were pleased to see Mitchum in good spirits laughing and telling stories. They hoped to catch the actor in good form for the next day's interview.

However, the two-hour interview was painfully slow with awkward silence. Robert Osborne said the struggle "seemed like two years in Beirut...Either because of illness or cantankerousness, he was about as pleasant to interview that day as Attila the Hun." He did offer interesting views on Marilyn Monroe and Howard Hughes and the network was able to squeeze out an acceptable 40-minute television program.

Feisty as ever, Russell related how she grew to understand the press's underhanded ways to get a good story. "When we were on location...[male reporters] they would go up on balconies and shoot down (in order to catch the actress at a busty angle). It was all over the magazines. Later, they'd say, 'lean over and pick up the pail, honey,' and I'd say, 'up yours, buddy!'"

Jane at a *Vanity Fair* party in 2005

Jane patiently endured Mitchum's moody demeanor and left the impression that their on-screen romance was in real-life more of a brother/sister dynamic. Mitchum died on July 1, 1997, of lung cancer and emphysema.

Jane Russell will always fall victim to speculations about her relationship with Howard Hughes, or lack thereof. But troubled family life, alcohol abuse and physical objectification only served to strengthen her faith in the Lord. She read the Bible daily and believed in Divine intervention.

She passed away on February 28, 2011, at the age of 89. Daughter-in-law Etta Waterfield told the press that Jane had been a "pillar of health" but came down with a bad cold and died of respiratory failure. Services were held at Pacific Christian Church and her remains were cremated.

Russell was always ahead of her time. The movies she made, the clothes she wore (or wouldn't wear), the causes she supported, and the pitfalls in life she sustained, all blended together to create the sexy, fiery and bitchy persona that made Jane Russell, Jane Russell. She believed in second chances and made no apologies.

# 8.
# DOROTHY DANDRIDGE:
## *Like A Lotus In Bloom*

DOROTHY DANDRIDGE, AWARD-WINNING FILM AND TELEVISION actress, as well as a popular singer and nightclub performer, believed she could have "captured the world" had she only been born white, and not interracial. A transcendent figure, she was dubbed "our Marilyn Monroe" by fellow performer Lena Horne and labeled "Hollywood's first authentic love goddess of color" by *Ebony* magazine.

Dandridge was the first African-American performer to appear at the Waldorf-Astoria Hotel and played the Cotton Club and the Apollo Theater. She received hundreds of fan letters a week. In 1954, she became the first woman of African descent nominated for a Best Actress Oscar. It wasn't until Halle Berry's win in 2002 that a woman of African heritage would actually take home the best actress statuette, and an actress of that racial makeup has not won the award since.

When Dandridge died suddenly on the verge of a comeback, it was unclear if her death had been a tragic accident or a self-fulfilling prophecy.

On November 9, 1922, entertainer Ruby Butler Dandridge entered Cleveland's City Hospital to give birth to her second child. She had just left her husband Cyril, vowing to give her children a better life away from what she termed a "mama's boy." When the baby was born, Ruby decided to give her an elegant name that she felt would look good on a movie marquee—Dorothy Dandridge—although the child would go by her lifelong nickname of Dottie. The infant had a light complexion, the result of a biracial father and a mother of Jamaican, Native American and Spanish descent, the latter born in Wichita, Kansas.

Ruby managed to erase Cyril from the lives of her daughters, Vivian and Dorothy, raising them to believe their father had no interest in knowing them. At one point, Ruby even told them he was dead. But Ruby took Cyril to court—an unheard of thing for a biracial woman to do in the 1920s. Though he was ordered to pay $10 a week in child support, Cyril still hoped to reconcile with his wife.

In adulthood, Dorothy would relay the story of when her father paid an unexpected visit to her home at Christmastime. Ruby told the girls that Santa Claus was coming and they needed to hide. But while upstairs, the sisters eavesdropped on their mother's conversation, and realized it was their father who was visiting. Ruby and Cyril argued intently.

"Vivian and I began to cry," Dorothy remembered, "We cried because it was fearful and violent below, and we didn't know what was going on or why." Cyril realized reconciliation was a moot point and filed for divorce in June 1924.

Dorothy wouldn't meet her dad until she was 16-years-old and a performer at New York's Cotton Club. After the awkward first meeting, daughter and father did not reunite until after the birth of her daughter.

Cognizant of the fact her girls possessed talent from a young age, Ruby arranged for them to sing and dance for some of Cleveland's churches and social groups. "Colored churches" were full of potential for exposing their young talent. Ruby herself started performing at church gatherings and at black women's groups. She recited poetry, sang and danced, doing whatever she could to make ends meet as a single mother.

The two sisters' singing venture was successful, and the newly formed "Wonder Children" were bound for a five-year tour of the South as young vaudevillians. Their mother arranged all routines and hired a pianist named Geneva Williams to also chaperone the girls. Williams soon moved in with the family and began teaching the girls singing, dancing and piano; she also proved to be a controlling woman who put restrictions on Dorothy's social life, obsessed with the young women's sexual exploits, which in reality were nonexistent.

The girls were too young to realize it at the time, but Geneva was their mother's lover. According to Dorothy's manager Earl Mills, the actress told him Geneva, whom she referred to as her "aunt" sexually assaulted her and was physically abusive.

In 1930, Ruby and her children moved to the Los Angeles suburb of Watts, hoping to advance the girls' careers. By 1934, Dorothy was appearing in bit parts in films, but she encountered sexual harassment and was barred from visiting the homes of her white childhood friends. She also witnessed the widespread use of alcohol and drugs in the slums, so traumatized by what she saw, that she became an avowed teetotaler.

In the late '30s, Ruby decided to send Dorothy and Vivian to a dance school. She also recruited Etta Jones to be the third member of the act. The group then became known as The Dandridge Sisters. When the girls learned that radio station KNX in Los Angeles was holding a talent contest, the trio decided to enter. As the only African Americans in the contest, Ruby had the girls emulate the popular white group, the Andrews Sisters.

The Dandridge Sisters won first place in the competition and were soon offered a six-

Dorothy (right) with sister Vivian; mother Ruby (left) and Geneva Williams

month gig in a traveling circus destined for Hawaii. It was while on the Islands that talent agent Joe Glaser saw them perform, and decided the sisters were ideal to be cast as singers in a string of films.

Their first motion picture was made in 1935 as part of the *Our Gang* series and was entitled *Teacher's Beau*. Next, they joined the cast of *The Big Broadcast of 1936* and the Marx Brothers' *A Day at the Races*, released in 1937. The Dandridge Sisters then appeared in the aptly entitled *Going Places*, starring Dick Powell, Anita Louise and Ronald Reagan. The film introduced the now classic tune *Jeepers Creepers*.

## America's First "Colored" Movie Star

Glaser was so impressed with Dorothy and her colleagues, that he booked them at the prestigious Cotton Club. Before they knew it, the girls, now young women at this time, were singing with Cab Calloway in his show and also appeared on radio and stage with Duke Ellington.

Dandridge then set her sights on Europe, where The Dandridge Sisters played the London Palladium, among other venues. When World War II broke out, many performers' tours were postponed or canceled, and the Dandridges were no different. Then Etta Jones left the group to get married.

In 1944, Dorothy made the acquaintance of Harold Nicholas, of the famed Nicholas Brothers stage act. They became fast friends, even though they ran in different circles. He was a notorious ladies' man and Dorothy rebuked his sexual advances.

The actress, dubbed "the lady" by her friends, not only didn't consume alcohol, she didn't smoke or drink coffee and rebuffed the Hollywood party scene. She preferred her favorite meal of chitlins and greens over a fancy meal out. She exercised frequently, including lifting weights and doing aerobics. As a homebody, Dorothy also spent time scrapbooking, saving various clippings pertaining to her career, and spent long stretches on the phone talking with friends.

When Vivian left to launch a solo career, Dorothy tried out and won a role in a Los Angeles stage revue entitled *Meet the People*. The play was such a big hit that Hollywood wanted to film a screen version. Dandridge, feeling she would be a shoe-in, lobbied to get a part. Upon speaking with MGM studio officials, she learned the film would instead feature an all white cast, consisting of Lucille Ball, Dick Powell and Virginia O'Brien.

One studio exec told Dandridge, "The South isn't ready for colored actors. The picture would get shut out of a lot of key spots if it were made like the play. I'm afraid there's no place for sentiment in this business. We'd like to use more people from the play, but it just can't be done."

Despite the bitter letdown, Dandridge was confident in her ability to get work on the stage and as a singer. By then, the actress was becoming cozy with Mr. Nicholas who asked her to marry him. Dorothy agreed to the proposal, but her lack of sexual experience (she was reputed to be a virgin on her wedding night,) caused an early manifestation of dysfunction in their marriage.

In later years, Dorothy told her manager Earl Mills of her fear of sexually intimacy, stemming from assaults at the hands of her "aunt" Geneva. Mills wrote of an incident when Dorothy was 16-years-old and was late coming home from a date. Geneva assumed that Dorothy had been delayed in getting home because she had had sexual relations with her date, but the teenager denied the accusation.

Geneva made Dorothy remove her clothing and get on her bed. "No one had seen her private parts since she was a child," Mills wrote. "That was sacred...she worked her fingers into Dorothy's behind and then down into her vagina...but her aunt didn't stop until she was satisfied. Then she got off Dorothy and said, 'All right, you're still a virgin. But then maybe it's because he didn't put it in all the way.'"

Dorothy knew that after her wedding ceremony on November 2, 1942, she would have to face the inevitable; her husband would assume the pair would consummate their relationship. But the couple's sex life proved tumultuous.

A few months into their marriage, the actress discovered she was pregnant. Because Harold traveled extensively in Europe, Dorothy filled her time by studying acting and socializing with friends including Marilyn Monroe and Ava Gardner.

When Dorothy went into labor on September 2, 1943, and as the contractions got closer together and the pain intensified, she made her way to the hospital, despite wanting to wait for her husband to return that day

With husband #1 Harold Nicholas

from performing in Europe. But the birth of their child did not strengthen the Nicholas' marriage.

Harolyn Suzanne Nicholas, or Lynn, as the child was called, was the wellspring of joy in Dorothy's life. But by the time her daughter reached preschool age, it became clear the child was cognitively impaired. She couldn't form words, only grunted and seemed to be in a world all her own. Devastated, Dandridge took her daughter to every doctor and specialist she could find, seeking answers that could mitigate her aching heart. The actress was told to try many useless home remedies.

Mother and daughter were turned away from all the places Dottie tried to have the child enrolled in school. She worried that her delay in going to the hospital may have harmed her child. But as she later learned, the surgical forceps used by the doctor during delivery damaged her child's head.

Finally, Dorothy received the answer to her questions about Lynn's slow development. The child was cognitively disabled and would have the mental capacity of a four-year-old for the rest of her life. Dottie carried the guilt that her daughter's condition was her fault. For Harold, the prognosis did nothing to change his attitude towards his family. He spent most of his daughter's early years touring extensively in Europe, living the life of a bachelor. Dottie wrote to him constantly, pleading with him to help her with Lynn and to come back home. She begged him to accept the child as she was, and to be content as a married family man. He never replied to the letters, and eventually, the mailbox no longer harbored his support checks.

When Dorothy finally succeeded in contacting him, he told her he liked his carefree life in Paris and that their marriage was over. Dandridge raised Lynn herself for many years, until the child became harder to handle. Dorothy, in desperation, sent her to go live with "aunt" Geneva and her mother Ruby. Later, Dandridge placed the child in a private institution, because in that era, there were not agencies that offered one-on-one support and care to families with children with disabilities like there are today.

Realizing she needed to work to sustain her lifestyle, Dorothy went back to acting. She appeared as a singer in *Hit Parade of 1943*, and a few uncredited roles, including a small part in the Claudette Colbert war tearjerker *Since You Went Away*. Her Hollywood career remained lackluster through the rest of the decade. In April of 1951, Dottie made the acquaintance of Earl Mills, a man who was to become her manager and life-long friend. He was impressed by her singing and beauty and became smitten with her immediately.

He told her he could help her career and propel her star higher than its current station in the Hollywood sky. Dottie, ever self-sufficient, told him she was making a film entitled *Tarzan's Peril* and that his services wouldn't be needed. In the film, she played an African Queen who needs saving in her own jungle.

The Baltimore Afro-American newspaper published an article praising the interracial actress, noting, "Newest glamour star among

Dorothy with Duke Ellington in *Hit Parade of 1943*

colored film actresses, petite Dorothy Dandridge, who went West from Cleveland is starring in one of her first major roles as an African princess in 'Tarzan's Perils' at the Met Theatre...It is expected that Miss Dandridge will supplant beautiful Lena Horne and exotic Acquanetta (an actress billed as the 'Venezuelan Volcano,' who claimed Arapaho Indian heritage) as Hollywood's choice for leading roles."

After realizing the role unfairly exploited her talents and looks, Dorothy decided to seek the services of Earl Mills after all.

She took a break from moviemaking and returned to the night-club scene. In May of 1951 she opened in Hollywood's top club, the Macombo with the Desi Arnaz Band. That same year she became the first African American to perform in the Empire Room of New York's Waldorf-Astoria Hotel. Dandridge also toured venues in Miami, being forced to stay outside the city limits due to racial segregation. At one of these engagements, when she asked where the restrooms were, she was handed a plastic cup.

Out West, things weren't much better. In Las Vegas, Dottie and Earl were appalled by the rampant racism. She was not allowed to use main entrances in hotels or talk to guests. She was asked to remain in her room while not performing and not use any public facilities. Her meals were delivered to her room. One day she and Earl ventured down to the swimming pool. Before she could get in, the hotel manager appeared and caused a scene forbidding her to use it. In retaliation, Dorothy dipped her foot in the water. The next time she went by the pool, she saw it had been drained and was being thoroughly scrubbed—ironically, by several black employees.

Soon after, Dandridge returned to Hollywood where MGM was making *Bright Road* using African Americans. She was cast in the film as an Alabama schoolteacher. Shooting of the movie began in August of 1952. Her co-star was an up-and-coming actor by the name of Harry Belafonte, and the two would become lifelong friends.

After the movie's release, Dorothy resumed her nightclub act, touring in South America where she found fewer instances of racial bigotry against her.

Dorothy ended up dating Gerald Mayer, the director of *Bright Road*, as well as actor Peter Lawford (before he married JFK's sister, Pat Kennedy). She also got involved with a millionaire from Rio de Janeiro named Christian Marcos, but the affair was short-lived.

With her career on the rise, she appeared on the covers of several magazines. She told *People Today* in 1953, "To be a siren of song, one needs more than talent, looks, and voice. One needs understand-

Dorothy Dandridge had the beauty to play a seductress...on screen or in real life

With Harry Belafonte in *Carmen Jones*

ing of people. At first I was afraid they wouldn't like me. Then I realized the first step in that direction was to like them, and to assume they would like me." The magazine referred to her as a "bronze bombshell" and featured her on the back, not front cover.

Earl Mills became aware that director Otto Preminger was casting his new film entitled *Carmen Jones*, an Americanized version of the Bizet opera with lyrics by Oscar Hammerstein. It was to be a big-budget film and musical with an all-black cast. Mills knew his client had to get in on the action. He arranged for Dorothy to meet with Preminger who only wanted Dottie to read the part of Cindy Lou, the quiet and submissive girlfriend of the male lead, who gets dumped for Carmen. Dandridge told him that she was only interested in the lead role. Preminger felt she was too sweet and innocent to play the rough and tumble seductress. Dottie took the script home and read it, determined to change Preminger's mind.

Her mother and manager insisted she take the role offered to her, but Dorothy had other plans. She purchased a sassy short wig, a billowy skirt and low cut blouse that she wore off the shoulder. She met with the director and read a few of Cindy Lou's lines in a provocative way. Preminger was shocked, but thrilled that he had found his Carmen.

Ironically, Dandridge then had doubts she could play the role. Always battling low self-esteem, she argued that now that she had proven she could get the part, she didn't need to actually play it. Otto and Earl finally convinced her to follow through with her commitments. By that time she was becoming intimately involved with Preminger.

Harry Belafonte was cast as Carmen's love interest, and Pearl Bailey and Diahann Carroll co-starred. Only Bailey would do her own singing, as the rest of the cast's voices were dubbed, despite Dandridge and Belafonte being professional singers. Instead of using Dottie's natural husky singing voice, it was dubbed by then-teenaged opera singer Marilyn Horne. Dorothy spent hours a day lip-syncing to Horne's records to obtain all the proper facial nuances.

The film was a major success, winning a Golden Globe Award for Best Musical Motion Picture of 1954 and an Audience Award from the Berlin Film Festival in 1955. The next few months would center on movie premieres and publicity shoots.

It was rumored that Dandridge would receive an Academy Award nomination for her performance. She only smiled at the notion, doubting it would come to fruition. Later that year, Dottie became the first woman to be featured on the cover of *Ebony* magazine, and she became the first African American to appear on the cover of *Life* magazine, gracing the cover on November 1, 1954.

Usually brash columnist Louella Parsons praised Dorothy's performance: "I have seen many Carmens, and Dorothy Dandridge compares with the best of them."

In February of 1955, Dorothy became the first woman of color to be nominated for an Oscar in a leading role. She was the third black performer to be nominated in general after Hattie McDaniel for Best Supporting Actress in *Gone with the Wind* (1939) and Ethel Waters in the same category for her 1949 role in the racially charged film *Pinky*. To ensure the nominees would attend the ceremony, all were made presenters throughout the evening. In fact, Dorothy was the first woman of color to be an award presenter. She handed the Academy Award for Film Editing to Gene Milford for *On the Waterfront*.

The women nominated for Best Actress alongside Dandridge were Audrey Hepburn in *Sabrina* with Humphrey Bogart and William Holden; Grace Kelly for *The Country Girl*, opposite Bing Crosby and Holden; Judy Garland for the musical masterpiece *A Star is Born*, co-starring James Mason and Jack Carson; and Jane Wyman in *Magnificent Obsession*, with Rock Hudson and Agnes Moorehead.

When it came time to announce the winner for best actress, presenter William Holden took the stage. Many assumed he would filibuster to keep the audience in suspense. However, when he reached the podium all the actor uttered was, "Because time is running short, the Best Actress Oscar goes to Grace Kelly, for *The Country Girl*."

20th Century-Fox studio head Darryl F. Zanuck pushed for the company to award Dandridge a lucrative film contract. However, she would only agree to appear in integrated motion pictures. "A smart young woman, who knows where she's going, the clause was inserted by the studio at her insistence...Motion pictures were the poorer because pretty girls like Miss Dandridge weren't given a chance 40 years ago," wrote the *Baltimore Afro-American*.

With her career reaching new heights, Dorothy was now commanding a salary as high as some of her white contemporaries. She bought a home overlooking Los Angeles and her name remained in the papers. But not all of the publicity was positive. In 1957, the tabloid magazine *Hollywood Confidential* ran a story about an alleged affair between Dandridge and a bartender in Lake Tahoe. She successfully sued the publication for libel.

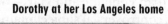
**Dorothy at her Los Angeles home**

Despite the acclaim for *Carmen Jones*, Dottie's personal life left something to be desired. She would often go out for a night on the town with best friend and former sister-in-law Geraldine Pate Nicholas Branton, who had been married to Harold's brother. Dorothy's sister Vivian would also dine out with them. However, her career was in the doldrums, and she resented being known as "Dorothy Dandridge's sister." She was jealous and drank heavily, often causing scenes in public. Dottie felt sorry for her sibling, and tried to help her financially.

Dorothy devoted herself to Preminger, who was married at the time. He claimed his current marriage was a loveless one and that his wife had open affairs too. Dandridge felt he was the love of her life and hoped they could someday get married and live in Europe where their relationship would stir fewer racial tensions. Instead, Preminger flaunted his wife at movie premiers and did not file for divorce.

Dandridge next starred in the movie *Tamango*, which was a minor hit. She then attended the Cannes Film Festival with Preminger, after which she returned to the States for more nightclub work as she awaited her next movie offer. The actress was then asked by Zanuck to play Tuptim in the big-budget musical *The King and I*, but Preminger convinced Dorothy she deserved more than a supporting role. Actress Rita Moreno won the part and the film was a huge success. This strained Dorothy's relationship with her lover, and the affair that had remained behind closed doors for several years, came to an end.

In 1957, Zanuck asked Dottie to play Margot Seaton in *Island In The Sun*. The movie dealt with two interracial relationships, involving Dorothy's character and white actor John Justin, as well as an affair between Joan Fontaine and Harry Belafonte. It was a successful picture due to its controversial subject matter, but critics dismissed it as simply dull.

In 1959, MGM mogul Samuel Goldwyn announced that he would shoot a silver screen production of George Gershwin's musical *Porgy and Bess*. The story was highly unpopular with some African Americans who found it to be a stereotypical portrayal. When Harry Belafonte and Dorothy were asked to star in the lead roles, Belafonte turned it down. Dorothy did not want to do it either, but reluctantly accepted because no other movie offers were coming her way. Sidney Poitier was cast in Harry's place with Sammy Davis, Jr. co-starring.

The director was to be Reuben Mamoulain, but Otto Preminger replaced him at the last minute, much to Dottie's chagrin. Otto was particularly harsh with his former flame during filming. He criticized her acting and her usage of artificial tears. His reprimands were often so cruel and embarrassing that Dottie would rush from the set—in tears. He began shooting one scene by sadistically saying, "Finally, real tears."

Despite the difficulties she faced with Preminger, Dorothy won a Golden Globe Award for her performance. She re-entered the nightclub scene, and soon met a down-and-out, yet debonair white restaurant owner named Jack Denison. He pursued her relentlessly and told her a sob story of how he had been involved with a black woman who died tragically. In reality, he had abandoned her and their child, leaving them destitute.

Dottie's friends tried to convince her not to marry Denison, telling her he was just after her money. Despite the warnings, the two wed on June 22, 1959. He not only controlled her career, but also made her cut ties with friends, including manager Earl Mills. Denison would often beat her, causing movie makeup crews to work to cover up Dorothy's bruises.

On top of this, an oil investment that Dandridge had entered into with other Hollywood stars turned out to be a scam and she lost a large sum of money. Dottie also discovered that the people who were handling her finances had defrauded her of $150,000 and she owed $139,000 in back taxes. Her business manager at the time was a man named Jerome Rosenthal. Years later he would be found liable by a California court for a massive $22.8 million judgment in favor of a former client of his, Doris Day.

With husband #2 Jack Denison

In 1961, Dorothy appeared on the *Ed Sullivan Show*, but few other television appearances would follow. To alleviate her troubles, Dorothy began to drink heavily. She moved into a small apartment at 8495 Fountain Avenue in West Hollywood, California.

The actress did again appear on the cover of *Ebony* magazine, in June 1962. In the extensive interview she reflected on her life as a child performer, her career breaks, personal life and views of actors of color trying to establish careers in show business.

"She is well-read, well-traveled and—perhaps a skill initiated in her family's pre-show business days when her mother sold pastries and sandwiches to keep them going—a good cook," the magazine reported. "Her mind is kept sharp by a constant honing on everything from Sigmund Freud to Langston Hughes, and she confesses to a restlessness born of 'a never-ending curiosity about life.' She has said of such curiosity 'It may kill cats, but it keeps me alive.'

"I could play the part of an Egyptian or an Indian or a Mexican, and I'm certainly not the only one," Dorothy said. "There are other actors and actresses who can do the same thing. There is no reason why a Negro has to just play a Negro because he's a Negro. White people don't do it. They've even played Negroes."

Dottie did manage to land an appearance on a popular TV crime drama, *Cain's Hundred*, about an ex-con that turns against the mob and helps the FBI nail gangsters.

But on April 26, 1963, Dorothy filed for bankruptcy. She had to sell her home, two cars and owed 77 bill collectors nearly $128,000. Her daughter Lynn was also dropped on her doorstep by authorities, because she was unable to pay the costs of her private institution. The child, then 17, did not respond to her mother and would only play one note on the piano, for hours straight, while Dorothy sobbed in her bedroom. She was now faced with the hardest decision of her life—what to do about her daughter's care? Dottie agreed to drop her parental rights and made her daughter a ward of the state, placing her in an institution in Camarillo, California.

Dorothy continued to drink to excess and would call friends at all hours of the night, unable to sleep and hopelessly depressed. She finally filed for divorce from con man Jack Denison and tried to get her life back on track. Doctors prescribed her an antidepressant, which seemed to help. Also a

Dorothy in bankruptcy court

blow to her self-confidence was losing the film role of Cleopatra to Elizabeth Taylor, a role she had coveted.

In 1964, Dottie reconciled with manager Earl Mills, who helped to resurrect her flagging career. She attended a health spa in Mexico, performing in that country and in Japan. Dandridge had plans to go to New York, but sprained her ankle, fracturing her foot instead.

## A Self-Fulfilling Prophecy

On the morning of September 8, 1965, Dorothy had an appointment to have a cast put on her foot. Mills phoned Dottie early in the morning, but she requested he call back later, as she had been up all night. He phoned again in the afternoon, but there was no answer.

Finally, a concerned Mills went to Dottie's apartment, but she did not answer the door. He returned around 2 p.m. and forced his way into the residence. He found his client lying nude on the bathroom floor with only a blue scarf tied around her head. He called out her nickname, "Angel Face." But Dorothy Dandridge had expired several hours before. She was 42 years old.

In May, Dandridge had written a cryptic note to Mills, which read: "In case of my death—to whomever discovers it—don't remove anything I have on—scarf, gown or underwear. Cremate me right away. If I have anything, money, furniture, give it to my mother Ruby Dandridge. She will know what to do. (Signed) Dorothy Dandridge." She gave Mills the note, saying, "You keep it Earl, because I know you will be the one who discovers me."

Because Dorothy had made no prior arrangements, the note became her Last Will and Testament. But commissioner Victor Donatelli ruled that her handwritten will, requesting that she be cremated in whatever clothing she wore in death, was not valid because it was not dated. Donatelli decided the estate would be split between her mother, age 60, and daughter, age 20.

It was first believed Dorothy died from a blood clot caused by flanks of bone marrow clumping in her ankle. The question of suicide was posed, mainly due to the note and her history of depression. But an autopsy revealed that the cause of death was due to an overdose of Tofranil, the antidepressant she had been taking at the time. The coroner ruled her cause of death as drug overdose, undetermined causes.

Her estate consisted of $4,000 worth of furniture and she had only $2.14 in her bank account. Dottie was cremated and buried at the Little Church of the Flowers at Forest Lawn.

"She had contracted to give for the aid of mentally retarded children most of the proceeds of an autobiography to be published soon," Mills told the press. "Much of Dorothy's money over the years went to help Lynn and other retarded children."

In 1970, Mills released a biography on Dandridge entitled *A Portrait in Black*. Posthumously, the actress received a star on the Hollywood Walk of Fame and was inducted into the Black Film Hall of Fame in 1977. Her mother Ruby died in 1987, and is interred next to her. Father Cyril passed away in 1989, and sister Vivian in 1991. Dorothy's daughter, Lynn, was still in an institution at last report.

Ann Dandridge, a cousin of the actress, who works as a publicist in California, said she paired with Mills to help turn his book into a film. Ann grew up in Chicago and was 12 years old at the time of Dorothy's passing. She told this author, "We spent ten LONG years seeking funding to turn this book into a motion picture. Earl Mills' final project became the 1999 HBO Movie *Introducing Dorothy Dandridge* starring Halle Berry. I enjoyed working with Earl Mills who had great admiration for Dorothy Dandridge." The film is marketed with the tagline: "Right woman. Right place. Wrong time."

Berry, a fellow Clevelander, described what it took to play Dandridge as having "to find a way to be sad on every day, in every scene, in every moment. And always try to hide the sadness. And (then) you'll

get the essence of who she was."

The movie took home five Emmys and Berry walked away with a Golden Globe Award and a Screen Actors Guild Award for her performance.

Berry became the first African-American woman to win a Best Actress Academy Award for the 2001 film *Monster's Ball*.

In Halle's acceptance speech, she honored the women of color who had come before her. "This moment is so much bigger than me. This moment is for Dorothy Dandridge, Lena Horne, Diahann Carroll. It's for the women that stand beside me—Jada Pinkett, Angela Bassett, Vivica Fox. And it's for every nameless, faceless woman of color that now has a chance because this door tonight has been opened. Thank you, I'm so honored, I'm so honored and I thank the Academy for choosing me to be the vessel for which is blessing my flow."

(On April 13, 1964, Sidney Poitier became the first African American to win an Academy Award for Best Actor, for his role in the 1963 motion picture *Lilies of the Field*.)

The saga of Dorothy Dandridge is much like the life story of the lotus flower, a plant that despite being rooted at the bottom of a muddy, murky pool of water, finds the strength to rise to the surface of each day to display its prepossessing blossom.

According to the sacred Buddhist text, the Lalitavistara, "The spirit of the best of (wo)men is spotless, like the lotus in the muddy water which does not adhere to it."

# 9.
# ROCK HUDSON:
## *Unraveling the Myth*

ROCK HUDSON WAS ARGUABLY THE MOST CLASSICALLY HANDsome man to ever grace the silver screen. He stood six feet four (some sources add two more inches), had a head of thick wavy hair, a toned physique and a trademark deep, sexy voice. Hudson was the epitome of the "tall, dark and handsome" prototype.

In 1957, he was voted the number one "Name Power Star" in the movies—a title he held for seven years straight. His films with Doris Day captured the essence of the changing sexual mores of the late 1950s and early 1960s—Day with her virginal girl-next-door image and songbird voice; Rock with his suave, roughish playboy ways. These "bedroom comedies" seem tame by today's standards, but women swooned when Rock took his leading lady in his arms or when he took off his shirt.

Rock led a private existence shunning fans and the press. He enjoyed throwing elaborate parties for his close circle of friends where he could be the center of attention. Music was his passion, and he owned thousands of records. His hobbies included needlepoint, gardening, landscaping and barbequing, (or as friends would note, more like burning steaks, but he tried).

He turned a blind eye to conflict, and simply lived in denial when the truth was too painful to deal with. For years, the fan magazines published articles dubbing Rock Hollywood's Most Eligible Bachelor and explained he had not yet wed because he hadn't found the right woman or he was too busy making movies to settle down. He accompanied beautiful actresses to award ceremonies leading to frequent rumors that he was engaged to one starlet or another. Oftentimes, these women were dates set up by the studio or the relationships were platonic. His marriage to Phyllis Gates in 1955 was a sham.

By 1985, the once debonair and youthful movie/stage/television star was unrecognizable. It was first reported that he was suffering from liver cancer and indeed he had a serious drinking problem. He no longer weighed the 225 pounds of his prime, but had dropped to a skeletal 140 pounds. Rumors of anorexia swirled. But in reality, Hudson was being ravaged by a horrific, newly discovered disease. After over a year of hiding his prognosis, the truth was announced at a press conference that made front-page news across the world. In that instant, the myth Hudson had spent a lifetime perpetuating had unraveled. The heartthrob of the 1950s and '60s was dying of AIDS — Acquired Immune Deficiency Syndrome, an incurable and ravaging disease usually associated with homosexual behavior. For decades, Rock Hudson had guarded his sexuality from the public with unparalleled stealth. Now he was cast in a new role as the face of a global and much misunderstood pandemic.

He was born Roy Harold Scherer, Jr. on November 17, 1925 in Winnetka, Illinois, a town located 16 miles north of the heart of Chicago. Five years after his birth, his father walked out on the family.

Decades after the abandonment mother Kay dropped the bombshell that Roy Sr. had left the family because there was doubt he was the boy's biological father.

As a youth

A year after being deserted, the young boy got a stepfather named Wallace Fitzgerald. But Wallace was abusive and beat both his wife and stepson. Kay would divorce Wallace, remarry him, and divorce him again.

Rock grew up impoverished and he did poorly in school. His outlet was the movies. He secured a job as a theater usher in order to see films. His favorite star was Lana Turner. Rock was so inspired by the actors he saw up on the screen that he tried out for school plays. However, he could never remember his lines. Also, the young man was insecure about his height; by age 14 he was already six feet tall. After barely finishing high school, Rock entered the Navy and worked as an airplane mechanic from 1943-1946.

After being discharged from the service, Rock—who at that time was still known as Roy Fitzgerald—decided to move to Long Beach, California to live with his father and break into acting. Roy Sr. had remarried and adopted a daughter, and the presence of his first-born was not welcome. Rock worked as a vacuum cleaner salesman, truck driver and mail carrier trying to support himself after leaving his father's home. While living in Long Beach, he discovered that the city had a gay subculture where he could associate with other homosexual men. Hudson met radio producer Ken Hodge who took the budding actor under his wing and into his bedroom.

Rock then met Henry Willson, a talent agent who found attractive young men and banking on their sex appeal, made them into stars. He bedded most of them and Rock was no exception.

Willson is often credited with selecting Hudson's stage name. Seeking a manly sounding name, Willson thought the Rock of Gibraltar and the Hudson River exuded strength. Others cite that the name Hudson came from the car company, or that even the name was picked at random from the phone book. For a while, the "k" was left off the name for aesthetic purposes, and he went by Roc Hudson. Willson arranged for his client to meet Warner Brothers director Raoul Walsh. Hudson received a minor role in the movie *Fighter Squadron*. Allegedly, it took Rock 38 takes to get his one line correct and it was ultimately simplified due to the flubs.

Unimpressed with Rock's acting abilities, Walsh sold the actor's contract to Universal-International Pictures in 1949. Universal was no MGM, the Cadillac of all studios, but Rock immersed himself in his craft at the B-movie studio. He learned to fence, ride horses and even studied ballet. Some actors found the Studio System stifling but Hudson appreciated that Universal pampered him, "The Studio took care of everything. They could get you a house, a car, airline tickets, special shoes. All you had to do was concentrate on your performance. There was no better method of training," he said.

While his career was picking up, his personal life was blossoming. In 1951, Rock met two men who would become his lifelong friends. Mark Miller and George Nader were a gay couple, also in show business. Three men out socially did not draw as much suspicion as two, so the trio often went out together. Mark taught Rock how to play bridge, advising the up-and-coming actor that he could meet the Hollywood movers-and-shakers at bridge parties. He later became Rock's personal secretary. Rock next appeared in the movie *Iron Man*, where he depicts a boxer.

Then he made *Bend in the River*, a Western starring Jimmy Stewart, which struck a chord with female moviegoers. At the premier in Portland, Oregon the crowd cheered for Stewart, but they mobbed Hudson who was visibly surprised, "It went to my head—I was floating! Me over Jimmy Stewart? I went back to the hotel that night and got

**Rock was surprised by the enthusiasm of the fans for him**

drunk. I couldn't sleep, I wanted more!" the actor enthused.

Rock made a string of pictures and caught the attention of fan magazines that marketed him as the "beefcake king" giving its readers tips on what it took to become Mrs. Hudson and "how to handle Hollywood's 'Big Rock.'" One caption read "Bachelor on the Loose: What kind of romance does he want?"

Hudson was painted as a persnickety movie star hunk for whom no woman would ever meet his standards. In February 1952, Hudson told columnist Bob Thomas that when his dates want to get more serious he simply gives them the cold shoulder. Rock didn't chase women—they went after him. Rock found women attractive and was actually bisexual, but preferred men.

In 1954, Rock starred in a film that could best be described as his break-through role. He was teamed opposite Academy Award-winning actress Jane Wyman for *Magnificent Obsession*. In the movie, Rock Hudson plays the hedonistic and wealthy Bob Merrick whose boating accident makes local paramedics take their only equipment to save him, thusly making emergency services unavailable to aid local hero Dr. Wayne Phillips, who dies as a result. Hudson befriends the widow Helen, played by Wyman, with whom Merrick has fallen in love. But his overzealousness leads to an accident that causes Wyman to go blind.

He goes back to medical school, in an attempt to make amends and win her love.

Hudson's gal pal Betty Abbott and Agnes Moorhead also starred. The film was Universal's most profitable motion picture up to that point and Hudson became its top star, receiving 3,000 fan letters a week, mainly from women who had fallen in love with his image. *Life* magazine did a cover story on Hudson but one can read between the lines: "Fans are urging 29-year-old Hudson to get married—or explain why not." There was trouble, indeed. Hudson wasn't in the closet; he was in the dungeon.

The studio was in a conundrum because the pressure cooker was about to explode. The tabloid *Confidential* had approached several friends of Hudson's including his "roommate" Jack Navaar asking them to expose him as homosexual. George Nader shared the same concern of being outed. "We lived in fear of an exposé…Every month, when *Confidential* came out, our stomachs began to turn. Which of us would be in it? The amazing thing is that Rock was never nailed…he seemed under supernatural protection."

Rock's agent Henry Willson casually suggested that Rock would enjoy the company of a pretty brunette named Phyllis Gates. She was Willson's secretary. Hudson was hesitant, but when he finally went out with Gates he found her hu-

**Rock married Phyllis Gates**

morous, unpretentious and fun to be around. She even charmed Rock's gay friends and was absorbed into their inner circle. The two became infatuated with each other and Rock asked Phyllis to move in with him. However, in 1955 it was regarded as "living in sin" for a man and woman to reside at the same address without being married.

Willson pressured Rock to ask Phyllis to marry him. The wedding took place in Santa Barbara without any fanfare. However, to stay in the good graces of Hollywood's top gossip columnists, Rock phoned

Hedda Hopper and Phyllis dialed Louella Parsons to give the ladies the scoop on the spontaneous nuptials. Phyllis Gates was envied by Rock's legion of fans, yet she may or may not have known Hudson was gay.

### The Lavender Marriage Keeps Rock's Career Red Hot

Finally, Rock Hudson had a personal life to match his public image. In 1956, he starred in the epic film *Giant* alongside Elizabeth Taylor and James Dean. He was paid a whopping $100,000 for his role

**Rock Hudson lived the good life with all its hedonistic pleasures**

and was nominated for a Best Actor Oscar. He and Taylor grew close while filming and the two often required numerous re-takes due to their constant laughter. Rock was a hard drinker and he had met his match with Liz. She made the claim that one night the two were experimenting and ended up combining chocolate liqueur with vodka and invented the chocolate martini.

They wouldn't make another film together until 1980 with *The Mirror Crack'd*, but the two stayed friends. Elizabeth publically supported Rock when he announced he had AIDS and she raised money for AIDS research.

*Something of Value* and *A Farewell to Arms* were minor hits in 1957 but his popularity swelled with the 1959 comedy that became one of his signature movies—*Pillow Talk*. In the light comedy, Rock plays womanizing songwriter Brad Allen who shares a party line with prim interior designer Jan Morrow, played by the infectious Doris Day. She despises him and to win her over, he poses as a different man, naive Texan Rex Stetson, but she finally catches on—and seeks revenge. Thelma Ritter and Tony Randall co-starred. The film was the start of a bond between Hudson and Day that the two would foster. "Shooting *Pillow Talk* was like going to a party. It was like a day's work of fun," Rock joyfully reminisced.

**Rock nervously smoking, studying his *Pillow Talk* script**

From the start of filming that February, Rock and Doris had a rapport that erupted on the screen. They looked and acted like a real couple. However, Hudson was not fond of the script and the storyline was a departure from his earlier roles. "I was quite apprehensive, nervous and scared, because I'd never played comedy," Rock revealed.

Director Michael Gordon told him that to be humorous, an actor had to take the lines seriously because, "If you think you're funny, nobody else will," he said.

After three years of marriage, Phyllis filed for divorce on April 22, 1958 citing "extreme mental cruelty," a cliché term before no-fault divorces. She described her husband as disinterested in making the union work and claimed he was never home.

Hot on the trail of what was certainly a juicy story—if anyone ever revealed the full facts—gossip columnist Louella Parsons wrote of the dissolution of marriage in her syndicated column. She told her readers how Phyllis had demanded Rock remove himself and his belongings from their home. "Something, of course, led up to that," Parsons hinted. "But neither has ever discussed what is the basis of all this trouble."

Rock hired Machiavellian Hollywood attorney Greg Bautzer who worked out a settlement. Phyllis received $250 monthly as alimony for a period of ten years, a house, a Ford Thunderbird and stock in Rock's film compan —7 Pictures. In 1961, Phyllis filed suit to increase her monetary allowance. She was given a lump sum of $130,000. There was talk that the ex-Mrs. Hudson was planning to write a tell-all book. It wasn't until the mid-'80s when Hudson was dying that Phyllis went public with her story and later released a memoir called *My Husband, Rock Hudson*.

After licking his wounds from the messy divorce, Rock did what he always did; he acted as though his problems were not real and that Phyllis Gates didn't exist. In the summer of 1959, Rock relocated from Malibu to Newport Beach where he spent time sailing and out with friends.

In 1960 he headed to Mexico to shoot the Western *The Last Sunset* with Kirk Douglas and Dorothy Malone. He then jetted to the Italian Riviera to shoot *Come September* wherein he plays a wealthy man who strings his Italian girlfriend along—played by the brunette bombshell Gina Lollobrigida—only seeing her in September. Upon arriving earlier than expected to his Italian villa, he discovers that his home operates as a hotel when he is away. In addition, a quartet of hormonal American college boys, one of them being played by Bobby Darin, try to make the moves on a group of teenage girls, led by Sandra Dee. Besides being remembered as a scenic romantic comedy, the film was the first movie shown on transcontinental and intercontinental flights.

Again, Rock proved himself a capable comedian and audiences and critics made the film a hit. *Variety* magazine swooned, "Comedy appears to be his forte, which should make him an even more valuable leading man in Hollywood film." Indeed, Rock's next teaming with Doris Day proved more successful than his first. In early 1961, Rock, Doris and Tony Randall went back to the studio to shoot a movie using the same blueprint as *Pillow Talk*. In *Lover, Come Back*, Rock plays Jerry Webster, an advertising executive who steals an account from Carol

Templeton, a woman at a rival firm, played by Day. She begrudges his tactic of plying the client with booze and women while she went after the account by more assiduous means. In split-screen fashion Doris confronts Rock:

"*I don't use sex to land an account,*" Carol affirms.

"When do you use sex?" Jerry asks coyly.

"*I don't.*"

"My condolences to your husband."

"*I'm not married.*"

"That figures."

"*What do you mean?*"

"A husband would be competitive. There's only room for one man in a family."

"*[Growing flustered] Oooh. I wish I were a man right now.*"

"Keep trying. I think you'll make it."

On February 16, 1962, Rock appeared on the cover of *Life* magazine. "Like any movie star, Rock Hudson has to lead a double life — he lives in reality yet works in make-believe," the magazine reported.

**The chemistry between Doris Day and Rock Hudson on screen was magic**

"On one hand there is Rock Hudson, Hollywood's most valuable star, tall, gay, insouciant. He owns three homes, gets his hair pulled and his coat ripped by admirers, and collects 8,000 adorning fan letters every week."

The article paralleled the hero-worship image with that of Rock's real-life persona as a shy, introverted music and antique lover who was a fan of chess and who dabbled in astronomy.

*Lover, Come Back* surpassed *Pillow Talk* at the box office and became Hudson's favorite pairing with Doris. Believing the old adage that the third time's the charm, Rock and Doris poured over scripts for yet another film. They didn't find a suitable storyline until 1963 when they made *Send Me No Flowers*. The formula for this flick varied from their prior two. Rock and Doris start the film already married and living in the suburbs. Rock's character believes he is terminally ill and Doris' character misinterprets her husband's behavior and assumes he is having an affair. Once more, Tony Randall added to the cast.

While Rock preferred his secretive rendezvous with men, he did date women. The woman who came the closest to becoming the second Mrs. Rock Hudson was singer/actress Marilyn Maxwell. The pair became friends in the early 1950s and when Marilyn divorced her husband in 1961, she and Rock began a relationship.

A little known fact about Rock Hudson is that he enjoyed singing and playing the piano. When he was first starting out, he was advised to go out in a remote area and scream at the top of his voice, while sick with a cold, to permanently lower his voice. Whether or not that is how he achieved his smoky sound, his singing voice was never the same. Nonetheless, he and Marilyn—whom he called Max—would sit at the piano and play and sing to their hearts' content. They also

**Marilyn Maxwell captured Rock's heart**

**A happy domestic life eluded Rock**

danced, laughed and played jokes on each other.

When Rock asked her to marry him in 1962, he made it clear that he could never be monogamous and still desired boyfriends. Marilyn Maxwell thought Rock's interest in men was just a "fad" of the time and that once he married her, he would be content in a heterosexual relationship. She told Hudson if he could not be faithful they would have to stay friends, although she was in love with him. Rock later confessed that while he loved her, he wasn't in love. Their dynamic could be compared to that of the sitcom *Will & Grace*.

Nevertheless, Rock stepping out with a vivacious blonde caught the eye of the press. Louella Parsons reported, "The Rock Hudson—Marilyn Maxwell romance is still on." In her usual manner, she schmoozed, "When Rock called to say he was going to New York, he said, 'Don't print that until I am on my way. I want to surprise Marilyn. She has no idea I'll be there.'"

Maxwell never left Hudson's life, calling him "without question the best friend I've ever had." Since Rock never had any children of his own, he befriended Marilyn's son Matthew, becoming a surrogate father. When Marilyn passed away in 1972, Rock took in her 15-year-old son and seriously considered adopting him, but the boy ended up going to live with his father.

Rock made several motion pictures a year as the 1960s came to a close. Hollywood has never lacked for young attractive males to star in lead film roles, and thus, Rock's position as the top male star in the world slipped. In 1971 he starred in an X-rated porno entitled *Maids All in a Row* alongside Angie Dickinson. Film critic Roger Ebert quipped at the time, "Rock Hudson sex comedies sure have changed since *Pillow Talk*."

Biographer Sara Davidson worked with Hudson the last month

of his life to record his life story with the help of friends and associates. She described Hudson's disdain for the new crop of younger actors, "In the last 10 or 15 years of his life, he drank a lot. It wasn't easy, going from the Number One box office star in the world to Number Two, Number Six, and then dropping off the list altogether. The irony is that he just started to hit his stride as an actor in the 1960s, when handsome leading men like him were on the way out. He looked at the new stars like Dustin Hoffman and called them the 'Little Uglies.' He hated them because they didn't have perfect faces. Rock Hudson never took a bad picture, Davidson wrote.

With film roles dwindling, Rock experienced another potential blow to his career—one that rattled him to the core. That summer, members of a gay group in Manhattan Beach, California sent out invitations to their annual party, citing the theme as commemorating the nuptials of Rock Hudson and actor Jim Nabors, who was also a closeted homosexual. (Nabors is best known for his role as Gomer Pyle on *The Andy Griffith Show*). It was meant in good fun, but a columnist got a hold of one of the invites and wrote an exposé. While the actors were not named, the writer made a lame attempt at revealing their identities by reporting how two male actors had wed and that, "One is like the rock of Gibraltar; the other is like your neighbor." Television, radio and print media picked up the story. Rock used his wit to charm the press into dropping the story by joking, "It's over. I've returned all the emeralds and diamonds Jim gave me." Urban legend has it that the men were married in the home of Carol Burnett, a close friend of Rock's. After the incident, Nabors ended their friendship.

Rock figured that if the gay marriage rumor hadn't made much of an impact on his image, then having men live with him at his home would fly under the radar. He became romantically involved with a man named Tom Clark who worked as a publicist at MGM. Years later, Rock would say that Clark was "the most important person who was ever in my life." Clark acted as Hudson's publicist, travel companion and all-around best friend. By 1973, Clark was living with Hudson and even told Davidson about their romantic relationship for the book, but when Tom Clark published his own memoir in 1990, *Rock Hudson: Friend of Mine*, he omitted any references to a physical relationship with Hudson. Rock also pursued a man named Jack Coates who also lived at Hudson's estate, but he later moved out to live a life outside of the movie star's shadow. Coming to terms with the changes in the motion picture business, Rock channeled his creativity and embarked on a new career path.

## The Big Screen Couldn't Contain Him

Hudson believed television work was beneath him, but he finally capitulated by agreeing to star in an NBC movie of the week called *Once Upon a Dead Man*. The pilot was developed into a series and *McMillan & Wife* was born. Running ninety minutes, the show rotated airtime with *Colombo* and *McCloud* as part of the network's Mystery Movie cycle.

From 1971-1977 viewers tuned in to watch a revamped version of "The Thin Man" series, wherein Hudson portrays a San Francisco police commissioner whose wife helps him solve crimes. He earned $120,000 per episode—the highest amount paid for a television role up to that point. Susan Saint James was cast as his much younger wife. Hudson did not enjoy the hurried atmosphere of television and as the show wore on, he felt the scripts grew inferior.

**Rock with Susan Saint James**

There was also a different director hired for each episode and Rock was frustrated by the lack of continuity. He also ruminated about how the plots never completely made sense, and how the final scene of the show was always shot first. His character explains the mystery in great detail, but Hudson never knew what he was talking about.

More than television, Rock loved appearing on the stage. In the 1970s, he starred in *I Do! I Do!* with Juliet Prowse on the London stage and with Carol Burnett in the States. In 1976, he went on tour with *John Brown's Body*, followed by a rendition of *Camelot* where he played King Arthur.

After *McMillan & Wife* came to an end, NBC offered Hudson the lead in *The Delvin Connection*, where he played a man who solves crimes with his son, played by Jack Scalia. Production began in the autumn of 1981. In November, Hudson had a severe heart attack, requiring emergency quintuple heart bypass surgery and blood transfusions. He started smoking again right there in the hospital recovery room.

The show was stuck in limbo for a full year and upon its debut, critics who dubbed the program "McMillan & Son" panned it.

Hudson continued to make television appearances and a few movies including 1984's *The Ambassador* alongside Robert Mitchum and Ellen Burstyn. It was to be his last film. Years of heavy drinking had destroyed his liver and his heart condition forced the star to transition out of show business. But Rock was suffering from symptoms that could not be traced to his known health issues. Something had gone awry.

Rock couldn't keep food down, he sweated through the night, developed itchy body sores and most telling, he developed a spot on his neck known as Kaposi sarcoma, a tumor caused by human herpesvirus 8. In June 1984, Rock Hudson learned he had AIDS. He flew to Paris to receive HPA-23, an experimental drug. By November, Rock was in better health and his blood tested negative for AIDS. However, one needed treatment every few months, but Rock refused to go back for nearly a year. He told friends he had beaten the disease.

Despite his declining health, Hudson accepted a recurring role on the highly popular nighttime soap *Dynasty*, in which he appeared in nine episodes as Linda Evans' love interest. One episode required Hudson to kiss Evans, sending the actor into a panic. He feared that his saliva would expose her to the disease. When the scene was shot,

**Rock was aging rapidly and his health declining**

**The famous kissing scene with Linda Evans in *Dynasty***

one can see an awkward Hudson barely brush the side of Evans' lips, giving her a closed mouth kiss.

In Linda's 2011 memoir she wrote, "In retrospect, it was incredibly touching how hard he tried to protect me." He was let go from the show due to his struggles with remembering lines. In addition, he suffered from the mouth infection Vincent's disease, which impaired his speech.

Since developing AIDS, Rock had lost 50 pounds. It is unclear as to how the actor acquired the disease. It is possible that when Rock had bypass surgery in 1981 he was exposed to it through blood transfusions. However, Hudson also admitted to having unprotected sex. In the summer of 1985, Doris Day invited Hudson out to Carmel, California to tape an episode of her newly launched show *Doris Day's Best Friends*. Against the pleading of friends and associates, Rock did the show.

On July 16th, Rock appeared at a press conference with Day to promote her new show, revealing how gaunt and sickly he'd become. How fitting that his last role was with Doris Day. "It was his final thing, and it was with me, and I really cherish that," Day opined.

Sara Davidson was hired to record Rock's life story. She interviewed the movie star, his friends, associates and lovers, piecing together a puzzle having only weeks to speak with the dying man. "A lot of people said it was so brave of Rock to admit that he had AIDS," Davidson commented. "But actually he wanted it to be hushed up. He thought of AIDS as the plague. It made him feel unclean, and he felt it would destroy the image he had carefully built up over 35 years. If he had collapsed in L.A., he would have been taken to a place like Cedars-Sinai, a hospital used to hushing up the details of movie stars' illnesses...but he collapsed in Paris, and the officials at the American Hospital were enraged. They didn't accept AIDS cases in the hospital, and they said either he would have to announce it, or they would."

**A sad ending to an amazing man**

On July 25th, Hudson's press agent Yanou Collart made a statement to the French media that the film idol of the 1950s and '60s was dying of a disease mostly associated with homosexuality.

Rock decided he would rather live out his final weeks at home, and he was flown back to the States. On October 2nd, 1985, he passed away due to complications from AIDS. He was 59-years-old. As per his wishes, Hudson was cremated and his ashes were spread at sea. Before his death, he founded the Rock Hudson AIDS Foundation where he donated $250,000 as well as the advance and royalties from the book he co-wrote with Davidson. But his image would receive another layer of tarnish when in 1985, scorned lover Marc Christian sued the estate.

Beginning in 1983,

Rock was romantically involved with Christian who remained a resident of Hudson's estate long after the relationship ended. Rock grew to distrust Christian and worried that if he informed his former lover that he had AIDS, Christian would go to the tabloids. When the announcement was made that Hudson was dying of AIDS, Christian worried that he might have it, too and he went and got tested. The results were negative, but he filed a lawsuit anyway citing "intentional infliction of emotional distress." It was the first case of its kind.

In 1989, Marc received nearly $22 million in damages, later dropped to $5.5 million by the court. In 2010, Robert Park Mills, the lawyer who represented Hudson's estate in the lawsuit, wrote a book entitled *Between Rock and a Hard Place: In Defense of Rock Hudson*, documenting his experience handling the first case dealing with a former lover suing for exposure to AIDS.

More than 30 years after his death, Rock Hudson is still remembered for his romantic comedies and remarkable good looks. But fans are quick to add how shocking it was to learn that someone so desired by women preferred men and would later die of AIDS.

Rock had mastered the art of compartmentalizing his life—separating gay from straight friends—wearing whatever mask was required for the occasion.

It was said that he even had a secret "love child" whom he never knew. The boy's name was supposedly Richard, and Hudson admitted on his deathbed that one of the biggest regrets in his life was not getting to know him.

As George Nader, one of Rock's best friends for 35 years offered to biographer Sara Davidson, "There is no Rock Hudson. There are many Rock Hudsons."

# 10.
# MARILYN MAXWELL:
## *The Forgotten Marilyn*

WHEN ONE THINKS OF A FAMOUS BLONDE ACTRESS named Marilyn, most people envision Marilyn Monroe. But before Monroe ever made a film, Marilyn Maxwell was an established singer, dancer, actress and performer for our troops overseas. While her career ebbed and flowed, Maxwell starred in some of the most iconic movies and sang some of the most recognizable tunes of all time. Her private life was stormy; she dated powerful, volatile men that broke her heart.

She was born Marvel Marilyn Maxwell on August 3, 1922 in Clarinda, Iowa. The southwest Iowa town, situated halfway between Omaha, Nebraska and St. Joseph, Missouri, stakes two major claims to fame. Bert W. Gray is said to have started the first hamburger business in the country when he opened a café at the turn of the 20th century, located on the east side of Clarinda's Courthouse Square. The town is also the birthplace of Big Band musician Glenn Miller, who was born in the town in 1904.

Marvel's father Harry sold insurance and her mother Anne was a pianist. Marilyn had an older brother, Lelland, and a brother, Paul, who died young. The Maxwells divorced when Marvel was a baby. Left to support herself and two children, Anne took her offspring on the road with modern dancer Ruth Saint Denis, for whom she played piano. Marilyn made her stage debut at age three doing a butterfly dance at the Brandeis Theater in Omaha. At her mother's urging, the young girl took dance and singing lessons. She began her singing career on a radio program in Des Moines, Iowa. "[My mother] tried to fulfill her ambitions through me," Marilyn later opined. Former classmate Sally Presley recalled, "She had a very pushy mother, one of those stage mothers like you read about."

When Marilyn was fifteen, her family moved to Indiana. Cathy Katz, the daughter of Marilyn's brother Lelland and wife Kitten, says Anne "played the organ in the Embassy Theater in Fort Wayne for the silent movies." Amos Ostot, a regional bandleader, heard the girl sing on a local station and hired her to tour with his band for thirty-five dollars a week.

Maxwell quit school her sophomore year and took the job. Soon after, actor Charles "Buddy" Rogers signed her for a one-year-long tour across the Midwest. While at an Indianapolis nightclub engagement in 1939, Ted Weems recruited the teenager to perform with his musicians on *To Beat the Band*. She was also asked to record *Monstro the Whale* with Fred Foley.

Maxwell told Motion Picture magazine Weems "suggested that I go to the Pasadena Community Playhouse, and he'd finance me and pay my salary for a full year. It would be an investment for him. Then, when I was signed by a studio — as he was so sure I would be — I could pay it all back." She sang on an amateur radio program in Des Moines. For two and half years, she sang with Weem's band alongside then-unknown Perry Como. In 1961 the *The Milwaukee Journal* reported, "She prefers to forget her association with Como because apparently he has." Maxwell complained, "I don't know what's with him. He's never had Ted or me on his program. I've asked Perry about it, and he tells me it's a fine idea and gives me the name of the man for my agent to call, but when he does call, nothing happens."

In 1942, Maxwell took a screen test at Paramount studios. That year she was cast in *Stand By For Action* with Robert Taylor. It bombed at the box office, so the starlet went on a U.S.O. tour instead of rushing back into films. When she returned, she discovered the most prestigious movie studio in Hollywood wanted to put her under contract.

MGM recognized that the young bubbly blonde had potential. "When I was signed by Metro, Louis B. Mayer said 'Marvel' sounded too phony," she told syndicated columnist Earl Wilson in 1952. "They were tossing all possible names around and I ventured meekly that Marilyn was my real [middle] name." Mayer liked the idea, but Marilyn's mother was disappointed. Ironically, she had chosen "Marvel Marilyn Maxwell" as her child's name because she believed that it would look perfect on a theater marquee.

The newly deemed "Marilyn Maxwell" was featured in *Salute to the Marines* in 1943. Later that year her role opposite Van Johnson in Dr. Gillespie's *Criminal Case* proved a moderate success and the film starred Lionel Barrymore. Maxwell appeared in two subsequent installments of the Barrymore series. In *Swing Fever*, also released in 1943, Marilyn played alongside Kay Kyser. She sang *One Girl and Two Boys*, *Mississippi Dream Boat*, *I Planted a Rose*, and *I Never Knew*. Marilyn also appeared in the Judy Garland/Van Heflin musical *Presenting Lily Mars*. In 1943, the young actress appeared in a total of tens films.

Following these flicks, Marilyn made *Three Men in White*, the second in the Dr. Gillespie series. Also in the film was Ava Gardner, who became her rival off the set.

Marilyn met her first husband on the set of the 1944 Abbott and Costello picture, *Lost in Harem*. While not a lucrative endeavor, Marilyn did sing the notable song *What Does It Take to Get You?* Her character teased, "I can even get as far as second base with Frank Sinatra too."

## She Swooned over Sinatra, But Married Another Man

Although Marilyn would soon develop a genuine interest in Mr. Sinatra, it was co-star John Conte who pursued a romance with her. She and Conte married after filming wrapped but were divorced in two years.

As if foreshadowed by the song, Marilyn began spending a great deal of time with Frank Sinatra and was the first guest on his radio program. It was rumored Marilyn and Frank had become an item. In fact, Marilyn's niece Cathy Katz, told this author the story of when her parents met Sinatra for the first time.

"For their honeymoon they went to Chicago. My aunt Marilyn met them there with Frank Sinatra, whom she was friends with for a while. I remember the four of them went out to dinner. And my mother was pretty excited about that!"

Nick Sevano, a friend of the singer, said Marilyn "was gorgeous, simply gorgeous, and nice too. She spent hours showing me around Hollywood when I first came out because she knew that I had once been associated with Frank, and they were crazy about each other." Sinatra wanted to divorce his wife, Nancy for his new love interest, but was advised against it by associates.

On one occasion, Mrs. Sinatra found a diamond bracelet Frank purchased as a gift for Marilyn. She confronted the actress when she arrived at the Sinatras' New Year's Eve party, demanding she leave her husband alone. After Sinatra divorced Nancy, he married Ava Gardner, but his flings with other women didn't end. In a 1952 incident at Bill Miller's Riviera in Fort Lee, New Jersey Marilyn came to hear Sinatra. Consequently, her presence upset his new wife, who was convinced he was singing to his old flame. Ava left in a huff, and then sent a terse note to Frank, along with her wedding ring. Ava later admitted she had overreacted.

In 1945, Ms. Maxwell made her final Dr. Gillespie flick entitled *Between Two Women*. In the picture, Marilyn vied for Van Johnson's affections once more. In one scene she states, "I admit that girl (played by Gloria DeHaven), isn't exactly repulsive, but anything she's good at I can do better, quicker, and cheaper!" Van and Marilyn's characters eventually wed at the end of the film.

Marilyn was excited to be cast in the now iconic 1946 *Ziegfeld Follies*, but her songs performed with the likes of Lucille Ball and

Jimmy Durante were cut from the final film. Her luck changed when she was asked to become a regular on Bing Crosby's popular *Kraft Music Hall* program and she signed on for additional U.S.O. tours. Also that year, Maxwell was cast in the film *The Show-Off*, playing Red Skelton's wife. The pair sang the familiar tune *I've Got You Under My Skin*.

On Bing Crosby's radio show

Made in the summer of 1946, but shelved until 1948, *Summer Holiday* was Maxwell's preeminent role for MGM. "That was my real introduction to acting," she reflected. "For although I'd been in pictures before I played the role of Belle, I certainly hadn't been an actress. I'd been Marilyn Maxwell, going through some necessary motions for the camera, and luckily getting by."

In 1947 she made yet another movie with Van Johnson, *High Barbaree*, but Johnson's movie "other half" June Allyson, stole the show. "With the studio cutting down its planned schedule...it didn't seem as though there was anything left for me; so I went to Mr. Mayer and asked him to release me from my contract. The whole thing was very friendly, and the studio finally agreed to let me go," Marilyn reflected.

Now on her own, she freelanced and landed a role at RKO studios after darkening her blonde hair. She played in the 1948 film *Race Street*. Afterwards, she appeared with Jack Benny in his London Palladium Show.

Benny's daughter Joan wrote about her encounters with the

actress in her book *Sunday Nights at Seven*, "The engagement at Palladium was a great success and sold out every performance... Marilyn Maxwell sang and did a skit with my father as the 'sexy dumb blonde,' similar to the role Marilyn Monroe later played.... 'Max' never made it big, but her name was well-known, she had a nice singing voice and fair amount of talent... Sexy and glamorous — yes, very — but hardly dumb. I liked her because she was one of the few of many people who came in and out of my life who paid attention to me... I enjoyed knowing Max for a short time. She was a neat lady."

By 1949 Marilyn finally starred in a motion picture that received mass attention. The film noir *Champion* teamed her with Kirk Douglas and was a raw, earthy picture that propelled Douglas's career. *Key to the City*, made in 1950 alongside Clark Gable and Loretta Young, was a motion picture wherein Maxwell's star was outshone by Gable and Young. Looking for love yet again, Marilyn remarried on New Year's Day 1950 to 31-year-old Anders McIntyre, owner of the Encore Room. They wed in a cottage at the Santa Barbara Biltmore Hotel. She wore a gray suit and hat, not a gown. The marriage dissolved after one year amid allegations of affairs and domestic abuse.

Marilyn bounced back quickly and began another tour of entertaining the troops. In June of 1950, Marilyn became the first female performer to go to Korea. She told friends upon returning how "conditions were rugged — once they shot a sniper right near where I was standing."

That year her father died, followed by her mother a year later. She missed the funerals of both her parents because she was on U.S.O. tours for American servicemen overseas. The other celebrity on the tour was Bob Hope. Interested in each other early on, the two began an affair while touring.

In 1951, they made a film together entitled *The Lemon Drop Kid*. The now ubiquitous holiday tune *Silver Bells*, was introduced to the world with the Hope/Max-

**Bob Hope and Marilyn Maxwell**

well duet in the movie. Their affair was not kept under the radar, despite their claims of being merely friends. In fact, on the Paramount lot Marilyn was even referred to as "Mrs. Bob Hope."

Louella Parsons interviewed Hope's wife Dolores about the rumors of her husband's infidelity, hoping to acquire juicy fodder for a column. "Our marriage is stronger than ever," Mrs. Hope maintained. Yet according to Arthur Marx, who wrote an unauthorized biography on the comedian, Dolores and her mother begged Bob to end the affair.

Their pleas fell on deaf ears and overseas it was common knowledge that Bob and Marilyn were romantically involved. Maxwell's personal secretary Jean Greenberg told Marx, "Bob asked Marilyn to marry him when they were in Ireland together. But she turned him down because she knew Dolores would never give him a divorce" (due to her Catholic faith).

When Marilyn Maxwell was the mystery guest on the May 10, 1953 episode of the popular network television program *What's My Line?*, she used a high-pitched baby voice that threw off the panel. Asked by a blindfolded Bennett Cerf if the mystery guest was a female, Marilyn quipped, "The last time I looked," getting a big laugh from the audience. But then host John Daley casually brought up Bob Hope's name. Maxwell kept her cool, not betraying just how intimately she knew the famed comic.

Marilyn then appeared in *New Mexico*, a classic cowboys and Indians tale alongside Raymond Burr and Lew Ayres. Although low budget, Maxwell again was allowed to show off her best talents: singing and dancing. Her next role came in 1953 opposite Hope and Mickey Rooney, who was strangely cast as her nephew, even though the actor was a year older than Maxwell. Her singing redeemed the picture. Also that year, Maxwell was featured in *East of Sumatra* with Jeff Chandler and Anthony Quinn.

In Bob Thomas' 1953, "About Hollywood" column he noted, "She now has myopia in one eye, and astigmatism in the other. She always keeps four pairs of glasses — two dark and two clear — in case she loses one."

Asked if it made her feel less glamorous to wear glasses she replied, "It used to be hard at MGM because I couldn't see the chalk marks on the floor that showed where I was supposed to stand. So the boys worked up a system for Esther Williams and me — she can't see either. They put a couple of small boards on the floor. When our feet hit them, we stopped." She blamed dimly lit dressing rooms, bright

**Marilyn Maxwell was a pin-up girl before Marilyn Monroe came along**

spotlights and smoky clubs that she performed in during her youth for her vision problems.

Often confused with another attractive blonde, Marilyn Monroe, Maxwell recalled for Bob Thomas that back in 1948 when she threw a Christmas Eve party at her Hollywood home, Marilyn Monroe showed up uninvited. The two women chatted about the similarity of their names, with Monroe falsely claiming that "Marilyn" was her birth name. Maxwell advised her guest (actually born Norma Jean Baker), that perhaps she should take a different stage name so they wouldn't get mixed up with one another.

Five years later, Marilyn Monroe had become the bigger star. "I was the only Marilyn in pictures until she came along," Ms. Maxwell stated. "I suppose she is subject to the same confusion, but people often call me inadvertently 'Miss Monroe.' My answer is, 'No, I'm the Marilyn with her clothes on.'" Even friends would poke fun at the mistaken identity. As a prank, classmates from high school took the Monroe calendars and pasted Maxwell's head on the body.

Despite the comparisons with the younger blonde actress, Maxwell claimed to have no qualms with her counterpart (younger by a mere four years). "I think she has done a great deal of good for the movie industry. She is just what the business needed — someone to put some glamour and magic back into Hollywood. I think we have gone too far in promoting stars on the 'girl next door' level. We need a return to excitement and allure [like in] the days when Garbo was a reigning star," Maxwell affirmed.

**An Unconventional Romance**

While making films for Universal, Marilyn Maxwell was introduced to a man who would become her best friend — Rock Hudson. "Big Sam," as she called the Illinois native, was three years her junior.

**Rock Hudson and Marilyn Maxwell visit her grandmother**

Actress Lori Nelson believed Marilyn wanted to marry Rock and start a family with him. But Marilyn was also seeing writer/producer Jerry Davis, having met on a blind date. She and Davis, five years her senior, tied the knot on November 21, 1954 in New York City. Stepping in as matron of honor was her sister-in-law Kitten Maxwell. The honeymoon was in Acapulco, Mexico.

Davis was suspicious of Hudson from the start. He wondered why this man always seemed to hang around the house. Cathy Katz remembers, "In the early '60s, [Aunt Marilyn] came to the New York area to do theater. She got sick, and so she had to come and stay at our house, to recover. Rock Hudson came to visit her. He stayed at our house. Needless to say, we were pretty excited. I remember making pancakes for him one morning thinking he was a handsome guy, but he was also very down to earth and friendly."

Cathy added, "I know they saw a lot of each other. They were very good friends. The two of them loved to sit around the piano and play songs and laugh. [Rock] was actually pretty musical."

On April 28, 1956, Marilyn gave birth to her only child Matthew. In the book, *Rock Hudson: Friend of Mine*, longtime Hudson companion Tom Clark wrote of Rock's relationship with Marilyn, "I could certainly understand why Rock fell for her. But I think he loved Marilyn's son, Matthew Davis, even more...he and Rock had a great relationship. Matthew was the son Rock had always wanted." Hudson loved playing football with the boy and doing other father/son activities.

In 1958, Marilyn made the comedy *Rock-A-Bye Baby* with Connie Stevens and Jerry Lewis. Maxwell played movie star Carla Naples, who — recently widowed — finds herself pregnant. She decides to return to her hometown to lay low and figure out what to do next. There she meets a former boyfriend, played by Lewis, whom she recruits to be the father of her triplets, despite the fact that Lewis marries her sister, played by Stevens, instead.

In 1960, after six years of marriage, Maxwell filed for divorce, citing "extreme cruelty" and accusing her husband of being jealous of her leading men and having a gambling problem. She told the judge that Jerry Davis had said to her the day after the two wed, that he had married her "because I was a glamour girl and could help support him. I thought that was an odd sense of humor, but later I found out he wasn't kidding."

Marilyn was granted a divorce, receiving $500 a month in alimony and $150 for child support. Former agent George Ward stated, she "picked the wrong men, always. She brought on her own problems."

Nationally syndicated columnist Dorothy Kilgallen wrote of the alleged affair between Marilyn and Rock Hudson. "Marilyn Maxwell's estranged husband, screenwriter Jerry Davis, has been getting his kicks by telling friends he expects Marilyn to waltz down the aisle with Rock Hudson as soon as she gets the divorce," Kilgallen reported. "Marilyn says she has no such plans, she and Rock are just good friends, and she wishes Jerry would stop being such a wise guy with his wedding flashes."

In April 1960, when asked about her health habits, the actress gave diet and exercise advice. "When I am home and not working, I spend an hour a day at a gym...I have a stationary exercise bicycle at home," she explained. "It isn't easy for me to resist myself because I love to eat [not sweets], but I could live on pasta, spaghetti, lasagna, macaroni au gratin." She recommended exercising with hand weights and eating a high protein diet. For ten cents readers could send for a copy of "Marilyn Maxwell's Sensational 30 pounds in 30 Days Diet."

For an interview, the actress spoke of her new starring role in the television version of the Marilyn Monroe picture *Bus Stop*. Maxwell played Grace Sherwood, owner of Grace's Diner, the place where travelers stop. The plot for this hour-long drama was set in Colorado, and aired for 26 episodes on ABC between 1961-62. Marilyn effused, "I get to play Grace as a young widow still interested in men, and I want to keep it romantic. What I don't want them to do is make me a kind of mother for everybody, or the big fixer of everybody's troubles."

Cathy Katz says of *Bus Stop* that Marilyn "was hoping it would lead to some other roles. She was feeling encouraged that she could continue her career even as she got older."

After 13 weeks on *Bus Stop*, Marilyn left the show. She told reporter Bob Thomas, "There was nothing for me to do but pour a second cup of coffee and point the way to the men's room."

Marilyn decided she wanted to return to the big screen. She found out her pal Rock was working on a script for a film entitled *Lover Come Back*.

"I thought I was a cinch for [the role], especially since it was Rock's own production," she told Thomas. "But Rock wouldn't let me do it. He wants me to get away from Marilyn Maxwell roles. He even wants me to let my hair go brown, so I can get away from the limitations that every blonde actress has."

The article also reported that Maxwell and Hudson were

steady daters, to which the actress demurred, calling the relationship merely a good friendship. Doris Day was cast in the role instead.

Marilyn spoke of her disdain for not having been selected to be one of the year's inductees for a Hollywood Star of Fame. "I have to admit I was puzzled and mad when I couldn't find my name [on the list], especially after I saw all those rock n' rollers were there. Conway Twitty?" Marilyn said, bemused.

She had also complained of being stereotyped by producers as "the other woman," asking, "Do I look like a blonde menace?"

Bob Hope cast Marilyn in his 1963 comedy *Critic's Choice* in which she plays his ex-wife, a movie star. Hope, a film critic who must now go easy on current spouse Lucille Ball, who has written a manuscript he is sure he will dislike, still butts heads with his first wife, saying, "I miss you too. On my masochistic days."

In 1964, Maxwell made the film *Stage to Thunder Rock* depicting a woman recovering from life on the streets. Four years later, she made *Arizona Bushwhackers* in which Howard Keel plays a captured Confederate riverboat gambler and gunfighter, who is given the opportunity to join the Union Army and help bring law and order to the West.

**The fetching Ms. Maxwell**

In 1970 she made her last movie, appearing alongside other celebrities in a cameo role in the cult classic *The Phynx*, wherein a rock and roll band is sent to Albania to rescue hostages.

Taking a break from motion pictures and entertaining soldiers, the aging blonde spent the late 1960s and early '70s appearing on television and in burlesque shows, mainly for the money. She supplemented her income selling household cleaning products. Despite yearly requests from Bob Hope to resume U.S.O. tours, Marilyn declined, since the tour schedule would mean spending Christmas away from her son. "Ever since I divorced Jerry I've decided to remain with Matthew for Christmas," she explained.

Marilyn Maxwell's last role was as an aging stripper past her prime on an episode of the television series *O'Hara — United States Treasury*, starring David Janssen. By 1972, she was planning a nightclub act for Chicago and had been offered a role in the film *Mama's Boy*, and a recurring part on the soap *Return to Peyton Place*. Overjoyed with job offers, Marilyn phoned Rock Hudson with the news.

The following day, March 20th, Marilyn collapsed in her closet while getting dressed, the result of a heart attack and a battle with pulmonary disease and hypertension. Her 15-year-old son Matthew found her lifeless body after returning home from school. She was 49 years old. At a neighbor's house, he called Rock Hudson. "He was wonderful to my cousin Matthew, who was her only son," says Cathy Katz. "Rock came right over, and took care of Matthew."

Jerry Davis, Matthew's father, was in Mexico at the time and not able to be reached for several days. In the meantime, Clark and Hudson made the funeral arrangements. As soon as Davis returned home he reclaimed his son. In his book Clark wrote of the funeral, "It developed into one of those Hollywood circuses, complete with shoving photographers and screaming fans and all that hysterical nonsense."

After her death Hudson became obsessed with his own mortality and wanted Clark to promise, "Don't ever let them turn my funeral into a circus like poor Marilyn's."

Bob Hope delivered the eulogy. "If all her friends were here today we'd have to use the Colosseum," he said. "Marilyn had an inner warmth and love for people...and the thousands of servicemen she entertained over the years felt this. Who would have thought this little girl from Clarinda, Iowa would do this much and go as far as she did? Who knows why some of us are called earlier than others?" Hope somberly continued, "Maybe God needed a lovely gal to sing and cheer Him up, and so He called her...I must say it was a great job of casting." Marilyn was cremated and her ashes were scattered at sea.

After her passing, Maxwell's brother, Lelland Maxwell of Armonk, New York, filed a petition in Los Angeles Superior Court seeking probate hearings on her will. The late actress had reportedly left all of her $104,000 estate to her 15-year-old son, Matthew, and her brother Lelland—whom she had named as executor—nevertheless sued to contest it.

"I just remember her as my glamorous aunt. Sometimes we would get to see her in live shows. She had a great sense of humor. I remember she loved to laugh. She was a very warm, affectionate kind of person," Cathy Katz reflected. "I wished we had lived closer and been able to see more of her. I think she regretted that too. My father was her only family, really. Even though we didn't see her very often, she always made us feel special. My aunt loved performing. It was what she wanted to do. It seemed to me that it was just a natural thing for her to pursue. I wish she had the chance to be in some more movies that utilized her talents more. It's a difficult business."

# 11.
# JANE WYMAN:
## *Not Your Average Jane*

J ANE WYMAN CAME INTO PROMINENCE AS A PLEASING CHARACTER actress during the Golden Age of Hollywood. Longing to be freed from typecasting, she would slowly receive recognition as having leading lady potential. Wyman would succeed playing strong-willed, and sometimes unglamorous heroines. She even won a Best Actress Oscar without uttering a single word. Wyman wed five times—twice to the same man. She saw the loss of two children in her lifetime.

Jane appeared in over 80 films, had two successful television shows, and has two stars on the Hollywood Walk of Fame: one for motion pictures, and one for television. But perhaps her most memorable role came in the form of matriarch Angela Channing in the hit 1980s nighttime soap *Falcon Crest*. The show dominated television while her most famous ex-husband's political career reached its apex.

But Wyman avoided political notoriety at every corner. She was the only member of the "ex-wives of a U.S. president club" until Ivana Trump and Marla Maples joined her, with the election of Donald. J. Trump as President of the United States in 2016. Wyman is also the only spouse of a president to win an Academy Award.

Despite being hounded by the press for the remainder of her life to comment on her ex-husband, she considered it to be in "poor taste" to kiss and tell.

Press releases sent out from studios in the 1930s preferred embellishment and enchantment when marketing their contract players. For whatever reason, Jane did not dispute false stories or claims about her early life. In fact, she seemed to be at the helm of the re-creations.

Jane's exact date of birth has been under speculation for decades. Some accounts claim she and her daughter Maureen have the same birthday of January 4th. Different years, earlier and later, have also been listed as her year of birth. There is a general consensus that Jane was born Sarah Jane Mayfield on January 5, 1917, in St. Joseph, Missouri.

Wyman's birth parents were Manning J. Mayfield and Gladys Hope Christian. In 1921, her mother filed for divorce, and Mayfield died the following year of pneumonia. Gladys moved to Ohio, and placed her young child with her Missouri neighbors, Emma and Richard Fulks.

In later years, the actress commented on her rigid upbringing by the Fulks.

"I was reared under such strict discipline that it was years before I could reason myself out of the bitterness that I had brought from a childhood hemmed in by rigid rules, many of which I broke without knowing it and was punished long afterward by being denied something I had joyously anticipated."

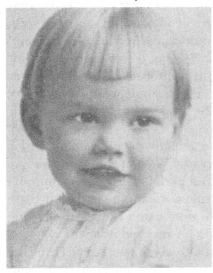

Jane at age three

Mr. Fulks, who had served as chief of detectives in St. Joseph, died when the child was 11 years old. Jane and Emma moved to Los Angeles where the adoptive mother had two grown children residing. The pair moved back to Missouri in 1930, but two years later returned to California.

Like many other well-known actresses, Jane started out as a chorus girl at 20th Century-Fox. "I couldn't do the steps but I looked all right," Wyman later reflected. "I had those skinny long legs and that was what they wanted." Her first film role came in the mold of such a dancer in the 1932 film *The Kid From Spain*. She lightened her brunette hair to get noticed and played alongside other blonde hopefuls such as Betty Grable, Paulette Goddard and Lucille Ball.

The following year, Jane wed Ernest Wyman, although she never publicly discussed this union. She only claimed to have been married once before Reagan. In *Dutch*, the authorized biography of Ronald Reagan, author Edmond Morris claimed this early marriage is on record with the state of California. In addition, Morris stated that Reagan alluded to Wyman's first marriage when he told him in 1989,

"What you have to look at [is] that there were a few husbands before me." Another answer to how Jane claimed the last name of Wyman was due to the fact that Emma Fulks' one-time husband had been named Dr. M. F. Weyman, a man the actress had known in her youth.

Jane believed she could go on forever playing the button-nosed, fast-talking, not-a-brain-in-her-head secretary,

Jane became a blonde to get film roles

chorus girl; or the leading lady's sister/best friend/confidant indefinitely. In the 1936 movie *Stage Struck* for instance, Dick Powell asks Jane's character what her name is. "My name is Bessie Fufnick. I swim, dive, imitate wild birds, and play the trombone," her character replied.

Wyman made a whopping ten films that year, including a brief appearance in the Carole Lombard/William Powell flick *My Man Godfrey*. "But you have to look fast to see me," Jane later said.

The actress made eight movies the following year, including her first top-billing role for *Public Wedding*, opposite William Hopper, columnist Hedda Hopper's son. The still popular *Mr. Dodd Takes the Air* followed. *Smart Blonde* was the first motion picture whereby Sarah Jane Fulks was credited as Jane Wyman.

In 1937, Wyman married "officially" for the first time—to a man twice her age. She wed a dress manufacturer, Myron Futterman, on June 29, 1937. They separated three months later after Jane discovered her new spouse already had a teenaged daughter and did not desire more children. The divorce was finalized on December 5, 1938. But before she became unattached, Jane set her sights on a handsome contract player she would invite to sit with her at lunch. Although he was more interested in Wyman as a friend, she nonetheless pursued a romance with a popular young actor by the name of Ronald Reagan, affectionately known as Dutch by his friends.

By 1938, Wyman got her chance to make a picture with Reagan, a man she was beginning to fancy. They co-starred in the flick *Brother Rat*, which also featured Wayne Morris and Priscilla Lane. Jane finally persuaded Reagan to go out with her, and a courtship ensued. The young actor was born on February 6, 1911 in Tampico, Illinois. In the 1989 memoir *First Father, First Daughter*, the couple's eldest child

Maureen Reagan wrote, "The movie magazines called them the ideal Hollywood couple, and in a way I suppose they were, at least in the eyes of their studio bosses; for a while, at least, theirs was a match made in press-agent Heaven.

"My parents had announced their engagement on stage during one of Louella Parsons' 'vaudeville-style' tours—a routine that wasn't exactly in the script—and from that moment on 'Aunt Lolly,' had taken credit for bringing them together."

In her October 24, 1952 column, Parsons wrote about the friendship, or what she deemed a "mother/daughter" dynamic with Wyman.

"I had known that Janie worshipped Ronnie, but I hadn't realized he was falling seriously in live [sic] with her," Parsons wrote. "I announced the engagement that night from the stage and in the newspapers, and later in Hollywood I gave them their wedding reception. By then they had become almost like a son and daughter to me."

"Like my father," Maureen continued, "[Louella] was another Hollywood transplant by way of Dixon,

Ronald Reagan and Jane Wyman

Illinois and she was pretty much a fixture in our household during the early years of my childhood. I still have some clippings in which Aunt Lolly figured publicly that my parents should have named me after her, because of the history they all shared."

### Life As The First Mrs. Reagan

The "All-American" couple married on January 26, 1940. Her engagement ring was a 52-carat amethyst ring; Reagan later gave her a matching brooch.

Both continued pursuing acting roles with Ronald advancing faster than his wife. He wanted to play George Gipp in the film *Knute Rockne, All American*. He went to friend Pat O'Brien to help him get the role, as O'Brien was set to play Knute Rockne. Having been successful at lobbying for the part, Reagan scored "one for the Gipper."

Jane on the other hand, was struggling to get parts she could be proud to play. The couple made a movie together entitled, *Tugboat Annie Sails Again.*

While Wyman's career was lackluster, she did get involved in the war effort. Jane entertained at the Hollywood Canteen and proved herself a pleasant singer. She also loved to sing for friends at cocktail parties and other get-togethers. She appeared in the comedy *You're in the Army Now* in 1941. Jane holds the record for the longest screen kiss, which was done with Regis Toomey, clocking in at three minutes and five seconds.

In 1942, Jane made the comedy/gangster picture *Larceny, Inc* with Edward G. Robinson and Broderick Crawford. Wyman regarded her big break as being cast in the 1943 film *Princess O'Rourke*, starring Olivia de Havilland, Robert Cummings and Charles Coburn. The comedy *Make Your Own Bed*, wherein Wyman and Jack Carson play detectives posing as a maid and butler in order to apprehend some criminals, followed. *The Doughgirls* (made with friend Ann Sheridan and Alexis Smith) and the star-studded *Hollywood Canteen* were other prominent film roles that followed.

On January 4, 1941 the couple welcomed their first child Mau-

Jane with Phil Silvers (left) and Jimmy Durante (right), in *You're in the Army Now* in 1941

Jane with newborn Maureen

reen, into the world. Now the "Ben and J. Lo" of the '40s, as son Michael would later describe them, this power couple had settled into domestic bliss with the fan magazines and newspapers following their every move. They adopted Michael in 1945 when the child was only a few days old.

Wyman's breakthrough role was soon to come. When producer Charles Brackett and director Billy Wilder screened the actress' 1943 film *Princess O'Rourke*, they agreed she had the "it factor" to star in their upcoming film *The Lost Weekend* alongside Ray Milland.

The film presented a raw picture of the damning repercussions of alcoholism, chronicling the several-day-long "lost weekend" of a writer battling chronic alcohol addiction. It is regarded as the first film to tackle alcoholism head-on and not merely view the disease as a vehicle for comic relief.

"Until then, I'd really never had anything dramatic to say," Wyman said in an interview in the 1980s. "I had to be either terribly funny, terribly dumb or not even all there. But this little scene stood out and that's how Brackett and Wilder picked me. I guess you'd have to call it luck."

The movie won Best Picture that year.

Jane made the poignant period piece *The Yearling* in 1946, a tale based on the novel by Marjorie Kinnan Rawlings about a boy in post-Civil War Florida and his bond with a fawn. Wyman was nominated for an Oscar for her performance.

The Reagans then discovered there would be a new addition to their family, but alas, the child, later named Christine, died the day after she was born prematurely, in 1947. The actress gathered up her grief and mourned the loss of her child the best way she knew how—

returning to the film studio.

She achieved a career milestone with her starring role in the drama *Johnny Belinda*. While studying the movie script and developing her character, her home life grew more and more volatile.

In Michael Reagan's book, *Twice Adopted* he described the day his mother asked his father for a divorce. "One day in mid-1948, Dad came home, and Mom told him the marriage was over. He was stunned...Dad blamed himself and his busy schedule with the Screen Actors Guild for the failure of his marriage." (Reagan was elected to a full term as the SAG president a month after their divorce.)

In *Johnny Belinda*, Jane plays a deaf/mute teenager who is raped and becomes pregnant in a seaside village in Nova Scotia. While preparing for the role, Miss Wyman studied at a school for the deaf for six months, learning sign language. She memorized the lines

A deglamorized Jane in *Johnny Belinda*

of the other actors and performed with her ears plugged. Her friends assured her she would be nominated for an Academy Award. They were right. She went up against Olivia de Havilland, close friend Barbara Stanwyck, Irene Dunne, and Ingrid Bergman for the statuette.

The night of the ceremony, Jane took home the Best Actress Oscar. On stage, she made the shortest acceptance speech on record, "I accept this very gratefully for keeping my mouth shut. I think I will do it again."

This film was one of only a dozen on record at the time to be nominated in the best actor and actress and best supporting actor and actress categories. Barbara Stanwyck, assured she would win that year for *Sorry, Wrong Number*, kidded Wyman that she would allow "her award" to be kept at Wyman's home.

Ronald Reagan reportedly cracked to a friend, "Maybe I should name *Johnny Belinda* as co-respondent [for the divorce]." But Wyman cited other reasons for the split at the divorce hearing, "Politics built a barrier between us. I tried to make his interests mine, but finally there was nothing to sustain our marriage."

Reagan told Hollywood writer Gladys Hall, "It's a strange character I'm married to, but—I love her...Please remember that Jane went through a very bad time when, after the strain of waiting for another baby, she lost it. Then perhaps, before she was strong enough, she went into *Johnny Belinda*. It was a taxing, difficult role. Perhaps, too, my seriousness about political affairs has bored Jane."

He was right. On December 14, 1947, Jane made their separation final in the midst of allegations of an affair with *Johnny Belinda* co-star Lew Ayres. Wyman denied this accusation and the former power couple would slowly divert public attention away from their marriage. Archer Winsten, writing in *The New York Post*, called her performance "surpassingly beautiful. It is all the more beautiful in its accomplishment without words."

While Jane was in the spotlight receiving one A-Movie role after another, Ronald was re-building his life.

### Enter Nancy Davis

On November 15, 1949, a young starlet by the name of Nancy Davis approached Reagan, then sitting president of the SAG, with a little problems. She had been wrongly placed on the Hollywood blacklist. She contacted Reagan in hopes of having the tarnish removed from her name. Reagan told her that she had been confused with another actress of the same name. A friendship forged, and the two began casually dating. Nancy enjoyed Reagan's daily musings about world affairs and politics far more than Wyman had.

Davis made her first film in 1949, and appeared in *East Side, West Side* starring Barbara Stanwyck. Marriage seemed the natural step for advancing their relationship, but Ronald had his doubts, as did Jane. But in her 1989 memoir *My Turn*, Nancy wrote, "I could see that Jane knew how to play on Ronnie's good nature. She had convinced him that he shouldn't get married until she did. It took me a little time, but I managed to unconvince him." Nancy and Ronald exchanged vows on March 4, 1952.

Also in her memoir, the second Mrs. Reagan noted, "Maureen and Michael lived with their mother, and Ronnie would often drive over to Jane's big house on Beverly Glen to see them—especially on holidays. Sometimes he'd ask me to come along, and I did, although this wasn't exactly my idea of pure joy. Jane was perfectly nice to me, but these visits were awkward. Not only had she been married to Ronnie, but she was very much 'The Star' and it was her house and her children. I felt out of place, and I was a little in awe of her."

Despite being, "a little in awe" of Wyman, in her memoir, Nancy had no qualms about criticizing the parenting skills of her husband's first wife. "Jane Wyman sent Maureen and Michael to Chadwick, a boarding school in Palos Verdes, about an hour from Los Angeles. Michael was only five and a half when he started at Chadwick, and I found that appalling. Ronnie did too, to the point where he thought seriously about filing for custody."

Nancy continued her assessment, writing,

**Michael and Maureen craved maternal attention**

"Michael went through a turbulent adolescence, and when he was 14 his relationship with his mother had deteriorated to such an extent that a psychiatrist recommended that he would be better off moving in with us." At age 16, Michael asked Nancy if she could help him track down his birth mother. Nancy added, "Ronnie and I had the same business manager as Jane Wyman, so I called and asked him to find out." Wyman was furious.

However, in his memoir, Michael Reagan recalled his childhood differently, "I had succeeded in getting out of Mom's house, only to discover that I was just as uncomfortable and unhappy in Dad's house." But despite being the adopted child of two celebrities, Michael took the chance in the book to be at peace with his parents, "It was easier to blame Mom for putting me in boarding school, even though that was the best she could do as a single mother...I blamed Nancy and Dad for making me sleep on the couch in [their home in] Pacific Palisades."

Wyman starred in *The Glass Menagerie* in 1950, which garnered mixed reviews. The following year, Jane made *Here Comes the Groom*, with Bing Crosby. The duo sang the Carmichael/Mercer song, *In the*

*Cool, Cool, Cool of the Evening*, which debuted in the movie, and won an Oscar for Song of the Year in 1952.

Released in 1951 was *The Blue Veil*, in which the actress was aged from 20 to 75 throughout the film, spending 14 plus hours a day wearing thick rubber makeup that was taken off with gasoline. "My face looked like raw beefsteak," she later quipped. The film also features Joan Blondell, Agnes Moorehead and a young Natalie Wood. Wyman won a Golden Globe for Best Actress. Her next significant role was starring in *Magnificent Obsession* opposite Rock Hudson. *The New York Times* called her performance in this film about redemption, "Refreshingly believable throughout."

In 1953, Wyman appeared in the Barbara Stanwyck film *So Big*. A string of well-known movies such as *All That Heaven Allows*, *Miracle in the Rain*, and *Pollyanna*, would see Wyman's career through the end of the decade.

Jane began making frequent television appearances on *General Electric Theater*, *Summer Playhouse*, *Lux Playhouse*, *Westinghouse*, *Desilu Playhouse*, *Bob Hope Presents* and *The Chrysler Theater*. She hosted her own series and was nominated for an Emmy in 1957. While popular in the beginning, the show was canceled after three seasons.

Maureen Reagan wrote of her mother's time working in television, "It wasn't until I got to be a teenager and she started doing *Jane Wyman's Fireside Theater*, a 1950s television anthology series that allowed her to play a different depressing character each week, that I realized what was happening...Movies in those days took about three to six months to shoot, which meant we had to live with Mother's wide personality swings for months at a time, but television dramas were often cranked out in less than a week. By that time we would sit around and wonder whether Mother would come home from work as a Maryknoll nun or an ax murderess, but we'd learned to accept her sudden about-faces as part of the territory when it came to Mother and acting."

While home from Chadwick for Halloween, Maureen and Michael met their mother's new beau, bandleader Fred Karger, three years their mother's junior and his daughter, Terry. The kids went out to go trick-or-treating. When they returned, Fred and Jane told the youth of their plans to marry. Maureen recalled this revelation with less than fond feelings. "Boom! Instant extended family! Just add water and stir." She went on to say, "I can't tell you how odd it was to meet someone one minute and then to find out he was marrying your mother the next...Mother and Fred didn't waste any time. They eloped the next day."

Maureen recalled being handed bags of rice to throw at the bride and groom when they returned home. "I'm not sure, but I think I might have pelted Fred with clumps of rice a bit harder than tradition called for."

A week before her mother's surprise wedding, Maureen and Michael's half-sister, Patti was born. Maureen somberly recalled witnessing her father play with the new baby, throwing her in the air and catching her. He called the new baby Shorty. "Well, I died a thousand deaths," the eldest daughter opined, "Because of course that was the name he used to call me." Maureen cited a visit eight or so years later when Michael had gone to live with their father and Nancy. It was only when the young man showed up at the door that Patti was even told she had a brother.

"So Patti came up to me at one point during my visit and said, 'Did you know that Michael is my brother?' And I said. 'Yes, of course I know that. And do you know what that makes you and me?' 'No, what?' 'That makes you and me sisters.'"

Patti was quite upset by this news, cried and told Maureen that she was not her sister. When Maureen confronted her father as to why she had been so overtly left out of her half-sibling's life, he replied, "Well, we just haven't gotten that far yet."

Even Nancy admitted their relationship with Reagan's first children left something to be desired: "Maureen liked me better when I was her friend Nancy Davis than she did when I became her stepmother, Mrs. Ronald Reagan." A second child, Ronald Reagan, Jr., was born on May 28, 1958.

Jane's marriage to Karger did not last long. The couple separated on November 7, 1954, and the pair received an interlocutory divorce decree. The union officially dissolved

Jane with husband Fred Karger

on December 30, 1955. Possibly seeking some kind of solace from the divorce, Jane converted to Catholicism after she and Fred split. She also insisted her children become Catholics, too.

In an interview with *Coronet* magazine in January 1956, writer Richard G. Hubler commented, "Miss Wyman has the typical specialist memory of an actress; She forgets the names of her closest friends and her own telephone number, while remembering every word of a script and, as she puts it, 'every shadow on a face.'" Wyman also commented on how she preferred to not discuss her ex-husbands, and instead liked to focus on movie roles that are relatable to other women.

Even though she vowed marriage was not in her future, she was often spotted dating younger men. However, she and Karger did try to rekindle their romance and remarried on March 11, 1961. This reconciliation lasted four years. Jane received a special dispensation from a bishop to receive Holy Communion as a divorced woman. Reflecting on her five failed marriages, Wyman explained, "I guess I just don't have a talent for it. Some women just aren't the marrying kind— or anyway, not the permanent marrying kind, and I'm one of them."

In a 1968 newspaper interview, Wyman was inevitably asked why she never commented on her marriage to Ronald Reagan, who was then governor of California. She reasoned, "It's not because I'm bitter or because I don't agree with him politically. I've always been a registered Republican. But it's bad taste to talk about ex-husbands and ex-wives, that's all. Also, I don't know a damn thing about politics."

Reagan was also tight-lipped on his former union with Wyman. In Reagan's 1990 autobiography *An American Life*, the original "Mr. Family Values" only briefly mentioned his first wife. "That same year I made the Knute Rockne movie, I married Jane Wyman, another contract player at Warners. Our marriage produced two wonderful children, Maureen and Michael, but it didn't work out, and in 1948 we were divorced."

While Michael Reagan formed rocky bonds with his mother and his stepmother, both women have been criticized for their parenting methods, as well as Ronald's skills as a father, or lack thereof.

Observers of Nancy and Ronald found it curious that his second son would be his namesake and not his first. Michael said that while he campaigned for his father for president, he hypothesized that his dad did not like appearing with his two older children, stating, "Headquarters may feel it's embarrassing if Maureen and I are in the forefront and the real kids [Ron and Patti] are not."

The two sets of Reagan children never became close, and the

ally Michael had in Nancy devolved after the birth of her own children.

In an interview with Scott Ross of *The 700 Club*, Michael said his time at boarding school was an isolating experience. "All of us so-called 'rich kids' and 'lucky kids' [whose] parents were rich and famous would be dropped off at 7:00 Sunday night and not picked up 'till two weeks later on a Friday and taken home to be back Sunday night at 7:00," he said. "If you could stand outside our dorm at Chadwick, you would literally hear us all crying ourselves to sleep at night."

Michael has spoken publically and in print about his experience of being sexually abused by a day-camp official as an eight-year-old child. "He owned me and started the process of sexually molesting me three days a week for the rest of the year. Even though I knew it was wrong, I couldn't put my mind to it. Who do I tell? I had no relationship with my parents to be able to tell them. I felt that I was doing something terribly, terribly wrong."

The man took a nude photograph of the boy, threatening to give a copy to his mother.

"I will never forget that photograph, because it changed my life," Michael said. "I knew I had to get away from my mother. I had to get away from God. I thought God had abandoned me, and I knew then I was going to hell."

Michael became Born Again due to his wife Colleen's influence. He believes his father wouldn't have been president being married to Jane Wyman. "He needed a Nancy, who was willing to give up her career to be there, by his side."

Jane's daughter Maureen followed in her father's footsteps. She was active in the Republican Party and worked as a radio talk show host, health care reformer, a supporter of the Equal Rights Amendment and was pro-choice (issues over which father/daughter clashed). She also served on the California World Trade Commission and was chairwoman of the United Nations' "Decade for Women Conference" in Kenya in 1985. Maureen was the first daughter of a president to run for political office, campaigning for senator of California in 1982, and for representative of that state's 36th district in 1992. She became a member of the Alzheimer's Association in 1994, influenced by her father's struggle with the disease.

The youngest Reagan child, Ron, Jr. became a professional ballerina, as well as a Liberal pundit and Atheist. In 1980 *Time* magazine reported, "It is widely known that Ron's parents have not managed to see a single ballet performance of their son, who is clearly very good, having been selected to the Joffrey second company, and is their son nonetheless. Ron talks of his parents with much affection. But these absences are strange and go back a ways."

Wyman accepted only a handful of film roles throughout the 1960s, the most famous being *Pollyanna*, and only appeared in made-for-television movies in the 1970s.

"I left the movies because I didn't like the kind of pictures they were making in the 1960s," Wyman said in a newspaper interview in the early 1980s. "I wouldn't throw away my reputation on the odd things they were doing in those days."

### The First Lady of Primetime Television

The year 1981 marked a turning point for both Reagan and Wyman's careers and legacies. Ronald Reagan was inaugurated as the 40th President of the United States. Wyman's career would not be eclipsed, nor would she quietly fade away. She was about to star in one of the most popular television shows of the decade—*Falcon Crest*.

"I liked the concept of the series," Wyman noted. "When you read a script, you can see the future possibilities of a show. My role as Angela Channing is fascinating. There are five different sides to her."

Made in the mold of *Dynasty* and *Dallas*, the show was set in the fictional Tuscany Valley, California. The evening soap opera centered on matriarch Angela Channing (played by Wyman) and her family's vineyard. The drama ran for nine seasons on CBS, from 1981-1990, and featured 228 episodes. Wyman won a Golden Globe for Best Actress in 1984, at age 67.

Wyman was known for her love of glamorous outfits and glittering if not gaudy jewelry, once leading Louella Parsons to refer to the actress as a "walking Christmas tree." In a 2014 interview Wyman's Falcon Crest co-star Morgan Fairchild recalled how the actress never lost her love of 'statement making' accessories.

"[On the show] Jane

Jane as Angela Channing on TV's *Falcon Crest*

Wyman was much more conservative, and one day I came down [to the set] and I was supposed to be dressed for a party or something. I was in a red leather miniskirt suit with the big shoulder pads and my Wendy Gell big jeweled cuffs and big necklace and big earrings and spiked heels, and somebody said, 'Oh my God, you have to go change. Jane will hate that!' Before I could go, Jane walks on the set in an A-line dress and pearls and comes over and looks me up and down and says, 'Now this is what the show needs—a little damned glitz!'"

In retirement, Wyman stayed busy oil painting and working for the Arthritis Foundation for more than 20 years and served as its national chairwoman. She declined to star in theater productions, saying "I never did any stage work in my life. I just don't like the theater, and I don't enjoy going. I can't tell you why."

Maureen passed away in 2001 from melanoma, age 60. *Frasier* actor David Hyde Pierce, a fellow volunteer for the Alzheimer's Association, told mourners at her funeral on August 19, 2001, "When she was given lemons, she did not make lemonade. She took the lemons, threw them back and said, 'Oh, no you don't.'" A feeble Jane went to Maureen's funeral, but Reagan was too ill to attend.

When Ronald Reagan died on June 5, 2004, Wyman released this statement: "America has lost a great president and a great, kind, and gentle man." However, she did not attend his funeral.

Jane passed away on September 10, 2007 at her California home. She had been battling diabetes and arthritis but died in her sleep from natural causes.

Son Michael told the press, "I have lost a loving mother, my children Cameron and Ashley have lost a loving grandmother, my wife Colleen has lost a loving friend she called Mom and Hollywood has lost the classiest lady to ever grace the silver screen." A devout Catholic, Wyman was a member of the Dominican order at the time of her death, and was buried in a nun's habit.

Nancy Reagan passed away on March 6, 2016, at the age of 94.

Jane Wyman wasn't an overnight success. She made 40 films before she won an Academy Award. She struggled with typecasting, and instead of seeking out any old role to play, she waited patiently for the right ones to come along. Wyman believed that there was no reason a husband and wife couldn't both be wage earners, even if it meant spending less time with her children. Jane triumphed in television at an age when most actresses retired.

# 12.

# LOUELLA PARSONS:
## *The Titan of Tinseltown*

OMNIPOTENT MALE STUDIO HEADS, DIRECTORS AND PRODUCERS dominated Hollywood during the Studio Era of the 1920s-1960s. Actors were at the mercy of the whims of such tyrants as Samuel Goldwyn, Louis B. Mayer, David Selznick, Irving Thalberg, Jack Warner and Darryl Zanuck. Filmmaking was "a man's world" with few opportunities for women to advance up the ladder. Despite the money, influence and control these powerful men wielded, there was one figure they all kowtowed to without hesitation. Her name was Louella O. Parsons.

Louella broke the most controversial, scandalous and tantalizing Tinseltown stories of her day. She blackmailed some of the most celebrated and famed names in the industry. She played matchmaker but also destroyed marriages. She elevated mediocre actors to fullfledged movie stars and let established actors fade into oblivion due to personal vendettas. And she did this all with her typewriter. At the height of her career, Parsons was syndicated in 1,200 newspapers with readership in the tens of millions. A newspaperwoman for over 60 years, it was her contract with the Hearst papers that allowed her gossip column unmatched readership until Hedda Hopper became a formidable opponent.

Parsons tried to end the career of Orson Welles when she found out his masterpiece film *Citizen Kane* was based largely on the life of her boss, William Randolph Hearst.

If stars didn't cooperate with her demands for an exclusive, she spoke ill of their personal lives and careers in her column, or worse— she had them blacklisted from the Hearst syndicate. Big name actors appeared on her various radio shows—free, of course. At a time, Parsons was handed major news stories from the studios with a 48-hour exclusive over her competitors. With a network of spies infiltrating every level of the movie industry, along with her own on the ground techniques, few noteworthy events got past Parsons. She often plied her subjects with booze to loosen their tongues and she would act distracted or disinterested as people spoke to her in order to not appear that she was hanging on their every word. Inevitably, the conversation would be reported in detail in her column the next day.

If a source was of questionable origin but the scoop too big to pass up, Louella simply cautioned her readers that "a little bird" had told her the story. When you were her ally, she would spare you embarrassment and keep your reputation pristine in her column. But if you were uncooperative, the columnist proved the saying that "the pen is mightier than the sword."

Louella Rose Oettinger was born on August 6, 1881, in Freeport, Illinois a town 20 miles south of the Wisconsin border. The Oettingers, a German-Jewish American family, consisted of Helen and Joshua, and their four children. To blend in with the predominately German Protestant citizens of the agricultural-based community, the family attended an Episcopal Church.

After Joshua died, Helen married a man named John Edwards and the family relocated to Dixon, Illinois. With a love of writing, public speaking and reading, Louella wanted to become a journalist. However, when the young woman graduated from high school in 1901, few women wrote for newspapers.

She was encouraged by her family to go to college to become an elementary school teacher. Not enthused with this career pathway, she secured a part-time position with the *Dixon Star* in 1902. The column paid $5 a week and her name did not appear on the byline. While writing in the society pages was not her ultimate goal, Louella broke the glass ceiling by becoming the city's first female journalist. The next year, she finished college and secured a position teaching in a country school.

On Halloween 1905, she wed real estate developer John Parsons. That December, the couple moved to Burlington, Iowa. At the local Garrick Theater she saw vaudeville acts and a new innovation called "flickers." In 1909, the Lyric Theater opened up in town and it was there that Parsons saw her first short film. From then on, she was a movie buff. August 23, 1906 saw the birth of her only child, Harriet, who would later follow in her mother's ambitious footsteps by becoming a columnist, screenwriter and a Hollywood producer. Unfortunately, John and Louella had little in common, and he abandoned his young family to pursue an affair with a woman named Ruth Schaefer.

Lonely and alone in Iowa, mother and daughter packed their bags for the Windy City.

The *Chicago Tribune* hired Louella for $9 a week—a sum not nearly enough to get ahead in a major American city. While hoping to become a reporter, instead she found herself doing clerical work. In the spring of 1911, she left the paper to work full-time as a "scenario editor" for Essanay studio. This position earned her $20 a week. If the 1920s and '30s are regarded as an era of cheap, mass-produced motion pictures, the 1910s saw the rapid-fire release of flicks because these early attempts lasted only 15 to 20 minutes, and theaters needed studios to send out several films at a time. Her task was to pour through mail sent to the studio in which everyday citizens wrote in and described a "scenario" they felt would make a good plot. Louella selected the entries with the most potential and sent the winners checks for $25. As many as 100 of these "scenarios" flooded into the studio daily.

Louella at the start of her career

Besides determining the plot of a film, Parsons often lent creative input to the productions and would even provide props and costumes from her personal belongings. It was while working for the Illinois-based movie studio that Louella met actors who would later become big names in Hollywood: Francis X. Bushman, Gloria Swanson, Bebe Daniels, Harold Lloyd and most notably, Charlie Chaplin. Many of these actors would remain her life-long friends.

Having lived apart for years, Louella and John's marriage came to an end on September 29, 1911. John married his mistress, and died in 1918. Ashamed to be a divorcée, for the rest of her life, the columnist told friends and associates that she had been widowed. Being a single mother with a small child, she took on another job and was hired by the *Chicago Herald*. She was able to combine her two passions: journalism and motion pictures. Her Sunday column "How to Write Photo Plays" first appeared on December 20, 1914. "The world was my oyster," she wrote in her memoir, "And Chicago was providing the cocktail sauce."

Parsons quit her job at Essanay in January 1915 due to creative differences. Luckily, she secured a second column with the *Herald* called "Seen on the Screen" which ran daily. On January 9th of that year, Louella wed Jack McCaffrey in a whirlwind romance only a month in the making.

In a stereotypical fashion, stage actors were regarded as immoral and not fit for proper society. Seeking to avoid comparisons with the theater, moviemakers tried to present their actors as virtuous and nothing like the "filth" produced on the stage. Columnist Parsons was eager to write about films as being educational, wholesome, entertaining and a positive influence on the youth. Her early columns dealing with the film world sought to portray actors and other movie folks as "just like the rest of us."

By November 1917, Parsons was not only an established newspaperwoman, but was being recognized as a key figure in the movie business. Her publisher James Keeley sent her to New York, all expenses paid, to report on a convention held by the Motion Picture Theater of America. Parsons later wrote that this experience made her believe she was now a woman with clout. "Always a ham at heart, I felt every eye in the place was on me as I registered 'Miss Louella Parsons, columnist, Chicago Ill.' I felt I had come into my own."

Despite securing such a coup, when she arrived back in Chicago she learned that the *Herald*, which had been in financial trouble, had been sold to one of the most hated men in the country—William Randolph Hearst.

The paper was renamed the *Herald Examiner*. Arthur Brisbane told Louella that his boss Hearst did not want a film columnist for his paper. On April 30, 1918, her last column in a Chicago paper was published. Discouraged, but not defeated, Louella headed for New York. She convinced the theater-focused newspaper *Telegraph* to hire her stating that covering the movie world would increase advertising revenue. With her claim deemed valid, she was awarded a column named "In and Out of Focus." Her salary jumped to $150 a week. In 1919, Louella made the acquaintance of a young actress named Marion Davies. Her film, *Cecilia of the Pink Roses* was released in a blitzkrieg of publicity in the papers. Intrigued by the praise the film and its actress were receiving, Parsons set out to interview Davies. The two quickly became pals, and as a token of their friendship, Louella mentioned Davies in her column constantly. If Parsons' friendship with Marion Davies seemed innocent at first, by 1922, with the release of Davies' *When Knighthood Was in Flower*, it became obvious that Louella was trying to catch the eye of the man who was footing the bill for the production and promotion of Davies' films. It was no secret that the 25-year-old starlet's career was being propelled by her married lover, a man 34 years her senior. His name was William Randolph Hearst.

Hearst owned over 30 newspapers at the time with a readership of seven million. One out of four families in the nation read a Hearst paper. To Louella Parsons, a column with the newspaper tycoon would cement her footing as the leading reporter on movie news. Louella asked Marion to speak with Hearst about the prospect of joining one of his papers. Hearst was impressed with the columnist's praise of his mistress, yet it took a few meetings for the mogul to agree to add Parsons to his payroll. Once he made her an offer, Parsons consulted a lawyer—one also used by Hearst—to make sure she secured a cushy deal.

Finally, on December 8, 1923, Louella was signed to be the motion picture editor of the *New York American*. Impressed with her moxie Hearst quipped, "I'm disappointed in you. You forgot to ask for hairpins." Parsons clearly had proved herself a capable and experienced journalist suitable for the job. Her lauding of Davies also helped her integrate into Hearst's inner circle. In less than a year, Louella's syndication expanded greatly and she went on to work for the Hearst syndicate until her retirement in 1964.

Parsons' column was never edited. Her viewpoints, and even typos, were never altered. Only once was her column changed. A review she had written about the silent film *The Ten Commandments* was dramatically re-worked by an anonymous source, leading Parsons to go to the boss and complain. From then on, Hearst vowed to never allow her column to be re-written. Years after the fact, Hearst revealed he himself had made the edits.

Speculation as to how this mere mortal secured such a lucrative deal with one of the most powerful men in the country is tied to what this author terms the "Ince Incident."

Ever involved in his mistress' film career, Hearst began negotiations on another movie in the spring of 1924. He recruited Hollywood mogul Thomas Ince, regarded as "The Father of the Western" to produce and direct a film in which Marion Davies would star. Ince was one of the earliest and most successful producer/directors in Tinseltown, a real pioneer of silent movies, who had released 100 films.

By the autumn, Ince and Hearst agreed to team up for the production of *The Enchanted Isle*. To celebrate reaching a deal on the movie, as well as Ince's birthday, Hearst took Ince and several friends out on a weekend cruise to San Diego on his yacht Oneida, beginning

**A case of mistaken identity? Thomas Ince (left) and Charlie Chaplin wore their hair the same way, had similar facial features and were of the same height and build.**

on the 15th of November. Davies and several others in show business, including Charlie Chaplin, were fellow guests. According to the official story, Ince suffered a heart attack and was rushed back to the mainland, where on November 19th he passed away at his home. His death certificate reads "heart failure as the result of an attack of acute indigestion." He was 42-years-old.

Hearst barred his papers from mentioning the yachting trip in reporting on Ince's death, leading to speculation as to what really occurred. Since no autopsy was performed and Ince was immediately cremated, it was assumed that Ince had met with foul play. Also, the guests onboard the boat refused interviews with the press. Legend has it that Ince and Davies were having an affair and Hearst—finding them in a romantic tryst—shot and killed Ince, thus accounting for the rushed funeral arrangements and lack of a thorough investigation.

However, another version claims that it was Marion and Chaplin who were caught in a compromising position (the two *were* lovers), that Hearst saw the two together, ran to get his gun, (a diamond-studded revolver with which he was known to shoot at seagulls), and when he came back, Chaplin had gone, and Ince happened to be standing near her. Hearst killed Ince by mistake, then covered it up by paying everyone off with money or jobs or acting roles. It is intriguing that Ince and Chaplin were of similar build and appearance. In this scenario, the guests were told to go along with the story that Ince took ill, left the boat, and died elsewhere.

There is no disputing that the first stories in Hearst's newspapers about Ince's death were outright fabrications. It was claimed Ince had taken ill while visiting at Hearst's ranch and had been rushed home by ambulance, dying in the arms of his family. This story quickly fell apart, because too many people had seen him board the Oneida in San Diego. Allegedly, Charlie Chaplin's secretary, Toraichi Kono, claimed to have seen Ince being carried off the yacht and that it appeared as if Ince's head was "bleeding from a bullet wound."

Initially it was reported Louella had also been onboard. Vera Burnett, a confirmed guest, claimed that Parsons had indeed been one of the passengers. Supposedly, Louella helped plan the cover-up. To reward her, Hearst made her column a permanent staple in his papers.

Nell Ince, the widow, received a trust fund from Hearst who also paid off the mortgage of a home belonging to the Inces. After her husband's death, Mrs. Ince also built—supposedly with money from William Randolph Hearst—the lavish Villa Carlotta Apartments and the Chateau Elysee, an even more upscale luxury long-term residential hotel where people like George Burns, Cary Grant, Bette Davis—and Louella Parsons—lived.

Those who do not buy into a conspiracy theory tend to surmise that Hearst had nothing to do with Ince's demise and probably wanted no mention of the party on his boat in the papers because alcohol had been aboard.

Although Hearst was a teetotaler and intolerant of drunkenness, he was already under suspicion for bootlegging with liquor—illegal due to Prohibition—so it may have been sagacious to not speak of the party. Regardless of how or why Thomas Ince died, the talk of Parsons and Hearst being co-conspirators was slow to die down.

Adding to the suspicions were the lies and denials that Hearst's guests began telling plus the fact that Mr. Hearst never even attended Thomas Ince's funeral.

In 1996, Patty Hearst (William Randolph Hearst's granddaughter, who'd gained her own notoriety through her kidnapping and subsequent bank robberies) and Cordelia Frances Biddle, published a novel called *Murder at San Simeon*, in which Chaplin and Davies were depicted as lovers and Hearst as the jealous old man unwilling to share his mistress with anyone else.

In 2001, Peter Bogdanovich released a film called *The Cat's Meow*, which made the case that Ince had been murdered. Bogdanovich said Orson Wells told him the true story, having heard it from Marion Davies' nephew.

Filmmaker D.W. Griffith, known for his controversial classic *Birth of a Nation*, said of the mysterious death, "All you have to do to make Hearst turn white as a ghost is mention Ince's name. There's plenty wrong there, but Hearst is too big to touch."

## Give Her An Ince, She'll Take a Whole Column

It was the summer of 1925 when Hearst recruited Louella to be his eyes and ears when he and Marion Davies were apart. He correctly suspected his young mistress was unfaithful. Parsons was now assigned the task of monitoring the extracurricular activities of Davies, which meant following the actress out to Hollywood. Soon after, the columnist contracted tuberculosis and ended up spending several months out West recuperating. By the time March rolled around, Louella phoned Hearst to inform him of her recovery. It was then that the newspaper tycoon told his star columnist that she was now to be stationed out in Hollywood—permanently.

Her salary increased to $350 a week. Her writing now appeared in all of her boss' newspapers, as well as the Universal News Service. Parsons supported and belonged to several female writers groups. In 1925, she was elected president of the Newspaper Women's Club. By the autumn of 1926, she had a readership of six million and she received 1,000 fan letters a week.

When talking pictures came into vogue in 1927, Marion Davies flew into a panic. With a pronounced stutter there was concern that her career would die alongside silent films. To circumvent this obstacle, Hearst told Parsons to speak disparagingly of the "talkies" in her column in order to turn the public away from this new form of entertainment. However, by late 1928 all of the major studios made the transition. And fortunately for Davies she was able to stay in the movies thanks to work with a speech therapist.

It was at this time the columnist obtained her 48-hour exclusive. Studios funneled her stories in exchange for maintaining clean images of their stars.

With her marriage to McCaffrey on the rocks, Louella began an affair with a politician named Peter Brady, whom she referred to as the love of her life. She ended up divorcing McCaffrey in 1927 but a wedding with Brady did not come to fruition. A man named Dr. Harry Martin Watson won her heart instead. The two wed on January 5, 1930. Louella became interested in her husband's faith and decided to convert from Judaism to Catholicism. Their marriage proved more successful than Louella's previous ones, although the couple was known for their binge drinking and gambling and were often the butt of jokes due to these vices.

Harry, also known as Docky, proved a reliable informant for his wife. As a Hollywood doctor he treated the stars for venereal disease, performed abortions and had first-hand knowledge of pregnancies in their early stages.

Louella quickly became a Hollywood insider by frequenting popular hangouts such as the Brown Derby, Romanoff's, Ciro's and most notably, Hearst Castle at San Simeon. The "ranch" as Hearst's guests called it, is situated 250 miles equally from San Francisco and Los Angeles in San Luis Obispo County. Hearst threw extravagant parties, which would sometimes last all week, at his palatial 165-room residence. While Hearst could be an eccentric host, refusing an invitation to one of his parties was unthinkable. To be regarded as a major star one only needed to be on Hearst's guest list.

One of the easiest ways to become a foe of Parsons' was to refuse to be interviewed for her column. Not every celebrity enjoyed speaking freely with the press about such sensitive topics as their health, marriage, or childhood. When the stars did not cooperate, Louella retaliated. Louella had long-running feuds with the elusive Greta Garbo, Katharine Hepburn, Howard Hughes and Mae West.

Louella got a coast-to-coast radio show

Her cattiness towards the star of *The Thin Man* movies, Myrna Loy, was exemplified in a 1930 column that read, "Miss Loy is one of the best-looking girls on the screen, and maybe one of these days her acting will match her looks. Here's hoping." When enough animosity developed between Parsons and a star, Hearst would agree to bar that star from his papers.

In 1931, Louella broadened her influence by obtaining her own radio show, sponsored by Sunkist. The show didn't last through the year, but in 1934 she went out over the radio again with a program sponsored by Charis, a women's underwear manufacturer. After deciding not to renew her contract with Charis, Louella teamed up with Campbell's soup and got a show called *Hollywood Hotel*. Seventy-two radio stations carried her program. Again, the guests appeared free of charge. Stars did, however, receive a free case of soup.

Throughout her career she would move in and out of radio. Fellow columnists would also appear on the radio, but Parsons was the first. Despite conquering yet another form of media, she was criticized for her poor broadcast skills. *Life* magazine reflected in 1965, "She fell prey to stage fright at the very sight of a microphone and sounded, when she projected her reedy, middle-western accents over the air, somewhat as if she were standing before a firing squad dictating her last will and testament."

To the shock of movie buffs everywhere, 1936 saw the break-up of the marriage of Hollywood's power couple Douglas Fairbanks and Mary Pickford. Louella was the first to report on the "biggest divorce story in the history of Hollywood." Hurt at Louella's insistence in revealing the details of the split, Pickford distanced herself from her former friend for years. When movie star and Kansas City native Jean Harlow died of renal failure in 1937, Louella got to pen the magazine supplement about the actress' life. Staying up for three nights straight to make deadline, the publication sold one million copies.

Still loyal to Marion Davies, when the actress moved from MGM to Warner Brothers, publicity in the Hearst papers adjusted accordingly. Wherever Hearst's mistress made her movies, the films and actors at that studio reaped the benefits. From Warners, Hearst and Davies made the switch to 20th Century Fox.

It seemed that with her exposure in the newspapers and on radio Louella Parsons had solidified her position as the reigning Hollywood columnist. To her consternation, on February 14, 1938, the *Los Angeles Times*—the rival of Parson's flagship paper the *Los Angeles Examiner*—introduced their readers to a budding gossip columnist called Elda Furry. A Hollywood insider since the early days of filmdom, she was a former actress and fly on the wall of sorts. But with an eighth grade education and no experience in journalism, her appeal came largely from her chatty and no-holds-barred writing style. Billed under several different names during her career, it was after consulting a numerologist that she changed her first name and kept the last name of her ex-husband. Thusly, Elda Furry dubbed herself Hedda Hopper.

Bitter rivals: Columnists Hedda Hopper and Louella Parsons

## Is This Town Big Enough For the Both of Them?

Before Hopper became a columnist, she was a struggling actress who frequently called up Parsons when she had a story of interest. In exchange, Louella wrote glowingly of her and warmly dubbed the actress "Queen of the Quickies." Indeed, in 1925 alone, Hedda appeared in seven films. As a Broadway chorus girl Hopper was part of a theater troupe of a man named DeWolf Hopper, whom she married in 1913 and later divorced. No longer a fresh-faced twenty-something, by the late 1930s it became clear that she wasn't destined for movie stardom. Accepting her failure as an actress, Hedda decided that if you can't join them, beat them. At age 53, she made a drastic career switch and got into the newspaper business.

Her column *Hedda Hopper's Hollywood* grew in popularity as she revealed the inner workings of Hollywood and spoke freely of the personal lives of those in the industry. The individuals she wrote about were less than pleased to have intimate details of a divorce splattered across the pages of major newspapers, but Hedda's readers couldn't devour the columns quickly enough.

If naysayers doubted Miss Hopper's chances of becoming as famous as Parsons, October 21, 1939, was the day these individuals were served a plate of crow. Stopping the presses like a scene out of a movie,

Hedda got her exclusive story into the paper right before going to press. Jimmy Roosevelt, eldest son of the president, was leaving his wife to marry a nurse from the Mayo Clinic. The story ran on the front page with Hopper receiving full credit. For the first time in her career, Louella had been "outscooped."

Hopper soon signed with the *Chicago Tribune-New York News* Syndicate, which tripled her readership, leading *Variety* magazine to declare: THE QUEEN IS DEAD. LONG LIVE THE QUEEN.

Louella now saw the former actress as a force to be reckoned with. "She's trying to do in two years what took me 30," Parsons remarked. In her 1962 book *The Whole Truth and Nothing But*, Hedda wrote, "Louella prepared for a fight. She had an intelligence service that included telegraph operators, telephone switchboard girls, beauty-parlor assistants, hotel bus boys, doctors' and dentists' receptionists."

*Life* magazine published a feature on Hopper in its November 20, 1944 issue. Francis Sill Wickware wrote, "Until the ascendancy of Hedda Hopper there was the unique phenomenon of a great American industry cringing and genuflecting before the redundant figure of Louella 'Lollipop' Parsons...And Hedda Hopper was largely instrumental in breaking Parsons' stranglehold on the studios. Louella Parsons is not a has-been, but neither is she any longer the ringmaster of the Hollywood circus. Hedda Hopper has a whip of her own and cracks it more expertly."

Wickware went on to say, "There was a large anti-Parsons audience ready and waiting when 'Hedda Hopper's Hollywood' first appeared and no one questioned that Hedda knew what she was talking about. For more than 25 years she had been soaking up memories of the triumphs and failures, the scandals and intrigues and idiocies of everyone in the business."

Hopper noted the influence that her rival had at the height of the Studio Era, "With the Hearst newspaper empire behind her, Louella could wield power like Catherine of Russia. Hollywood read every word she wrote as though it was a revelation from San Simeon, if not from Mount Sinai. Stars were terrified of her. If they crossed her, they were given the silent treatment; no mention of their names in her column."

Hedda, who rarely left the house without one of her signature hats, threw elaborate parties at her home and tried to befriend those in the business who had gotten on Louella's bad side. Despite the habit of getting the two columnists mixed up when speaking of them in conversation, the two women had very different styles and personalities.

Louella killed her subjects with kindness, had a dowdy appearance and drank too much. Hedda had a brash demeanor, used four-letter words and had a colorful wardrobe and regal look. And unlike Louella who was married several times, Hedda never remarried after divorcing DeWolf Hopper and claimed to lead a celibate lifestyle.

Because Louella and Hedda despised each other, the stars had to decide which woman was the better of the two in which to confide. "There were two factions. If you talked to one, you were no friend to the other," Marion Davies observed. Stars learned the hard way. "Double-planting," or giving a story to both columnists created nothing but trouble for the individual who committed such a faux pas.

In 1948, actress Gene Tierney was expecting a baby with her husband, fashion designer Oleg Cassini. Her first child Daria had been born mentally handicapped and was institutionalized. Happy to be pregnant again, and eager to share the news, she entrusted Hedda Hopper with the exclusive. However, the movie studio Gene was under contract to had already phoned Louella about the pregnancy. Feeling that the actress had double-crossed her, Louella confronted Tierney at a party, reducing the actress to tears.

Needless to say, after a while, the stars that had been disgruntled with Louella grew disenchanted with Hedda. When Hopper

**Louella hobknobs with Desi Arnaz and Lucille Ball**

began publishing stories claiming an affair between actor Joseph Cotten and his young co-star Deanna Durbin, Cotten demanded she stop the rumors, or else he would kick her in the ass. "It angered me and got my wife upset," Cotten told columnist Jim Bawden, "And later at a party I saw Hedda bending over to pick something up and I let her have it. She toppled and I walked away singing. Well, somebody had to do it."

Actress Lilli Palmer spoke of the contempt she and husband actor Rex Harrison shared for the two gossip columnists. "Hedda Hopper and Louella Parsons were the bottom of the bog. We cursed them collectively as 'Lulu Popper.' Louella looked like a very old tadpole; Rex called her an alcoholic illiterate. Hedda was just vituperative," she wrote.

David Niven wrote of a time in which he and his wife Hjördis, along with married couple, actors Ida Lupino and Howard Duff, were angered that the columnists published untrue claims of marital infidelity. To get even, Niven and Lupino booked a midnight table at the hotspot Ciro's, pretending to be on a secretive late date. Mrs. Niven and Duff entered the establishment and took a distant table for their fake date.

After a brief time, Niven and Duff spotted each other and began an argument. By then, the place was swarming with the press who had been tipped off by informants in the restaurant. Instead of punching each other, Niven and Duff grabbed each other and kissed then merrily danced around the floor posing as a couple. The next day, Hopper and Parsons phoned David Niven and scolded him for rudely having them roused in the middle of the night for a false alarm. "Neither of them was above a little gentle blackmail through the suppression technique," wrote David Niven in his droll memoir *Bring on the Empty Horses*. "People dreaded an imperious telephone message, 'Call Miss Parsons/Hopper—urgent'—but it was better to comply because at least there was a chance to stop something untrue or damaging from being printed; if the call went unanswered, the story was printed without further ado."

He added, "The great majority of us played a humiliating game of subterfuge and flattery, having long since decided that it was far less troublesome to have them with us than against us."

Yet, praise could be had—for a price. Both women took money from celebrities and press agents and in exchange would write whatever was asked of them. As long as the papers sold, it didn't matter how factual the columns were. The columnists' homes were flooded with sumptuous gifts at the holidays from folks trying desperately to stay in their good graces.

### Citizen Hearst

Louella received vacation time during the summer of 1940 and she and her husband went to Hawaii. Meanwhile in Hollywood, RKO pictures announced plans that Orson Welles and Herman Mankiewicz were collaborating on a screenplay and had begun shooting a movie called *American*. Originally, Welles and Mankiewicz wanted to make a film dealing with Thomas Ince's death and how William Randolph Hearst most likely had some involvement.

After mulling it over, the two men instead decided the script should be a biographical account of Hearst's life, told in flashback. The story would follow the rise to power and ultimate demise of the fictional character Charles Foster Kane, and the movie was re-titled *Citizen Kane*. It was obvious to the press that the movie was based on the life of Hearst, but with his top columnist out of the state on respite, Louella Parsons was the last to know that the much-talked about film was about her boss.

On January 3, 1941, the motion picture was ready for initial screening. Louella was not invited. Even when confronted about the nature of the flick, Welles lied to the columnist's face. Starting on January 9th, no Hearst-owned papers were to run any stories or advertising for any film or actor associated with RKO studios. Angered upon learning that the movie did lampoon Hearst, Parsons demanded to see the footage. Alongside two lawyers, she watched the screening and after it ended walked out of the room and phoned her boss.

It was bad enough that Welles portrayed Hearst as an egomaniacal newspaper giant, but the character of Kane's wife, Susan Alexander Kane, was based on Marion Davies. She was portrayed as a talentless lush. Of course, everyone knew of Davies' drinking problem and many believed that her career would have gone nowhere without her lover's money.

Xanadu, the mansion in which the reclusive Kane resides, was a take-off on the Hearst Castle. To most film historians, "Rosebud," the word Kane utters in the opening scene, was a representation of his childhood and lost innocence. In real life, Rosebud was the nickname Hearst gave to Marion Davies' private parts.

Desperate to prevent the movie from seeing official release, Louella contacted rival studios and recruited them to do her bidding. Louis B. Mayer, the head of MGM, was her biggest supporter. Along with fellow studio chiefs Joseph Schenck (20th Century Fox) and Jack Warner, Mayer contacted George Schaefer, the president of RKO and made him an offer. They would give him $800,000 to buy the film from the studio and have it destroyed. When Schaefer declined, the three studio heads refused to book the piece in their movie theaters. Louella

**Orson Welles in *Citizen Kane***

also told Schaefer that if he pushed the release of the motion picture, she would make sure that the Hearst papers published incriminating stories on the personal lives of the members of the board of directors. Henry Luce, one of Louella's harshest critics, and a rival to Hearst, offered to buy the film from RKO for $1 million and release it himself. Luce was the editor of *Life*, *Time*, and *Fortune* magazines and those publications often took pot shots at Parsons.

Not impressed with the offers—or threats—RKO decided to push ahead with the release of the movie on May 1, 1941. It went on to win the Academy Award for Best Screenplay, and often tops the list of the greatest movies ever made. Orson Welles, Agnes Moorehead and Joseph Cotten, the stars of the epic, were all blacklisted from the Hearst syndicate.

While she was unable to prevent *Citizen Kane* from commercial release, and with Hedda Hopper clipping at her heels, Parsons could have had a defeatist attitude. Yet on September 14th she boarded a train eastbound for her childhood town of Dixon, Illinois to celebrate Louella Parsons Day. Stars such as Bob Hope, Ann Rutherford and fellow Dixonite Ronald Reagan accompanied her. The columnist was treated to a parade attended by an estimated 35,000 people, a dinner in her honor and she did a local radio broadcast.

To boost her public image and enhance her likability, Parsons released a memoir in December 1943 entitling the book after a nickname she acquired (which wasn't too flattering, but one she came to embrace). *The Gay Illiterate* became a bestseller and 20th Century Fox purchased the movie rights, but a film was never made.

With Louella considered a media mogul, some speculated that

"Junior Parsons" as daughter Harriet was called, rode her mother's coattails. Not so. True, she wrote a column for Hearst and was a regular contributor to the fan magazines like her mother, but Harriet succeeded on her own merits. She produced the films *I Remember Mama*, *Clash by Night* and *Susan Slept Here*, among others.

In her magazine column "Louella O. Parsons In Hollywood" she interviewed her daughter about her career as one of the few women film producers. "Well, I think it's important to have some knowledge of writing and story values. I am glad that I was a writer before I became a producer, because it helps me to appreciate a good, sound story treatment. The second most important thing is to get the male animal to respect your opinions and judgment. Men are likely to have their tongues in their cheeks about women in the capacity of a 'boss.'"

Despite the feud with Louella, Hedda spoke highly of Harriet in her column. In return, Harriet arranged for Hedda and her mother to meet and put aside their differences. March 16, 1945, saw a détente of sorts between the rival columnists. They broke bread at the hotspot Romanoff's, setting tongues wagging. "Surely the world is big enough for us and the Russians," wrote one journalist. "Hedda Hopper and Louella Parsons had lunch together the other day!"

In the United States vs. Paramount Pictures, Inc. (1948) the Supreme Court ruled that the practice of movie studios, namely the Big Five, owning movie theaters violated antitrust laws. Studios were forced to sell their theaters, leading to relaxed film censorship, the rise of new, smaller studios and it gave actors more flexibility over their careers. The new crop of stars that came out of this era found the practice of reporting all their comings and goings to two aged columnists obsolete. Notwithstanding, Louella would blow the cover off one of the most talked about scandals in Movieland—the Ingrid Bergman debacle.

### Tell It To Louella

Swedish-born Ingrid Bergman was the darling of Hollywood. Best known for her role in *Casablanca*, she cultivated a wholesome girl-next-door image with her roles playing a nun and Joan of Arc, and often appeared in films without makeup (or so she claimed). In 1948, she contacted Italian director Roberto Rossellini and made plans to work with him on a movie to be called *Stromboli*. The two fell in love and tried to hide their romance due to the fact that both were married. By April of 1949 Louella was writing of the affair in her column yet tried to downplay the possibility that Bergman would divorce her husband Petter Lindstrom. With the romance trivialized by the press, the story grew complicated when in June Ingrid discovered she was pregnant. Hopper interviewed the actress who denied the rumor. However, an Italian newspaper revealed the truth. But since no columnist in the States would confirm the allegation, the public remained in the dark.

Finally, the house of cards toppled. Howard Hughes, the eccentric head of RKO pictures (where *Stromboli* was being shot), con-

**Louella shows actress June Allyson how she sends her column**

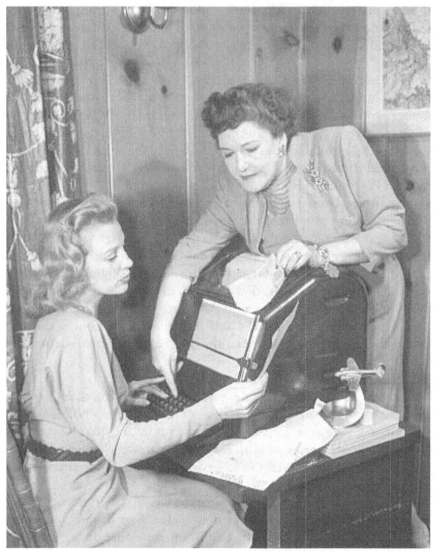

tacted Louella. He told her that Ingrid was indeed pregnant and that he decided to divulge the secret as a means of drumming up publicity for the film. On December 12th Parsons published the report. She told readers the movie star was hiding out in Rome and had left her husband and abandoned her daughter Pia. Bergman was denounced on the floor of the Senate for her "immoral" acts and the actress stayed in Europe for seven years before returning to American cinema. Hopper, abashed by her failure to see through Ingrid's deception, opted to not mention the pregnancy at all in her column.

Rita Hayworth and Prince Aly Khan's nuptials were regarded as the "Wedding of the Century." But when the Prince forbade the press from covering the celebration, Louella announced in her column that she had been personally invited and set off for Europe to crash the wedding. When Mari-lyn Monroe and Joe Di-Maggio wed in 1954, Louella was given the exclusive story—which dramatically increased her diminished readership.

With her husband Harry in poor health, Louella shifted her priorities to take care of him. Her drinking problem intensified in the process. On June 24, 1951, her spouse passed away from leukemia. That August, her boss/mentor/closest confidant, William Randolph Hearst died. His mistress of over 30 years, Marion Davies, was barred from the funeral on orders of his

**With Marilyn Monroe**

wife. Broke at the time of his death, Hearst Castle was ultimately donated to the state of California in 1957.

The columnist began dating Jimmy McHugh who wrote such classics songs as *I'm in the Mood For Love*, *I Can't Give You Anything But Love*, and *On the Sunny Side of the Street*. In addition to music, he was interested in managing the careers of actors. When he took blonde bombshell Mamie Van Doren under his wing, Louella sprang into action.

Van Doren recalled, "Jimmy sent me to one of the best acting schools in Hollywood—Ben Bard's Theater—personally gave me voice lessons, and got me screen tests at the major studios. However, there was never a quid pro quo between Jimmy and me...Louella, however, was unconvinced. She began a campaign of terror against my budding career. First she pressured Ben Bard to get me out of his acting school by threatening to boycott his plays and his students who were aspiring to stardom...I found out that Paramount had not turned me down because of my superficial resemblance to Marilyn. Louella Parsons had pressured them into not signing me by making it clear that if they did she would never again give Paramount, its pictures, or its stars a line of publicity in her column."

Van Doren also claims that a story published in the tabloid *Hollywood Confidential* was leaked by Louella. It reported, falsely, that the actress was a former prostitute. Due to her difficulties with Parsons, Van Doren befriended Hedda Hopper. "If Louella Parsons was the Bitch Goddess of my career, Hedda Hopper was my Guardian Angel," she wrote.

In 1961 Parsons published a second book called *Tell It To Louella*. But with the rise of television, tabloid magazines, the end of the Studio Era and the merger of newspapers, gossip columns faded into oblivion. By the next year, Parsons appeared in only 70 newspapers. Hopper was published in 130. In 1964, Louella turned her column over to her longtime assistant Dorothy Manners after over 60 years in journalism.

The following year, *Life* magazine writer Paul O'Neil did an 11-page spread on the now-reclusive former titan of Tinseltown. "Nobody understood better than she that Hollywood, for all its complaints, had an almost neurotic need to tattle or confess, and that she was the town's leading means of catharsis," he wrote.

Hedda continued her column until 1966, fulfilling her promise to "outlast the old bag." Despite appearing in newspapers after Louella's retirement, Hedda would not outlive her rival. Hedda Hopper succumbed to pneumonia on February 1, 1966. With heart, kidney and lung problems, Louella grew feeble. On December 9, 1972, Louella Parsons passed away at the age of 91.

"Louella was famous by virtue of her association with the famous," her biographer Samantha Barbas appraised. Yet Louella was a household name and a legend in her own right.

In 1985 a made-for-television movie was released about the stormy relationship between Louella and Hedda. The title of the film came from an anecdote wherein Hedda Hopper joked that one day she would call her memoirs "*Malice in Wonderland*." Although she wrote two books in her lifetime, she never used that title. *Malice in Wonderland* featured Elizabeth Taylor as Louella and Jane Alexander as Hedda.

Bette Davis, a proponent of the advancement of women in male-dominated professions, may have struggled with the intrusive nature of the gossip columnists, but she had respect for Parsons. In a 1971 broadcast of *The Dick Cavett Show*, the veteran actress acknowledged, "I had some very rough times, particularly with Louella. But she was probably one of the greatest newspaperwomen that will ever be. Let's hand it to her. She was a pro newspaperwoman. Nothing would stop her from getting a story if she possibly could. Well that was her business, wasn't it?"

Parsons and Hopper acted as the moral regulators of Hollywood. Their power and influence over the movie studios and the stars is a phenomenon that no longer exists. Still, in the 21st century, the public remains obsessed with the cult of celebrity, a concept Louella helped to gain momentum. "We can get along," Louella once famously said, "All you have to do is give me all the stories."

# Selected Bibliography

The works listed here include the key books, newspaper and magazine articles, websites and interviews referred to in the previous chapters. It excludes films, television shows, and musical works.

"A Kiss That Breaks Up Rock." *Life*, February 16, 1962, pages 65+.

Adams-Westin, Mark. Phone interview. 2015.

Andersen, Christopher P. "Lilli Palmer's Bittersweet Recall of Nazis, Madcap Hollywood, A Timid Cooper and Husband Rex." *People*. November 3, 1975. Pages 70-75.

"Anne Baxter Dies at 62, 8 Days After Her Stroke." *Los Angeles Times*. December 12, 1985. AP report.

Armstrong, Lois. "Anne Baxter Has a New Career in Hotel Management—and One More Debt to Bette Davis." *People*. June 11, 1984. Pages 141-144.

Arnold, Jeremy. "I Confess." Turner Classic Movies. N.p., n.d. Web.

Barbas, Samantha. *The First Lady of Hollywood: A Biography of Louella Parsons.* Oakland: University of California Press, 2006.

Barthel, Joan. "Jean Seberg Loses Her Innocence." *Cosmopolitan*, May, 1969, pages 110-13.

Baxter, Anne. *Intermission: A True Story.* New York: Putnam, 1976.

"Bobby sox to hard knocks." *Coronet*. February 1958. Page 12.

Brown, Vivian. "Author Describes Jean Harlow as First Blonde Glamour Girl" *Eugene Register-Guard*. August 16, 1964. AP report.

Bryant, Roger. *William Powell: The Life and Films.* North Carolina: McFarland & Company, Inc, 2006.

Busch, Noel F. "A Loud Cheer For The Screwball Girl." *Life*, October 17, 1938, pages 48+.

"Carole Lombard." Dear Mr. Gable. N.p., n.d. Web.

"Clarinda History." Clarinda Chamber. N.p., n.d. Web.

"Clark Gable Divorced by Lady Ashley." *The Milwaukee Sentinel*. April 22, 1952. INS report.

Clark, Tom and Dick Kleiner. *Rock Hudson: Friend of Mine.* New York: Pharos Books, 1990.

Curtis, James. *Spencer Tracy: A Biography.* Toronto: Alfred A. Knopf, 2011.

Dandridge, Ann. Email interview. 2015.

D'Arcy, Susan. "Adieu Tristesse." *Films Illustrated*, August 1974, pages 490-3.

Davidson, Sara and Rock Hudson. *Rock Hudson: His Story*. New York: William Morrow & Co, 1986.

Davis, Patti. *The Way I See It*. New York: Jove, 1993.

"Death of Jean Harlow Is Blamed on Sunburn." *The Milwaukee Sentinel*. June 21, 1937. Universal report.

Dirks, Tim. "The Lost Weekend (1945)." AMC. N.p., n.d. Web.

"Dorothy Dandridge Hailed as Newest Glamour Star." *Baltimore Afro-American*. March 27, 1951. AP report.

"Dorothy Dandridge Note Hints That She Expected to Die Soon." *The Milwaukee Journal*. October, 11, 1965. AP report.

"Dorothy Dandridge will ruled invalid." *Washington Afro-American*. November 9, 1965. AP report.

Ebert, Robert. "Birds in Peru Movie Review & Film Summary (1969) Roger Ebert." All Content. N.p., n.d. Web.

Eich, John Paul. Phone interview. 2016.

Fristoe, Roger. "The King and Four Queens." Classic Movie Guide. N.p.: Plume, 2005. N. pag. Turner Classic Movies. Web.

Frost, Jennifer (2011) *Hedda Hopper's Hollywood: Celebrity Gossip and American Conservatism*. New York/London: New York University Press.

Galt, Melissa. Phone interview. 2010.

Gehring, Wes D. *Carole Lombard: The Hoosier Tornado*. Indianapolis: Indiana Historical Society Press, 2003.

"George Hurrell, Jean Harlow, 1934." Laguna Art Museum. N.p., n.d. Web.

Golden, Eve. *Platinum Girl: The Life and Legends of Jean Harlow*. New York: Abbeville Press, 1991.

Graham, Sheilah. "Actress Jean Harlow: A Tramp Or A Lady?" *The Miami News*. January 10, 1965.

Hagen, Ray and Laura Wagner. *Killer Tomatoes: Fifteen Tough Film Dames*. North Carolina: McFarland & Company, Inc, 2004.

Hall, Gladys. "Why I Married Bill Powell." Motion Picture. December 1931.

Hamill, Pete. "Jean Seberg's Cinderella Career." *The Saturday Evening Post*. June 15, 1963. Pages 22-23.

Harlow, Jean (as told to Leicester Wagner). "Jean Harlow—Her Own Story." *The Pittsburgh Press*. December 4, 1934.

_____*Today is Tonight*. New York: Dell Publishing, Co, 1965.

"Harrison County." Appalachian Ohio. N.p., n.d. Web.

Henderson, Jessie. "Jean Harlow Movie Surprise." *The Miami News*. August 16, 1931.

Hepburn, Katharine. *Me: Stories of My Life*. New York: Random House, 1996.

"History - John Tracy Clinic." History - John Tracy Clinic. N.p., n.d. Web.

Hopper, Hedda (1952) *From Under My Hat*. New York: Doubleday.

————and James Brough (1963) *The Whole Truth and Nothing But*. New York: Doubleday.

Humphrey, Hal. "Marilyn Maxwell at the Crossroads." *The Milwaukee Journal*. August 6, 1961.

Hubler, Richard G. "Calamity Jane Wyman." *Coronet*. January 1956. Pages 92-96.

"Jean Harlow's Advice About Using Make-Up." *The Montreal Gazette*. September 15, 1934. AP report.

"Jean Harlow Hinted Death Was At Hand." *Sarasota Herald-Tribune*. June 9, 1937. AP report.

Kanin, Garson. *Hollywood*. New York: Viking Press, 1974.

Katz, Cathy. Phone interview. 2011.

Karbo, Karen. *How to Hepburn: Lessons on Living From Kate the Great*. New York: Bloomsbury USA, 2007.

Keavy, Hubbard. "Carole Lombard Gives Writer Rather Hectic Interview on 'This Screwy Picture Business'." *Reading Eagle*. August 7, 1938. AP report.

Keene, Dave. "Carole Gets Her Own Way." *Silver Screen*. May- Oct 1934 Pages 20+

Kendall, Elizabeth. *The Runaway Bride: Hollywood Romantic Comedy of the 1930s*. New York: Cooper Square Press,1990.

Kilgallen, Dorothy. "Broadway Bulletin Board." *New York Journal-American*. August 10, 1961.

Kramer, Stanley. "He Could Wither You With a Glance." *Life*, June 20, 1967, pages 69+.

"Lake Forest Ferry Hall." Illinois High School 'Glory Day.'" N.p., n.d. Web.

Leaming, Barbara. *Orson Welles: A Biography*. New York: Viking Penguin, 1985.

"Lemon Pie is Jean Seberg's Favorite Cooking Choice," *The Cedar Rapids Gazette*, February 19, 1970.

Lewis, Judy. *Uncommon Knowledge*. New York: Pocket Books, 1994.

"Loretta Young Now Is Mother—By Adoption." *The Milwaukee Sentinel*. June 12, 1937. Universal report.

"Lost Legend: Recalling The Tragic Crash That Claimed Carole Lombard." *Las Vegas Sun*. Jan 10, 2002.

Maltin, Leonard. "Overview for Carole Lombard." Classic Movie Guide. N.p.: Plume, 2005. N. pag. Turner Classic Movies. Web.

———— "Overview for William Powell." Classic Movie Guide. N.p.: Plume, 2005. N. pag. Turner Classic Movies. Web.

Mann, William J. *Wisecracker: The Life and Times of William Haines, Hollywood's First Openly Gay Star*. New York: Penguin Books, 1999.

Marx, Samuel and Joyce Vanderveen. *Deadly Illusions: Jean Harlow and the Murder of Paul Bern*. New York: Random House. 1990.

Matzen, Robert. *Fireball: Carole Lombard and the Mystery of Flight 3*. Pittsburgh: Paladin Communications, 2013.

Maxwell, Roger. Phone interview 2008.

McGee, Garry. *Jean Seberg—Breathless*. Georgia: BearManor Media, 2008.

McGee, Garry and Jean Russell Larson. *Neutralized: The FBI vs. Jean Seberg*. Georgia:BearManor Media, 2008.

McGee, Garry and Michael Coates-Smith. *The Films of Jean Seberg*. North Carolina: McFarland & Company, Inc, 2012.

Miller, Ron. "It's Back To The TV Grind For Jane Wyman." *Toledo Blade*. September 20, 1981. Knight News Service.

Mills, Earl. *Dorothy Dandridge: A Portrait in Black*. New York: Holloway House Publishing Company, 1970.

"Milwaukee Sewer Socialism." Wisconsin Historical Society. N.p., n.d. Web.

Morella, Joe and Edward Epstein. *Jane Wyman: A Biography*. New York: Delacorte Press, 1985.

Niven, David. *Bring on the Empty Horses*. New York: Putnam, 1975.

Nixon, Rob. "Hell's Angels." Turner Classic Movies. N.p., n.d. Web.

"Now Dottie Rocks Lena's Boat." *People Today* 23 Sept. 1953: 54-57.

O'Neil, Paul. "The Little Queen Hollywood Deserved." *Life*, June 4, 1965, pages 72+.

Osborne, Robert. Private Screenings: Robert Mitchum/Jane Russell. Turner Classic Movies. 2006. Television.

Ott, Frederick C. *The Films of Carole Lombard*. New York: Lyle Stuart, 1984.

Parsons, Louella O. "Driving Effort, Refusal to Accept Defeat Elevated Jane Wyman To Stardom." October 24, 1952. AP report.

———— "International News Service." *Palm Beach Daily News*. December 13, 1957.

———— *Jean Harlow's Life Story*. New York: Dell Publishing, Co. 1937.

———— "Rock Honor Set." *The Milwaukee Sentinel*. February 21, 1962.

———— *The Gay Illiterate*. New York: Garden City Pub. Co, 1945.

———— "Two Stars Expecting." *The Milwaukee Sentinel*. September 27, 1961.

Petersen, Anne Helen. *Scandals of Classic Hollywood: Sex, Deviance, and Drama from the Golden Age of American Cinema*. New York: Plume. 2014.

Reagan, Nancy and William Novak. *My Turn: The Memoirs of Nancy Reagan*. New York: Random House, 1989.

Reagan, Maureen. *First Father, First Daughter: A Memoir*. Boston: Little, Brown and Company, 1989.

Reagan, Michael. *On the Outside Looking In*. New York: Zebra,1988.

Reagan, Ronald. *An American Life*. New York: Simon & Schuster, 1990.

Richards, David. *Played Out: The Jean Seberg Story*. New York: Random House, 1981.

Robeson, Warren. "T-R City Editors Tells Nation about Marshalltown's Jean Seberg." *Times-Republican*. September 16, 1979. AP report.

Robinson, Louie. "The Private World of Dorothy Dandridge." *Ebony*, June 1962, pages 116-121.

Ross, Scott. "The Truth That Set Michael Regan Free." CBN.com CBN, n.d. Web.

"Russ Columbo Dies By Accidental Shot." *The Miami News*. September 3, 1934. AP report.

Russell, Jane. *My Path and My Detours: An Autobiography*. New York: Franklin Watt, 1985.

Russell, Rosalind. *Life Is A Banquet*. New York: Random House, 1977.

"Sarah Bernhardt." Bio A&E Television Networks. N.p., n.d. Web.

Scott, Vernon. "Testimony to 'second opinion' wisdom William Powell 90 Years Old." *The Bulletin*. July 28, 1982.

Seberg, Jean (as told to George Christy). "Jean Seberg's Confessions of an American girl in Paris." *Modern Screen*. October 1961. Pages 24+.

Server, Lee. *Robert Mitchum: Baby I Don't Care*. New York: St. Martin's Press, 2001.

Sheridan, Patricia. "Patricia Sheridan's Breakfast With...Morgan Fairchild." *Pittsburgh Post-Gazette*. N.p., Sept 15, 2014. Web.

Sheppard, Dick. "Wishing on a star." *Photoplay*. August 1957. Pages 67-70.

Shippy, Dick. "Jane Russell Unimpressed By Her Image." *Toledo Blade*. August 24, 1975. AP report.

Shuey, Mary Ann Seberg. Phone and email interviews. 2014/2015/2018.

"Simple Funeral To Be Held For Blond Actress." *The Evening Independent*.

June 8, 1937. AP report.

       Stenn, David. *Bombshell: The Life and Death of Jean Harlow*. New York: Doubleday, 1993.

       St. John, Adela Rogers. "Jean Harlow Tells The Inside Story." Liberty. N.p., n.d. Web.

       Strait, Raymond. *Bob Hope: A Tribute*. New York: Pinnacle Books, 2003.

       Swindell, Larry. *Screwball: The Life of Carole Lombard*. New York: William Morrow & Company, 1975.

       ——— *Spencer Tracy: A Biography*. New York: New American Publishing, 1971.

       Thomas, Bob. "Both Marilyns Doing Very Well in Films." *The Leader-Republican*. January 5, 1953. AP report.

       ——— "Marilyn Maxwell Disproves Old Couplet About Glasses." *The Tuscalossa News*. September 1, 1953. AP report.

       ——— "Marilyn Maxwell Just 'Rides Away From Show.'" *The Corpus Christi Caller-Times*. November 19, 1961.

       Thomas, Dan. "Jean Harlow, Rebel in School, Amazed Teachers by Her Speed in Learning Lessons Accurately." *The Milwaukee Journal*. September 12, 1932.

       Tornabene, Lyn. *Long Live The King: A Biography of Clark Gable*. New York: Pocket Books, 1977.

       Tracy, Spencer. "My Pal, Clark Gable." Dear Mr. Gable. N.p., n.d. Web.

       Welland, Gordon. "Bern Suicide Was Blow To Jean Harlow." *The Pittsburgh Press*. June 10, 1937.

       Wilcox, Grace. "So William Powell, Kansas City's 'Suave, Civilized and Elegant' Gift to the Ladies, Stirs the Hearts of America's Young Femininity." *The Milwaukee Journal*. September 29, 1934.

       "Woman Again Sues Clark Gable Estate." *The Tuscaloosa News*. August 31, 1962. AP report.

       "1942 Air Crash Widow Sues Clark Gable Estate." *The Desert News*. August 18, 1961. UPI report.

To order copies, comment or query:
**www.pageturnerbooks.biz**

Made in the USA
Columbia, SC
06 April 2019